Home *Before* Sunset

Home *Before* Sunset

The Sacred Journey of an Unordinary Life

Joseph G. Crowther

Middle Shelf
Publishing

This book draws upon the author's memories. In some instances, names of individuals have been changed to maintain anonymity or because a specific name could not be recalled. While not all conversations are intended as verbatim transcripts, the essence of all events and conversations are accurately represented.

Copyright © 2022 by Joseph G. Crowther

All rights reserved. No part of this book may be reproduced or used in any manner without the prior written permission of the copyright owner, except for the use of brief quotations in a book review.

To request permission, contact the author at www.JosephCrowther.com

ISBN 979-8-9854461-2-8
(Paperback: ISBN 979-8-9854461-0-4)
(Ebook: ISBN 979-8-9854461-1-1)

First hardover edition March 2022

Cover design by Brien Spanier
Cover photograph by Diana Foster
Author photograph by Peter Crowther

Middle Shelf Publishing
Olathe, Kansas

A portion of the proceeds from the sale of this book will be donated to The National Institute for Mental Health.

About the Author

Joseph G. Crowther has cycled the Rockies, climbed fourteeners, backpacked through Patagonia, snorkeled in the Caribbean, ridden a hot air balloon over Turkey, and hiked in nearly forty countries. Yet if you ask Joe to tell you about his most favorite or most meaningful adventures, he will share stories of parish ministry.

For thirty years, Joe served as pastor to congregations in the South and Midwest. His passion for preaching helped earn him a Doctorate in Homiletics from the Lutheran School of Theology in Chicago. His desire to reform the institutional church encouraged him to further post-graduate work in the area of missional leadership.

Joe currently travels the country consulting with pastors, church leaders, and nonprofit organizations. When off the road, he leads a missional community based out of a coffee shop in the suburbs south of Kansas City where he and his wife, Lori, live with Mabli, their overly rambunctious Welsh Springer Spaniel.

Contents

Preface xi
Introduction: Turning Around. 1
1. The Problem 5
2. A God with Skinned Knees 14
3. Sifted Like Wheat 21
4. Whispers & Storms 29
5. The Sound of the Gun 39
6. The Gift of Suffering 49
7. So, Ask *(The Man Who Sowed Good Seed — Part I)* 57
8. The Incubator Lessons 64
9. Resetting the Table. 74
10. The Treasure Chest. 86
11. Calling Out the Enemy *(The Man Who Sowed Good Seed — Part II)* . 97
12. What Might Have Been. 103
13. 14 Norman Street 112
14. Deus Loquens 120
15. The Limoncello Revelation 130
16. I Have a Feeling We're Not in South Carolina Anymore . . . 135

17. Empathy for Father McKenzie......................145
18. The Report.......................................153
19. Waiting for the Spirit's Hail Mary................160
20. When the Preacher Doesn't Know...................168
21. At the Base of "The Trough".....................175
22. Fields & Floods *(The Man Who Sowed Good Seed — Part III)*......183
23. The Macchiato Revelation........................191
24. When the Father Comes Running...................197
25. The Road to Jump Off Rock.......................206
26. A Controlled Fall...............................216
27. Why Me? Why Not?................................223
28. Thin Places.....................................233
29. A God Who Shudders *(The Man Who Sowed Good Seed — Part IV)* .241
30. Repacking.......................................249
31. The Difference a Good Ending Can Make...........260
32. The Art of Salvation............................267
Epilogue..276
Gratitude...283

When we trust that suffering can be part of God's great pattern to change all things, and that God is in the suffering, our wounds become sacred wounds. The actual and ordinary life journey becomes itself the godly journey.

~ Richard Rohr, *The Wisdom Pattern: Order, Disorder, Reorder*

Our wounds are God's hiding place and hold our greatest gifts.

~ Simone Weil, *Gravity and Grace*

Preface

I grew up in a gallery of Norman Rockwell classics. It was an era of winsome fathers, rosy-cheeked mothers, and playfully mischievous children. Our elders received the respect they were due, and all dogs were cute as a button and well-behaved. Those are my recollections.

Routine was sacred during my growing-up years. Each weeknight, my father returned home from work, greeted my mother with a kiss, put on his slippers, lit his pipe, and kept company with the newspaper until Mom called, "Dinner is ready!" We all spoke the table grace together, shared the news of our days, and asked to be excused when we were finished. Life was predictable and rhythmic.

Each summer, in a manner befitting the cover of *The Saturday Evening Post*, my family loaded the white, wood-paneled, Chrysler station wagon, posed for a Polaroid picture, and struck out for North Myrtle Beach. Despite his disdain for driving, and the objections of the long line of motorists that would inevitably form on the two-lane highways behind him, my father always took the wheel. Mom rode shotgun.

Mike, my older brother, collected the back seat to himself. My kid brother, Pete, and I were thirteen months apart (still are) and inseparable. Although there was plenty of room alongside Mike, we were stowed in the rear of the wagon for the entire trip, untethered. When the weather permitted, Dad cinched our luggage to the roof rack directly above us using baling twine and knots that would put most Boy Scout leaders to shame. My father took great pride in his knotsmanship.

Unless we mistimed the drawbridge over the Intercoastal Waterway, the trip from our North Carolina farmhouse to the South Carolina sand was a reliable four hours. My brothers and I knew this, of course, but that didn't keep us from occasionally checking in with Dad to make sure we were on schedule.

In the summer of 1969, just before Mike, Pete, and I turned fifteen, five, and six years of age, respectively, the tires on the Chrysler had barely warmed up when the inquisition began.

"How much longer? Hey, Dad! How much longer?"

I don't know why we bothered to ask. Dad's response was always the same.

"Twenty minutes."

"But Dad," we protested, "you told us twenty minutes…twenty minutes ago!"

"Twenty minutes," he intoned again in his low raspy voice, then chuckled under his breath.

Pete and I didn't mind the back of the wagon. We rather preferred sitting there. The space became our private rocket ship or the tail gunning turret of a B-52 from which we strafed trailing enemy vehicles. And with Dad in the cockpit, there were always plenty of targets. Just past the midway point of our trip to the Atlantic — as my brother and I shot down Japanese aircraft over the Pacific — Pete casually said, "There it goes," then returned to his post.

To this day, I don't know why it took so long for those words to register with my father, but sometime later, his eyes peered above his sunglasses and flashed in the rearview mirror.

"Peter, what did you mean a little while ago when you said 'there it goes'? There *what* goes?"

Without looking up, Pete responded, "The suitcases."

I would wager my inheritance that, at that moment, we witnessed the only time my father ever left rubber marks on an asphalt surface. The Chrysler had not come to a complete stop before Dad determined that his famous trucker's hitch knots had failed him.

With his pinched fedora cocked back on the crown of his head, aviator sunglasses pulled to the edge of his nose, and curved pipe hanging from the corner of his gaping mouth, Dad leaned against the tailgate of the Chrysler and stared west back down the highway. In a low, defeated voice, he asked, "Peter…think hard. How long has it been since you saw the luggage fly off the car?"

My brother didn't hesitate.

"Twenty minutes."

Yet one more cover image for *The Saturday Evening Post* etched indelibly in my memory: My father stands watch as Mike dashes in and out of traffic to retrieve clothing and pieces of luggage strewn over a quarter mile of Highway 9 in the Sandhills of South Carolina. In the background, two tail gunners sit in their turret, pointing and giggling.

Introduction

Turning Around

If I had to name my disability, I would call it an unwillingness to fall.

~ Barbara Brown Taylor, *Leaving Church*

God comes to you disguised as your life.

~ Paula D'Arcy

My office seems as good a place as any to begin. Though they have few listeners these days, the walls here are marvelous storytellers. If you were to visit our home, perhaps have dinner with Lori and me, at some point in the evening, I would find a way to place you in front of them.

"You know…I believe I have a copy of that book we talked about earlier," I might say. "Let's go have a look in my office."

My photo projects would probably speak to you first. I chose several of my favorite images, had them infused onto metal sheets, then hung them a few inches proud of the wall, so they appear to float. The most striking image is a distant shot of the Perito Moreno Glacier in Patagonia, partially framed by brilliant red, Argentinean spring foliage. Pete and I spent the better part of a week backpacking there. I would tell you all about the trip, even if you didn't ask.

Immediately beneath the glacier hangs a closeup of a footbridge that spans the boulders and rushing whitewater of a mountain stream. I captured this image while on a solo hiking trip in the Cascades; I call it *Bridge Over Troubled Water*.

I asked Lori for her advice when I began planning the project.

"Which of your pictures makes you happiest?" she wondered.

Easy: the altar in the chapel at Chateau de Chenonceau, outside of Tours, France. That image now hangs by my office door, so I pass it dozens of times a day. It still makes me smile, though I can't tell you exactly why.

Making your way around the room, you would discover the sort of items one might expect on a pastor's wall — certificates, crosses, and other religious symbols. Since the Doctorate in Preaching diploma is distinguished from all others by its large, handmade frame, you might assume it is most dear to me. You would be right.

On each side of the diploma hang gold-leaf icons of Jesus and Saint Paul, hand-painted by an orthodox priest in Greece. I could remove them from the wall and show you the signatures and wax seals on the back — *To Father Joseph*. The artist gave them to me with a kiss on the cheek.

Like most people, I spent the first half of life selecting luggage and then packing it. I arranged the contents carefully, just as my parents, professors, and pastors recommended. Academic achievements. A stunningly beautiful family. An honorable profession and successful career. I made the right decisions and, for the most part, avoided the wrong ones. My journey was charted and resolute — straight, smooth, and ever upward.

I was successful. The items on my office walls will tell you so. Every image, diploma, and symbol I have chosen to hang here has a common purpose — to show you the *me* I want you to see. These are the mountains I climbed, the degrees I earned, and the places I traveled. Here is evidence of my passions and achievements.

What these walls will *not* tell you is that something unexpected happened along the way. Life unraveled. One by one, my suitcases came unmoored. Marriage. Family. Vocation. Health. Everything I had so painstakingly packed took flight. I responded by doing what I knew how to do; I watched in the rearview mirror, winced, and just kept driving.

In the summer of 1969, my father turned around and left the shoulder of the highway to search for our belongings. Why not? Tread marks wash out of clothes, and tattered suitcases can be duct-taped or replaced. Besides, we were in the middle of an adventure that would make a great story one day.

Five decades later, my decision to turn around was not so simple. It would mean reawakening painful memories and grappling again with the large, unwieldy theological issues of suffering. Turning around would also signal to everyone watching that the debris scattered along the highway belonged to me and that I had not secured life as tightly as I should have. And in my line of work, there were always plenty of spectators.

Pastors are masters of image. We rarely survive for long in the fishbowl of ministry unless we learn which parts of our lives are display-worthy and which parts are best kept out of sight. There are images that we show no one, not even ourselves: unsuccessful adventures, relationships that failed, and dreams that remain unrealized. When it comes to our shortcomings, the world's advice is clear: Keep these storytellers stifled. And for heaven's sake, don't hang them on your walls.

Every weekend, members of my flock stood in long lines to shake my hand and tell me how much they appreciated the Norman Rockwell images of my youth. They would not be so eager to honor the vulnerability and self-disclosure necessary for this sort of truth-telling. The sheep become antsy when their shepherds share tales of personal failure or loss. We prefer our pastors' luggage to be well-anchored and free of duct tape.

So, I waited. And as time went by, the images in the rearview mirror became smaller and smaller until they eventually disappeared, at least from sight.

There are consequences for ignoring our suffering. Unresolved, unredeemed pain will eventually re-collect and embitter us. Until we find a sacred place for our wounds, we run the risk of transmitting our bitterness to those around us, most especially our loved ones. Moreover, we cannot transform pain that remains hidden, nor will we learn from suffering we do not confess.

It was for these reasons — and for others I cannot fully explain — that I finally abandoned the world's advice and made the transformative about-face. Eight years after removing my clerical collar and stepping away from traditional church ministry, I began a new journey.

Some refer to this turning as repentance. Others might say it marked the beginning of the second half of my spiritual life. While I am comfortable with both, I prefer to think of my turnaround as the moment I started repacking.

Suffering has much to teach us if only we will sit with our pain long enough to learn its lessons. Through this mosaic of stories, homilies, and reflections, I intend to share my journey with you, to ponder more deeply the insights and lessons that I learned along the way, and to encourage others who may be considering undertaking the journey themselves.

1

The Problem

Any discussion of the unfairness of suffering must begin with the fact that God is not pleased with the conditions of the planet either.

~ Philip Yancey, *Where Is God When It Hurts?*

We are always facing death. The time is urgent. For God's sake, talk to us. Does God love us? Show us how. Is there a good word from the Lord? Speak to us.

~ Thomas G. Long, *What Shall We Say?*

There is a God. God is all-powerful. God is all-loving. Innocent people suffer.

Most persons of faith can agree with each of these individual claims. The problem comes when we try to make the claims play nicely together. Theologians have historically defined this problem using various iterations of these statements.

If God is good and willing to prevent evil, but cannot, then God is not all-powerful.

If God is omnipotent but is unwilling to prevent evil, then God is malevolent.

If God is both omnipotent and willing to prevent evil, then how do we explain the ongoing presence of evil and suffering in the world?

Do you see the problem? For the statements to work, one of the four claims must be abandoned. Theologians refer to this quandary as the *theodicy problem*. Gottfried Leibniz, the French philosopher and mathematician, coined the term in 1710 by combining two Greek words, *theos* (God) and *dike* (justice). Theodicy initially sought to establish a defense for God in light of the existence of evil.

I am remarkably uncomfortable placing God on trial and am confident the Creator can prepare a defense without our assistance, as Job discovered. What *is* apt to be on trial these days is our faith in God. I have spent a career mounting *that* defense.

Most of my parishioners have no quarrel with (or interest in) lofty theological doctrines. They do, however, want assurance that their trust in God is not misplaced. Until we have an acceptable solution for the theodicy problem, each experience of suffering threatens to deliver us deeper into a place of crisis.

The older I get, the more I appreciate my father's accomplishments and eccentricities. After graduating from Brown University with a B.S. in chemistry, Milton Crowther spent his entire career in a research laboratory doing what he loved most — experimenting. I would proudly tell you more about Dad's work and the handful of patents that he has registered in his name if only I had the slightest idea how to interpret them.

Dad was a voracious reader and a veritable treasure trove of knowledge. If his hands weren't wrapped around a shotgun or fly rod, they were likely riffling through the latest *National Geographic*, newspaper, or some other piece of nonfiction. Bachelorhood gave my father forty-five years to exercise his passion for page-turning. By the time Louise Brown snagged him, Dad had acquired an IQ that measured somewhere north of 145. He got domesticated, and Mom got one heck of a Trivial Pursuit partner.

What Dad possessed in intellectual acuity, he lacked in coordination and dexterity. He occasionally worked up the gumption to join Pete and me in some athletic activity. We appreciated the effort, but the experiments were usually short-lived and involved a lot of awkward flailing about and ball-chasing.

Dad did not allow either of his left feet to keep him sidelined for long, however, nor did his lack of rhythm and pitch discourage him from boldly singing hymns at worship on Sunday mornings. His standard approach was to begin each verse one and a half beats ahead of the rest of the congregation, which would have been far less concerning had his preemptive solos been close to the correct pitch.

Dad unexplainably suffered from a different type of arrhythmia during Lent. For six long weeks, he sang each verse of the dirgeful hymns a little slower than the verse before. This caused my brothers and me to scribble on a worship bulletin one Sunday, "How many verses would a hymn need before Dad would never finish?"

Yet curiously, for all his challenges with coordination, Dad was an aerobic powerhouse. Until he turned seventy, my father could outwalk most men half his age, including me. Moreover, he handled a shotgun as if it were Excalibur. He was a left-handed crack shot with any weapon that had a barrel and a trigger. On several hunts, I watched Dad delay his shot just long enough for the flight patterns of two quail to cross. That way, he could drop two birds with a single pull of the trigger.

As children, Pete and I were interested in a different set of our father's attributes. He recovered lost baseballs more quickly than anyone we knew, asked stellar trivia questions during long car rides, and was willing to remove the especially squirmy fish from the hooks of our cane poles.

Our greatest fascination, however, was our father's ability to talk in his sleep. We theorized that he spent his slumber dream-inventing chemical formulas that would revolutionize life as we knew it. On the rare nights that our parents went to sleep before us, Pete and I grabbed the penlights, pencils, and notepads stashed in our nightstands, then sneaked into their bedroom and waited. Our mission was to capture our father's mutterings on paper. I still believe all our lives would be substantially different today had our preschool spelling skills been just a little more advanced and Dad's somniloquies a little less muddled.

Understanding our father wasn't necessarily any easier when he was awake. Nevertheless, we toted our notepads along on our visits to the laboratory. We were reporters in search of the next front-page scientific scoop.

"What is this purple solution over here?" "Hey, Dad. Tell us the longest chemical name that you know." "What are you working on now, Dad? Show us."

"You wouldn't be interested," he would tease.

"No! No! Tell us. Please. Come on, tell us."

"I'm developing a new process for manufacturing pentaerythritol tetra carbamate."

My brother and I would look at each other and swoon with clueless pride. "Cool!" The level of our astonishment was directly proportionate to the number of syllables Dad could pronounce without hesitating. We then moved on to more important matters, such as blowing glass swans and mixing up really smelly stuff.

All I truly know about my father's work is that red shirts maintain their redness, and bed sheets resist combustion because of his research with dyes and flame-retardant treatments of textiles. Ironically, Dad had no personal interest in clothing color…or clothing at all, for that matter. Mom was his self-appointed wardrobe manager and fashion advisor. On the days he left for work before she could conduct morning inspection, Dad was apt to return home in the evening wearing brown striped pants and a purple checked shirt.

"Milton! You didn't wear that all day!"

"Well, I didn't work any part of the day naked, Momma."

Dad's research may have been the only thing that spared his own wardrobe from incineration.

On at least one occasion, Dad did come home naked…sort of. As he told the story, during a lunch hour game of mad scientist ping pong, a bottle of toxic solution was knocked from the shelf and broke over Dad's shoulder. As his clothing began to smolder and dissolve, his coworkers whisked him quickly to the showers saving him from severe burns.

"It's an awkward feeling to have your husband show up at the door escorted by two of his snickering lab buddies and dressed in nothing but a lab coat," Mom said.

However, I think she preferred the flasher look over the brown pants and purple shirt ensemble.

Not all accidents at the lab were so harmless.

On the last day of summer in 1983, I was tooling around our farm when I heard a sudden, faint, percussive blast off in the distance. I assumed a jet had cracked the sound barrier overhead, or one of the local backyard mechanics had attempted to manufacture his own gasoline again and failed. But the sound set the dogs to yelping as if they knew something significant had happened and their master was involved.

A few moments later, Mom called frantically from the house, "Joseph! Come quick. There has been an explosion at your father's plant! I just heard it on the radio."

The blast took out the landlines at the lab, not that it mattered. Anyone who would have answered a call was busy sifting through rubble or helping manage the emergency. All we knew for sure was that something large and loud had taken place, and when something large and loud took place, Dad was usually involved, if not responsible.

In the pre-cellular, pre-internet world of the early eighties, we either waited for news to find us, or we went in search of it ourselves. I placed two calls. The first was to Mike, who worked in town at the time.

"See if you can get close enough to the scene to spot Dad."

The second call summoned Mom's best friend, Jane, who appeared within minutes, wrapped her arms around Mom, and led her on a walking vigil around the large gravel drive in front of the farmhouse. The two ladies circled and prayed, circled and prayed. When Mom trembled, Jane stopped and held her. After Mom calmed, they resumed the vigil.

I was not within earshot, but I could imagine their conversation. "Jane, if Milton is alive, he will be right in the middle of everything trying to help out. You know he will!"

"Louise, all we can do is pray. I am sure he's fine. Come, let's walk some more."

According to Saint Matthew, there was an explosion on the evening of Jesus' death. As soon as the Lord surrendered his final breath, the ground shook, rocks split, the Temple curtain ripped, and the graves of the saints opened. Everyone trembled. On Sunday morning, Mary Magdalene and the other Mary processed down the path to the tomb. As they walked and prayed, walked and prayed, the ground shook again. An angel of the Lord appeared and detonated Jesus' tomb. The blast frightened the guards to death…literally…and set the women to trembling once again.

I was twenty years and seventeen days old when Proctor Chemical Company exploded. It was the first time I had ever genuinely feared the death of a close loved one. My mother's father died eight years earlier, but Grandpa Brown had been so crippled by arthritis and racked with pain that those who loved him understood his passing as liberation. I had experienced no tragic or untimely deaths, no auto accidents or cancer or strokes, and certainly no explosions. The thought of losing Dad in any fashion was frightening. The prospect of his death resulting from such an event as this was unfathomable.

Using the railroad track to bypass the roadblocks and emergency personnel, Mike found Dad later that afternoon exactly where we predicted he would be — in the middle of the fray.

"It never occurred to me that anyone would be worried," he said, proving once again that IQ scores and common-sense quotients are not necessarily synchronized.

Dad created and calibrated small-scale chemical processes in test tubes and then translated his findings for large-scale production in ginormous kettle vats. He could spend years determining how best to keep blue threads blue so the company he worked for could help Levi Strauss keep America's blue jeans blue.

When a researcher muddles the process in the lab, glass shatters. If the same mistake is made during production, however, the consequence can be heard on our farm, six miles away. Someone failed to follow instructions or neglected to monitor pressure gauges or both. The resulting detonation sent one of the kettles rocketing skyward like the space shuttle. Seventeen people were injured. Astonishingly, no one was killed.

Our family huddled around the television that evening as Peter Jennings reported on *ABC World News Tonight*, "There was an explosion today at a chemical plant in Salisbury, North Carolina." Aerial camera footage revealed a tremendous scorched and cratered launchpad lying beneath the rubble that, earlier that morning, had been a building. The images set off yet one more round of trembling for my family. These tremors were the aftershocks of *what might have been*.

What if Dad had decided to check the status of the kettle at just the wrong moment? Or suppose the twenty-ton projectile had taken a different trajectory and crashed through the roof of his laboratory rather than landing in an empty field. Instead of watching television and fielding phone calls from reporters, we would have been receiving family and friends, each bearing casseroles and telling us what a good man my father was and how sorry they were for our loss.

Dad rarely displayed fear. He trembled privately, in his own ways. But his brusqueness with the reporters suggested he, too, was wrestling with what might have been.

"Listen!" he barked when he had finally heard enough. "I know you're looking for something you can use to sensationalize this story, but you're not getting it from me!"

But the story *was* sensational. And like the reporters, I also had a list of unanswered questions. How could a benevolent God allow this to happen? Was God preoccupied with another part of the universe when the explosion occurred? Was the Creator's power or will to prevent the tragedy somehow limited? What distinguished the wounded from the unscathed? Fate? Chance? What did the events of the day have to teach me about the heart of God?

The theodicy problem had become personal.

Pastors are drawn into the most painful moments of their parishioners' lives. I pray for patients as they are wheeled into surgery, mediate bitter family quarrels, and quietly bail offenders out of prison. I am the counselor who hears a couple speak "divorce" out loud for the first time, the initial call someone makes after receiving a cancer diagnosis, or the officiant who speaks the final words before a loved one is committed to the grave. And when those who are frightened, anxious, or lonely need to process their pain, they file into the pews, turn their attention toward the pulpit, and wait for God to do some explaining.

What are we to make of our suffering? Where can we place our pain? The need to understand our sorrow is as unavoidable as the experience of sorrow itself.

Some of my listeners have wrangled long and hard with their uncertainties. They are spiritually exhausted and stagger like boxers in the twelfth round of a badly mismatched fight. Others no longer look for answers, at least not from the pews. Sanctuary floors everywhere are covered with the towels of those who have given up the fight…if giving up the fight is possible.

But where are answers to be found if not in the realm of faith? Perhaps English writer Julian Barnes expresses the consternation of the weary when he begins his memoir, "I don't believe in God, but I miss Him."[1]

Explaining the presence of evil and unjust suffering has been every era's most vexing theological challenge. We have wrestled with the theodicy problem from the moment humankind first experienced pain and asked why — long enough to appreciate that solutions are hard to come by.

But those who suffer want more than simple solutions or pat answers

---

1 Julian Barnes, *Nothing to Be Frightened Of* (New York: Alfred A. Knopf, 2008), 3.

for their complex pain. They long for someone who honors their questions and understands their struggles, who has walked their valleys ahead of them and come out whole on the other side. They want to experience a God whose mercy is larger than their pain and whose grace will outlast their sorrow.

As we begin our journey together, it may be helpful for me to turn a few of my "faith cards" faceup on the table.

Faith Card #1: My primary allegiance is not to a set of rules, ethics, codes, or theologies; I follow a person.

Faith Card #2: To understand the heart, nature, and character of God, the best we can do is look to Jesus. He is the Image of God.[2]

Faith Card #3: God's plan for dealing with evil and suffering is expressed in Jesus' life and teachings.

Faith Card #4: Jesus' story is our story.

Faith Card #5: No one is immune to pain, not even God.

---

2 Colossians 1:15 NRSV. Unless otherwise noted, all scriptural references in this book are taken from the New Revised Standard Version of the Bible.

2

A God with Skinned Knees

This brief homily was given during a Christmas Eve service held at Kill Creek Barn in Desoto, Kansas.

In those days a decree went out from Emperor Augustus that all the world should be registered. This was the first registration and was taken while Quirinius was governor of Syria. All went to their towns to be registered. Joseph also went from the town of Nazareth in Galilee to Judea, to the city of David called Bethlehem, because he was descended from the house and family of David. He went to be registered with Mary, to whom he was engaged and who was expecting a child. While they were there, the time came for her to deliver her child. And she gave birth to her firstborn son and wrapped him in bands of cloth, and laid him in a manger because there was no place for them in the inn. (Luke 2:1-7)

If Saint Luke could have imagined the sort of airtime his Christmas story was going to receive, he may have told it a little differently.

Had the evangelist known that, even after two millennia, hundreds of millions of people all over the world would gather around candlelight every Christmas Eve and read his words, that his story would be acted out by shepherds in bathrobes and little angels in cutout cardboard wings, that Linus would borrow from his narrative to teach Charlie Brown and generations of *Peanuts* fans "what Christmas is all about," or that folks such as ourselves would worship in an out-of-the-way country barn just to experience his story more authentically, then surely Luke would have worked in a few more details.

Please don't mishear me. I am tremendously grateful for all Luke has given us. Were it not for the second chapter of his gospel, we would have no images of the Christ child lying in a manger. We would know nothing of the angels singing in the heavens above or their shepherd congregations quivering in the fields below. We could not sing "Silent Night," "The First Noel," or "Angels We Have Heard on High." Luke's story has shaped the way we understand and celebrate Christmas.

Still, I wish he had given us more.

Like any good storyteller, Luke provided the essential elements for his narrative but left out many of the details that listeners of his day would have assumed to be true. He did not mention, for example, that a good day's walk for a first-century Palestinian traveler was about twenty miles, but given Mary's advanced pregnancy and the hilly and treacherous terrain between Nazareth and Bethlehem, the holy couple probably only managed about half the typical pace. Their ninety-mile journey required at least ten days.

Luke also could have pointed out that Mary and Joseph's trip took place during the winter when the nighttime desert temperatures could be unbearably cold. And, since they traveled during a time of census, the roads and inns would have been unusually crowded, forcing the couple to endure more than a few long and sleepless nights exposed to the elements. The frozen Galilean ground can be terribly inhospitable, especially when sleeping for two.

Had Luke anticipated the way Italian artists of the Renaissance, or the Hallmark artists of our generation would interpret the story, he likely would have painted his own literary canvas more carefully. Dressing Mary in regal blue robes may sell Christmas cards, but someone of her lowly estate could not have afforded such luxury. Mary's maternity clothing was much simpler and more peasant-like. And don't place her on a donkey; Mary surely walked all two hundred thousand steps of her journey.

The details of a story become latch points for our senses. The more we see, hear, and feel what is happening in a story, the more powerful and relatable that story becomes for us. Why else would we drive out into the country to sit and shiver on hay bales in a simple, frigid barn? The experience helps us to connect with the Christmas story.

In the movie, *The Passion of the Christ*, Mel Gibson used his license as a director to provide details which he felt helped interpret Jesus' crucifixion. In one of the film's most poignant scenes, Gibson places Mary in the shadows of a Jerusalem alleyway where she watches Jesus carry his cross to the place of his execution. Jesus labors beneath the incredible weight of the crossbeam until he finally collapses in the street. As Mary runs to him, she flashes back in her memory to another place and time when, as a young boy, Jesus fell and skinned his knees. She remembers cradling her son and comforting him.

None of the gospel writers shared stories of the boy Jesus stumbling; they didn't need to. All children who run and play will inevitably fall. And when they do, mothers rush to care for them. That's just what mothers do.

We don't need Luke to remind us that stumbling children skin their knees, or that scrapes and scratches are painful. We know that empty stomachs grumble and unprotected bodies shiver in winter. We have all experienced pain, hunger, and cold.

But, until this night, our Lord had not.

Don't leave that statement too quickly.

The child lying in the feeding trough of a donkey is none other than the Author of all creation. He is the Word who, according to John, was "in the beginning with God. The Word was God." This infant helped fashion the stars and set the planets in their courses. But tonight, he lacks the power to care for or feed himself. This child helped speak each of us into being. But the most he can manage to produce on this night are a few coos and whimpers.

Tonight, God is cold. The Lord of the Universe is shivering. The Word has put on flesh.

Is there room in your imagination for a God with skinned knees?

My daughter, Lauren, recently shared with me that she had no photographs of her mother holding her. So, I set aside a week of evenings to rummage through old picture files in search of images I could use to make a collage for her thirty-first birthday.

The images I selected were quite dated — old prints from film and pictures of pictures that needed to be scanned and digitized. I found an old version of Photoshop, installed it on the laptop, and set to work enhancing the images' colors. I adjusted their vibrance, saturation, and hue levels. A fifteen-minute YouTube tutorial taught me to manipulate layers, erase scratches, and smooth out imperfections.

Rachael Lauren had barely entered the world before Carrie and I had her cradled in our arms. Those earliest pictures reminded me just how strenuous birth can be. Labor leaves its mark on everyone involved. But the blemishes and blotches on Lauren's tiny little cheeks were no match for the magic eraser tool.

In my favorite image of Lauren one of her beautiful newborn eyes was nearly shut. No problem. I simply made a copy of the open eye and transplanted it. Voila! Wink removed. I even softened Carrie's expression and dialed down the harshness of the delivery room lights.

If my pictures were your only exposure to the experience of childbirth, you might think labor was a delightful, painless process.

Over the years, we have made a similar project out of the images in Luke's story. Where the evangelist failed to provide details, we simply supplied our own.

To make the holy couple more comfortable on their journey — and to make ourselves more comfortable *about* their journey — we copied a donkey from someone else's photo and pasted it in the story for Mary to ride. We tidied up the maternity ward, removed the stench of the stable, and bent the wills of impertinent farm animals so every donkey, cow, and sheep bow in reverence before the infant.

Moments after delivering her first child, Mary kneels painlessly over the manger. Luke did not place her there; we did. Then we dragged and dropped Joseph immediately behind her. Both appear remarkably calm and collected for first-time parents. The child is perfect. The little Lord Jesus is clean and comfortable in the straw. He does not cry or whimper; that is what we sing each year.

Ultimately, we are left with a story that has no scratches, blemishes, or sharp edges. No skinned knees. The scene is flawless. We have photoshopped the authenticity right out of the nativity.

And that may be okay. If your life feels well-ordered and blessed now — if Christmas finds you without worry or grief or sadness or regret — then forgive me for suggesting an alternative version of the story you love.

But if your life is unsettled or a little messy, then finding your place in the photoshopped version of Luke's story may be challenging. If your Christmas doesn't seem to measure up to the Hallmark television specials or the perfect celebrations you watch through the picture windows of your neighbors' homes, then you're looking for Luke's original version of the story. You want details.

If you have the courage to delete at least some of the layers that history's imagination has added to the gospel, you will recover from both Luke and Matthew a story that is more relatable and human. You will read of a ruthless, jealous king who seeks to destroy this child. The angels may have brought tidings of peace and joy, but Herod brought bloodshed.

Delete a layer and you will see an oppressive government that is taxing the life out of the people of Palestine. Remove another layer and you will hear the whispers and gossip in Nazareth. Folks back home have not forgotten the scandal of this illegitimate pregnancy. Delete one more layer and now the faces of the holy couple show the terror and confusion that accompany first-time parenthood.

No passerby who peeked through the stable window on that first Christmas morning would have romanticized what they saw: A teenage maiden giving birth to a son she conceived out of wedlock; a group of no-account, lowly shepherds who, with tax collectors and dung sweepers, were at the bottom of the Palestinian social ladder; and, eventually, a clan of foreign astrologers who engaged in activities the Old Testament prophets found detestable. It would have been difficult for anyone in Jesus' day to imagine an odder or less-impressive congregation.

Yet these were the people God chose to witness the greatest moment in history. After centuries of waiting, the Messiah had finally been born. And while the gift tag on the manger may have read, "for all people," the only names on the invitations delivered that night belonged to a handful of people the world considered ordinary and unimportant and whose lives were unsettled and a little messy.

But no one in the congregation truly understood what took place in Bethlehem that night. The shepherds glorified and praised God for what they had seen and heard, but I imagine their hearts were still too aflutter with visions of angels to comprehend the significance of this child. Martin Luther claimed that of all the miracles of Christmas, the greatest was that Mary believed. She may have been obedient and faithful, but she did not fully understand. But then, neither do we.

But human understanding is not this night's goal. We are here simply to adore. The purpose of this night is for *God* to understand more deeply. The Eternal Word emptied himself of all glory and put on human flesh. For the first time, God understood our pain and trials.

So, don't fret if you haven't settled on a version of Luke's story or found your place within either. What's most important to remember this night is that God has seen fit to find a place in our stories.

On the evening before my father's funeral, our family decided to stray from the usual tradition of receiving guests at the funeral home. Instead, we arranged an area in the fellowship hall in Mom's church, next to the classroom where Dad taught adult Sunday School for decades. It was a beautiful evening. Folks came from all over the country to laugh and cry and celebrate Dad's life with us.

As the night grew late, Mom quietly stepped out of the receiving line and made her way through the sea of people to the other side of the room where she took a seat with friends. She wasn't tired; not at all. She simply needed to spend time in the widow's corner.

This was not an official church group. They wore no name tags. These sisters were bound to one another by the common pain of having lost a life partner. They were on the same journey; some were just a little further along the path than others. While everyone at church that night deeply cared about Mom's loss, these women also understood.

The child in the feeding trough may be newly born, but he has been around a while. Any emotion, difficulty, or pain that you are experiencing, he has experienced before you. On this night, God joined our little corners of the world. No one must explain to the Creator what pain feels like anymore. This child understands. Our God has skinned knees.

3

SIFTED LIKE WHEAT

> The great illusion of leadership is to think that man can be led out of the desert by someone who has never been there.
>
> ~ Henri Nouwen, *The Wounded Healer*

> Ah. I smiled. I'm not really here to keep you from freaking out. I'm here to be with you while you freak out, or grieve or laugh or suffer or sing. It is a ministry of presence. It is showing up with a loving heart.
>
> ~ Kate Braestrup, *Here If You Need Me*

It was early enough in January that Christmas lights still shone from one of the neighboring homes and glistened off the crusty snow, and late enough at night that most other houses in the cul-de-sac were dark and silent. Every few moments, the venetian blinds in the picture window next door separated and then closed. We were being watched.

A half hour earlier, I had been lounging in my pajamas in front of the fireplace at home, considering how fortunate I was not to be out on such a bitingly cold night. Now I stood at the end of a stranger's driveway huddled in a moonlight strategy session with two Overland Park, Kansas, police officers who I had known for all of fifteen seconds. I cupped my hands and blew into them to keep my fingers from numbing. For some reason, I thought that it made me appear confident and calm. I was neither.

"Watch yourself on the ice, Chaplain," the officer cautioned as we started up the drive.

None of us would have been there had it not been for the ice. The nineteen-year-old male who lived at this address would be sleeping in bed now instead of lying on the coroner's examining table had the day's snowmelt not refrozen. On the other side of town, a tow truck driver was unwrapping an automobile from a utility pole. Early reports from the scene indicated that the accident was not the result of recklessness or even carelessness; it was the ice.

The three of us stared at the doorbell as if *not* pushing it were an option. The little round button gave off the only light from the entire house, and we were about to put it out.

The first two rings produced no response. A part of me — a small, frightened, selfish part of me — hoped that the house remained still and that the officer in charge would say, "Well, gentlemen, we tried. Looks like we'll have to hand this job to the next crew."

But when the doorbell sounded the third time, the upstairs hallway light turned on. Then came the stairway lights, the foyer chandelier, and the sound of the deadbolts releasing. I loathed this moment. In the next ten seconds, we would meet someone for the first time and then share the news that would rip their heart out. The task was necessary...even sacred. But at that moment, I felt less like a chaplain and more like a nightmare delivery man.

When the door opened, we were greeted by the silhouette of a middle-aged woman still cinching the belt of her robe around her waist. As her face came into focus, I saw in her expression the sort of dread that anticipates something unforgettable is about to take place. She said nothing.

"Ma'am, we are very sorry to wake you at this hour. I am Officer Garver. This is my partner, Officer Simon, and this is Chaplain Crowther. Ma'am, I am afraid that there has been an accident." The woman's legs gave way, and she crumpled to the floor like a rag doll.

The victim was her son, who was home from college for his freshman Christmas break. He had ventured out earlier in the evening to see old high school friends.

"I went to bed early tonight," the mother sobbed. "I thought he was home. I couldn't understand why he wasn't answering the door."

The officers carried out their duties with empathy and decorum. There was an entire city in need of safekeeping and other doorbells to ring, so after they collected the information necessary for their reports and answered the mother's questions, they handed her care over to me.

"Chaplain Crowther will stay with you for a while if that's okay, Ma'am."

"Of course," she whispered.

I kept her company throughout the morning as others came and left. We placed phone calls and shared news of the tragedy with those who needed to know. But mostly, I just listened. As I prepared to leave, she asked for prayer and thanked me for everything I had done.

The sun was rising as I made my way down the drive. A voice called out after me, "Please be safe on the ice."

What do we say to people in times of tragedy? How can we speak to their pain? Ease their distress? Like the woman on that icy January night, the victims of suffering often thank me for everything I've done. But what did I do, exactly? The short answer is, I don't know. Ask the sufferer, "What did you need to hear in the midst of your grief?" and they will likely tell you the same; they do not know. So, how can we effectively help those who are hurting when we have no healing strategy and those who are in pain cannot direct us?

Jesus addressed our suffering by taking it upon himself. Instead of offering counsel from on high or sending prophets with a remedy for our condition, Jesus assumed our humanity and all the trials, pain, and heartache that come with it. The Lord of Creation became the servant who suffered. Jesus "bore our infirmities and carried our diseases, was wounded for our transgressions and crushed for our iniquities."[1] In the words of the renowned Dutch priest Henri Nouwen, Jesus became for us a *wounded healer*.

The disciples would not accept a wounded Jesus, however. There was no room in their imaginations for a messiah who suffered. So the Lord placed a gag order on the twelve. They were to reveal Jesus' identity to no one until after he had been raised from the dead.[2] The Lord would not permit the disciples to share a truth they did not yet understand.

In the same way, it is difficult for us to speak truth into the suffering of others until we understand that suffering. And, as God knows, the only way to understand suffering is to experience suffering.

Jesus told Peter, "Listen! You will be sifted like wheat."[3] Only after the sifting could Peter offer strength for his brothers. Spiritual guides can lead the sufferer into the wilderness only as far as they have traveled themselves. It is our scars that qualify us to sit with the wounded and our pain that prepares us to be with those who hurt.

"We need you, Pastor."

The voice on the phone was familiar. The dread in the voice was not.

"What's the matter, Dick?"

"It's Beth. We're at the hospital," he said.

Earlier that evening, with absolutely no warning, an artery in Beth's heart ruptured. She was alive when I arrived at the hospital, but only because

---

1 Isaiah 53:5
2 Matthew 17:9
3 Luke 22:31

of the mechanical heart that kept blood coursing through her body. There was no decision to make…except that there was a decision to make. The doctor needed authorization from the family to discontinue life support.

We prayed. Dick nodded his consent. Three days later, we celebrated Beth's resurrection.

I have been summoned to the front lines of suffering hundreds of times — to ICU waiting rooms, accident scenes, hospice homes, and police stations. Anyone who spends that much time in the foxhole learns how to survive under fire. I could develop a list of the *Dos and Don'ts for Ministering in Times of Crises*. I might even feel comfortable teaching a seminar on *Strategies for Attending to Those Who are Hurting*. But I cannot teach you how to be genuinely available to others' pain. The only instructor qualified to do that is pain itself.

When you visited my office at the beginning of our journey, you may have noticed the B.A. in Psychology diploma and assumed that anyone who has invested three years in studying the human psyche should know a thing or two about emotional distress. True enough. But helping assuage others' pain requires more than knowledge *about* suffering. A degree does not convey the capacity or authority to heal.

My professors where experts in modifying human behavior, counseling, and clinical work, but when it comes to crisis intervention, the most effective instruction comes from our own sifting. We help others by first attending to our journeys and sitting with our pain until it has surrendered its lessons. Only then can we begin to reach beyond the sufferer's head to touch their heart.

Most of us are empathetic to pain that is not our own. Empathy is the ability to accurately understand and psychologically identify with the feelings and experiences of others. Just as we can learn to drive a golf ball, repair a computer, or speak a foreign language, we can also learn to empathize. Empathy is a skill.

Compassion puts empathy into action. The word means *to suffer together*. If you have compassion for me, then you can feel and understand what it is like to walk in my shoes or live in my skin. Your joy is related to my joy. Your spirit will not be at peace while I suffer. Ultimately, if necessary, you will find a way to connect with my suffering and relieve it.

There are different schools of thought regarding the teachability of compassion. I believe that, as a virtue, compassion is conferred only through experience. I am empathetic towards soldiers, but I will not truly understand the horrors of war until I have stepped onto the battlefield beside them. I can take the hands of a husband and pray with him over the life of his wife or sit through the night with a grieving mother, and do so effectively, but my compassion will be incomplete until I have lost a dear loved one myself. Then, when I ring a doorbell in the middle of the night to deliver nightmarish news, the sickness that I will feel in my spirit will not come from nervousness but from my having *been there* before.

When the lights go out, we yearn for more than a teacher who knows our trials. We want a companion who has walked through the darkness before us, someone who has been sifted like wheat.

I cannot remember a time when I did not know who Jesus was. Before I could read the story for myself, others told it to me. My parents hoisted my brother and me onto their laps and explained the sea of letters underneath the Bible storybook pictures. On Sunday mornings, teachers helped me color the story. There were images of Zacchaeus in a sycamore tree, Noah herding pairs of hippopotami and giraffes onto the great ark, and Jesus multiplying the fish and loaves. While the preacher told his long Jesus stories to the adults, I listened to the images in the stained glass windows. I understood them better.

But something happened in my childhood that brought the biblical story to life. One fine spring day, God stepped out of the books and off the windowpanes and became part of *my* story.

The farm of my growing-up years was a veritable menagerie of birds and animals. It was also a magnet for stray creatures. Every spring and summer, Pete and I gave refuge to someone else's untagged, unwanted cats and dogs that somehow found their way onto our place. When I was five, one of the feline refugees disappeared for a while, then returned with a kindle of little refugees. I became particularly attached to a dark calico kitten with huge blue eyes. The two of us were inseparable.

When I noticed a sore on the kitten's stomach, I took her to Dad and, as was the case with most broken things, he fixed it. I assisted with surgery by handing the doctor whatever he requested — some alcohol, tweezers, and cotton swabs. After the short procedure, the patient was as good as new.

But several weeks later, it was Dad's turn to bring the kitten to me. "I'm sorry, Joe," he said. "Your kitten is dead."

Heidi, our rambunctious Weimaraner, had escaped her pen, captured the kitten, and brought it to Dad as a gift — at least that was his take. The kitten was still warm when I received her.

"I'll bury her," I said, fighting back tears.

What I wanted to say was, "Fix it!"

Pete and I had an agreement with Dad when it came to broken stuff: We handed him pieces and he gave them back whole. But on that day, I learned the meaning of *irreparable*. There was no backyard surgery for this condition. Death was final…or so I thought.

The following Sunday was Easter. The preacher's adult story that day was more interesting than usual. He spoke of something called resurrection. While his message did not make complete sense to me, from what I could determine, Jesus died. When we handed Jesus back to God, the Lord brought him to life again. As it turned out, death was fixable after all.

"This was how God loved us," the preacher said. At least, that was my take on it.

The Parable of the Birds was written in 1959 by Louis Cassels and popularized by Paul Harvey's regular Christmas retelling. The parable speaks of a kind, generous, mostly good man who could not believe the incarnation or buy into any theory that proposed God would become human. Accompanying his wife to Christmas Eve service seemed hypocritical, so he remained home.

Watching out the window that evening, the generous man spied a group of birds huddled together in the snow as they tried to stay warm in a sudden, unexpected storm. The man tried every way he knew to coax them into the safety of his barn, but the birds flew away, frightened of this strange, terrifying giant.

"If only I could be a bird," he thought to himself, "and mingle with them and speak their language. Then I could tell them not to be afraid. Then I could show them the way to the safe, warm barn. But I would have to be one of them so they could see, and hear, and understand."

At that moment, the church bells began pealing the glad tidings of Christmas. The man sank to his knees in the snow.

"Now I understand," he whispered. "Now I see why you had to do it."

4

Whispers & Storms

I think it would be well, and proper, and obedient, and pure, to grasp your one necessity and not let it go, to dangle from it limp wherever it takes you.

~ Annie Dillard, *Teaching a Stone to Talk*

"The wind doesn't scratch at doors...or whine to be let in."

~ Stephen King, *Cycle of the Werewolf*

Scripture offers two versions of Pentecost. In Luke's account, God's Spirit is noisy and raucous and sweeps like a mighty wind through Jerusalem and the house where the disciples have gathered.[1] Tongues of flame rest upon each person present and stir them to speak and understand strange languages. This spiritual outpouring is universal, touching someone from every nation under heaven. It even transcends time to include the Medes and Elamites, people who have been extinct for over five hundred years.

---

1 Acts 2

Amid this holy commotion and from this eclectic gathering, the church movement is born and given its first three thousand believers.

John's version, on the other hand, is so quiet and understated that a casual reader could easily pass over it unaware.[2] The Lord simply breathes upon a small, private gathering of his disciples and says, "What I've been doing…you continue to do that."

My call to ministry was delivered in Johannine fashion, so gently and unobtrusively that I almost missed it. No blinding lights. No pyrotechnics or angelic visitors. No exclamation points. Jesus did not rescue me from a life of crime or drugs or prison. No Hollywood producers phoned for the movie rights.

God summoned me with a whisper.

People who do not perceive God's call seem fascinated by the notion that others do. "How did you know?" they ask. "What made you decide to become a pastor?"

These inquirers are usually searching for a story that I cannot share. If God's call to ministry can ever be pedestrian, then mine was. Using children's sermons that I do not recall, Sunday school classes that I protested attending, youth group conversations, and pastors who took time to care, the Holy Spirit slowly prepared my heart for just the right time. All I needed was a nudge. Angels would have been overkill.

Through the years, I have resisted the temptation to either embellish or apologize for my version of the story. God comes calling when, where, and in the manner that God chooses. But folks are generally underwhelmed by whispers. There is a reason we remember Luke's version of Pentecost; we much prefer storms.

I, too, appreciate the call stories of colleagues whose souls were captured by a more animated Spirit. On July 2, 1505, Martin Luther was nearly struck by lightning while traveling from Erfurt to his home in Mansfeld in central Germany. Convinced that God had opened the heavens to take his life, Luther clung to a rock for safety and cried out, "Help me, Saint Anne, and I will become a monk." Brother Martin survived the storm

---

2 John 20:22

and kept his vows. A few days later, he traded his law books for a monk's tunic and changed the course of world religious history.

Luther believed that bolt of lightning was God's recruitment agent. I am skeptical. The Lord rarely lets a good tempest go to waste but whipping up a storm to bend our wills does not sync with my understanding of the heart, nature, or character of God.

I want to know more about Jesus' call story. How did he know it was time to lay aside his lathe and join the preaching, teaching, and healing circuit? None of the gospel writers tell us. The Lord just showed up knee-deep in the Jordan one day requesting baptism from his cousin John. Did he hear God's voice? Did God whisper or shout? Was there a holy and unmistakable tug at Jesus' heart? Was the carpentry business languishing? We are left to speculate.

I suspect the Spirit had been trying to capture my attention for some time before I finally answered. Even then, the voice was inaudible. Had you been there, you would have heard nothing. The whisper was more of a sensation than a sound, delivered over a season rather than in a moment.

The season was my first freshman semester at North Carolina State University. I landed in the School of Engineering mostly by default. "With your proficiency in math, Joseph, this is where you need to be." Aptitude test scores and the career guidance counselors agreed. But as I stumbled through my classes, unmotivated and unimpassioned, I began to pay attention to the guidance of another Counselor.

So, during Christmas break, I gave away my gently used science calculator and drafting equipment and applied to Catawba College, a small United Church of Christ liberal arts school in my hometown of Salisbury, North Carolina. By the second week in January, I had learned my way around the psychology department — all four rooms of it.

My folks rightly pointed out that, had I decided for ministry a few months earlier, there would have been a scholarship at Catawba with my name on it.

"Talk to God," I defended. "I didn't place the call. I just picked up the phone."

Martin Luther told clergy that the call to ministry is not based on merit but on election by a God who is a sucker for "sinners, evil persons, fools and weaklings."[3] Brother Martin was a colorful character. He was also spot-on.

When you consider God's penchant for tapping unlikely servants on the shoulder and pressing them into service, despite their deficiencies — stutterers who became prophets, a century-old man who fathered a nation, a persecutor of Christians who was struck blind and then converted into the greatest evangelist in history, and an unwed pregnant teenager who birthed the Messiah, to name a few of the more prominent examples — whispering into the heart of a frustrated and dispassionate engineering student and redirecting him into ministry so he might set the world on fire for the Gospel falls right in the Spirit's wheelhouse.

The lives of sinners, evil persons, fools, and weaklings become considerably more complicated after God shows up. There is evidence for this on nearly every page of Scripture, yet somehow, I missed it. Maybe I was absent from Sunday school the morning we discussed the prophets. The Old Testament seers clearly understood the consequences of saying "yes" to God. They bucked, pushed back, argued, even chartered transportation in the opposite direction when the Lord came calling. But God pursues what God wants, so in the end, saying "no" only further complicates life. Ask Jonah.

I embraced this new life path far more willingly and indiscriminately than Moses, Jeremiah, or Jonah. The Lord and I never argued, bargained, or talked about the fine print (or the large print, for that matter). Perhaps I should have asked more questions.

Dietrich Bonhoeffer, Lutheran theologian and World War II anti-Nazi dissident, said, "When Christ calls a man, He bids him come and die."

Daniel Berrigan, a renowned Jesuit priest and activist, added, "If you are going to follow Jesus, you better look good on wood."

---

3   Thesis 28 of Luther's Heidelberg Disputation

I was barely eighteen years old when the Spirit's whisper found me. What did I know about self-sacrifice? My impressions of pastoral ministry had been formed from the vantage point of my family's fourth-row pew in the congregation of my youth and had more to do with potluck lunches and directing Christmas pageants than picking up a cross and falling in line behind Jesus. My *yes* may have been mostly unexamined, perhaps even misinformed, but it was *yes*, nonetheless. My journey was underway.

One's pace quickens when life finds purpose. I immediately fast-tracked my education. For the next two and a half years, I delved into the study of the human psyche, researched what modifies and motivates behavior, ran biofeedback labs, served as an assistant to the head of the Religion Department, coerced a professor into learning Koine Greek with me, and prayed about which seminary (or as my psychology professors liked to call it, "angel factory") I would attend.

Some people refer to their undergraduate studies as a *career*. My experience was more of a frenetic blur. When I emerged from the whirlwind in the spring of 1984, Catawba handed me what I had come to collect — a B.A. in Psychology with a minor in Religion and Philosophy. I thanked my professors, stuffed the ticket to seminary in my back pocket, packed my bags, and had one foot out the door on my way to the angel factory when my pastor tackled me from behind.

"What's your big hurry, Joe?" Chris asked.

Everyone should have in their constellation of relationships at least one person who can help interpret God's call upon our lives, someone whose counsel can be trusted. During my undergraduate blur, Rev. Chris Heavner was that person for me.

"You're only twenty years old. Have you thought about delaying seminary for a year or two? The ministry isn't going anywhere. Travel. Go somewhere exciting and get your hands dirty doing volunteer ministry. I'll get you hooked up. Slow down for a while."

"Don't you think I'm ready for seminary?" I asked.

"I think you need to grow up a little."

Had anyone else delivered that message, I would have dismissed it out of hand and continued on my way. But it was Chris's counsel and friendship that had helped encourage me onto this path. He may have been the *only* person with the authority to hold up the pit stop sign. Besides, in my spirit, I knew he was right.

I unpacked my bags and agreed to ease off the accelerator for twelve months. During the evenings, I worked at a power company in town and dated Carrie, an adorable, way-out-of-my-league girl from the other side of the county. During the days, I played golf and, to stave off academic withdrawal, took a few classes at Catawba. And along the way, I managed to grow up a little.

Finally, in the stifling heat of the summer of 1985, I dropped my luggage on the dorm room floor of the Lutheran Theological Southern Seminary in Columbia, South Carolina. The sound reverberated through the empty hallways like a cannon. Either I was the first student to arrive for the term, or the rest of the class had taken Jonah's lead and opted for a resort in the South of Spain instead of the required summer crash course in New Testament Greek.

I surveyed my stark new institutional home and considered the *could haves*. I could have been arranging the furniture in my first house, growing a bank account, or planning a wedding. I could have been starting a family. Instead, I was starting over. Ahead of me were four more years of study and the prospect of a godly career that promised ungodly long hours in exchange for a nominal wage. Had I chosen well? Had God?

I introduced myself to the lonely room and asked the empty walls if those who had slept here before me shared the same misgivings and doubts on their first days. Had God made the offer, I may have traded my inheritance at that moment for another confirming whisper. A little holy commotion would have been even better. I closed my eyes and tried to envisage what lay ahead but thought only of Carrie.

It was impossible to imagine how the next four years would unfold. Carrie and I were married that October. Overnight, my seminary experience became *our* experience. We necessarily developed extraordinary packing skills as we loaded and unloaded our world seven times in four years — Columbia, South Carolina (twice), Gettysburg, Pennsylvania (thrice), Canton, Michigan, and Allen, Texas.

Each successive move required a slightly larger truck, mostly due to our slightly larger family. Joseph Grant and Rachael Lauren were born two years and twelve hundred miles apart in South Carolina and Texas. Following my first year of study, we transferred to the Lutheran Theological Seminary at Gettysburg, Pennsylvania, to experience a different culture, and because life apparently wasn't hectic enough.

Carrie organized and directed a childcare cooperative program for the school while I took classes on campus and at the theological consortium in Washington, D.C. When my nose was not buried in a book, our family became explorers. We scouted the Amish country and the Smithsonian, searched for covered bridges, and picnicked among the apple orchards of Adams County.

I spent Saturday mornings on my bike chasing down the double-decker tour buses as they roamed the battlefields, and on Sundays, I preached in the little two- and three-point parishes tucked away in the hills just north and south of the Mason-Dixon line. During the winter months, I offered my preaching to the local ski resort in exchange for a chaplain's winter jacket and lift pass. Each Sunday morning, I skied down to the little chapel on the side of the mountain where I stoked a fire and waited for no one to show for worship, then spent the rest of the day on the slopes.

Our lives were blessed not only with new places and experiences but also by a widening circle of relationships. Carrie was primarily responsible. Her beauty and Southern sweetness — the way she melodically drawled one-syllable words into two syllables, and occasionally three — collected everyone's attention as soon as she entered a room. When the administration needed a picture of the model student family for the school catalog, it was Carrie's magnetism that attracted the photographer to our door. In the photograph, I am leaning over the apartment counter to hand a baby bottle to Carrie as Grant sits patiently on her lap. We are all smiling, of course, because we are successfully managing family amid the seminary experience.

But we had not come to Gettysburg to chase tour buses or pose for catalogs. The primary goal of the angel factory was to prepare students for leadership in the parish. In those days, that meant four years of academics and spiritual introspection. Students spent their time either in the library, in front of a mirror, or under a microscope. Classes, chaplaincies, internships, psychological testing, and review boards were designed so that students would examine, reexamine, and test their sense of call. The result? Seminary cranked out a lot of cerebral pastors who were prone to spiritual navel-gazing.

The transition from student to pastor was sudden and harsh. In the parish, nothing is about the pastor. Clergy are servants, professional foot washers who preach, pray, and care for others. To make the transition even more challenging, each week the congregation hands the pastor a microphone, turns on the spotlight, and then lines up after worship to tell you what a fine job you're doing. Some clergy never manage the about-face. It took me entirely too many years.

I knew far more for sure about God in the spring of 1989 than I do today. That self-assurance, misplaced as it was, may have served me well as I sat before the final candidacy review board for ordination approval. Thankfully, the same Spirit who whispered me into this calling also graciously preserved me as I collected my bearings. Given my self-absorption as a student, the Spirit's hands were full.

Following all the necessary hoop-jumping and graduation, I accepted my first call to St. Luke Lutheran Church, a large rural congregation in the farming community of Bear Poplar, North Carolina. The township was originally known as Forty-Four, as it was forty-four miles from the town square (a location I never actually located) north to Winston-Salem and south to Charlotte.

During my first visit to the post office (the only building I recall in town), Patti the Postmaster informed me, "Now long about the time our forefathers was signin' the Constitution, ole Thomas Crown and his wife were walkin' about a mile from here one day when they spotted themselves an ole bear up in a poplar tree. That's how come we're known as

Bear Poplar."

It was good to be home.

Folks around those parts had a saying to describe what happened when a preacher stirred up a congregation and sent worshipers' spirits soaring.

"A storm done been preached up!"

I understood the image, but I was Lutheran. Those types of storms were not typically part of our tribal experience. When it came to worship, Lutherans generally took their cue from John, not Luke. We were whisperers. But on August 6, 1989, it felt as if anything might be possible. It was the day of my ordination.

The beautiful sanctuary at St. Luke was standing room only on that stormy afternoon. As the congregation sang the first hymn, "Praise to the Lord, the Almighty, the King of Creation," *CRACK!* God supplied the opening salvo of thunder right on cue. By the time the bishop stepped into that creaky old mahogany pulpit, the storm was on top of us, rattling the stained-glass windows.

Bishop Michael C. D. McDaniel tapped his notes into a neat stack, switched on the pulpit light, and surveyed the congregation. After an interminable pause, he eventually smiled, cleared his throat, and began with these words: "It is an amazing thing to me, Joseph, that God calls people like you to the ministry." *CRACK!* His timing was impeccable. His words…unsettling.

The thunder is my last recollection from that ordination message. By the time I recovered from the shock of Bishop Michael's opener, the sermon was pretty much over.

I manufactured an alternate version, which I much prefer. In it, the good bishop reshuffled his notes and discovered that he was working from the wrong manuscript (as happened to me a few months later in that same pulpit). He then spoke convincingly about my unwavering commitment to the Gospel, listed the rest of my inexhaustible gifts for ministry (beginning with humility), and wrapped things up by assuring my new flock of their good fortune to receive such a shepherd as I.

Following worship and the reception, Carrie, Grant, Lauren, and I crossed the steamy parking lot and collapsed in exhaustion on our new home's wrap-around porch. It had been a good day. It had been a good four years. My folks sat with the children on the porch swing and helped them count the cows in the field across the highway.

We all waved as the last parishioners pulled out of the parking lot. A gentle breeze drifted through the porch. John's Pentecost had finally decided to make an appearance. We breathed deeply.

There was dinner to plan, a parishioner in the hospital awaiting a visit from her new pastor, and a few random to-do tasks jotted on a scrap piece of the bulletin and stuffed in my pocket.

"Well…what's next?" I asked.

Without hesitating, Carrie responded, "Throw away the moving boxes."

5

THE SOUND OF THE GUN

I believe God made me for a purpose, but he also made me fast.
And when I run I feel His pleasure."

~ Eric Liddell, *Chariots of Fire*

Once a seminary student asked to shadow me for two days
to see what my life as a pastor was like. At the end, he said,
"Oh my gosh, you're basically a person for a living.

~ Nadia Bolz-Weber, *Pastrix: The Cranky, Beautiful Faith of a Sinner & Saint*

Runners, to your mark. Set…

My coach called it "the moment of truth," when a runner discovers if all the hard work has paid off. The months of training, the diet, the research, the after-school practice sessions which coaches monitored, and the extra weekend miles that no one knew about but me were evaluated at the start/finish line of the 3200-meter race. The runners leaned forward, elbowed one another, and jockeyed for position as if the six inches we gained by doing so would make the difference in the outcome of the next two miles of competition.

Then, the field became transfixed. We were hyper-focused on one thing — the sound of the gun. It signaled the end of training and the beginning of the race.

The gun changed everything.

Somewhere amid the thunder of ordination, life shifted. Time got recalibrated. All that took place prior to August 6, 1989, was *before ordination*. Anything that occurred later was *after becoming a pastor*.

Before ordination, I spent Sunday mornings bouncing like a pinball between the tiny churches of southern Pennsylvania and northern Maryland. If I planned well, knew exactly where I was headed, and didn't get too long-winded, I could manage three pulpits in a single morning. The cheap labor helped keep the doors of these struggling congregations open and allowed me to stretch my homiletical wings and experiment in ways our preaching professors might not have appreciated.

More importantly, Sunday mornings fueled my imagination. I stood tall enough in those little pulpits to see the future. I was someone's pastor. Even if only for a few hours, those borrowed congregations belonged to me.

Then, the gun sounded.

It was the moment of truth. The bishop placed that red stole around my shoulders and everything I had imagined became real. It was as if someone flipped a switch, and all the people I dreamed of serving suddenly appeared. Would the previous seven years of training pay off? Was I ready?

Ordination changed everything.

Unless they have been removed by the parishioners I offended through the years, my portraits hang in the Lutheran Rogues Galleries of Saint Luke in Bear Poplar, North Carolina, Saint Paul in Roanoke, Virginia, King of Glory in North Myrtle Beach, South Carolina, and Atonement in Overland Park, Kansas. My hair is light brown, and my eyebrows are nearly undetectable, so if dark mustaches or other alterations appear on any of these portraits, they were added after my departure. Please do me a favor and clean them off.

Like the pictures that hang upon my office walls, each of these congregational galleries has a story to tell. Any accounting of their histories would be incomplete without my picture and story. I must make room in my story for each of them as well.

The first stop on the call committee-conducted tour of Saint Luke's building was on the steps leading up to the front entrance. I had seen enough. There is much that you can determine about a congregation simply by looking at its doors. The raised light oak panels were striking and ornate, hand-carved by a woodworking artist in some exotic place, like California. But the doors' most remarkable feature was what they *lacked* — locks.

As much as I appreciated the symbolism of the lockless entry, the doors presented a problem when the next storm blew through Bear Poplar a few months later. Unlike the ordination day squall, this tempest had a name. Hugo was a Category 2 hurricane when it reached our little community in the early morning hours of September 22, 1989, two hundred miles from its point of landfall in South Carolina. Not only did the one hundred-plus mile-per-hour winds topple trees and propel acorns like musket balls through the old stained-glass windows, but they also caused the front doors to flutter like angel wings. By the time I fought my way to the church to lash their handles together, one of the wings had already ripped from its hinges.

The wind was still howling when members began gathering at the church. Before inspecting their fields or starting repairs on the roofs of their own homes, the farmers huddled in the parking lot, shook their heads, and began planning the cleanup.

What front doors do not reveal about a congregation, a good crisis will — especially when that crisis belongs to someone else.

When our farmers received word of a severe drought in Indiana, they not only ushered a hay collection initiative to help their colleagues in the Midwest, but they also loaded a relief caravan and delivered the offering personally.

"It's just what Christians do," they said.

Each fall, the bounty in Bear Poplar flowed in the other direction. Saint Luke identified a worthy in-house project, prepared a tremendous banquet, decorated the tables, and set out the collection baskets. The fellowship hall was standing room only as the members feasted, prayed, and gave their gifts. They called it *Ingathering*.

"It's just what Christians do," they said.

During our second Easter season together, I proposed to leadership that Saint Luke celebrate a *Blessing of the Fields* service. If ever there were a congregation that would honor prayers for the crops, it was Saint Luke.

The body language of the council suggested a slight miscalculation on my part, however. When Bear Poplar men remove their hats and begin scratching the backs of their heads, and the women raise their eyebrows and cut sideways glances at one another, then more explaining is clearly in order.

"Just pick a farm," I suggested. "We'll have a picnic following worship and then pray over the fields. How about your place, Buddy?"

Typically a *yes* person, Buddy seemed uncharacteristically uncomfortable with the idea.

"I don't know, Pastor," he stammered. "Last summer, you blessed our softball team, and we didn't do so good."

Johnny and Karen Moore stepped forward and offered their yard for the picnic and their fields for the blessing. That season, the Moore farm produced more abundantly than any other in the western part of the county. The following Lent, even the Presbyterian farmers lined up to volunteer as hosts.

The people of Saint Luke were simple, loving folks who appreciated a pastor who mirrored their character. "Love on us. Feed us when we show up. Check on us when we don't. And be on call when we need you." The unspoken directive was, "Don't fix anything that isn't broken. In fact, don't even tinker with it."

The short time we spent among these generous folks was filled with *firsts*. Grant began preschool and experienced his first love affair. Carrie eased into her first spotlighted role as pastor's spouse and did so with extraordinary grace. Lauren took her first steps. And, for the first time in our marriage, both sets of grandparents were close enough to experience our firsts.

The simplicity wore well for a few years. But as soon as my ministry teeth were sufficiently cut, my spirit became predictably antsy and longed for more tinkering.

I have a list of *ministry regrets*. The first entry: "Leaving Saint Luke too soon."

I kept my fidgety ambitions at bay those first years by studying. Once a week I commuted two hours north to Roanoke College in Salem, Virginia. One of the students in the Master of Theology course was Rev. James Mauney, assistant to the bishop of the Virginia Synod.

"Any ministry opportunities in your synod, Jim?" I asked in passing one week.

"I'll check," he promised.

Several days later, a handwritten, two-sentence note arrived in the mail from Bishop Richard Bansemer. "Lunch on Tuesday. Come hungry."

Saint Paul in Roanoke was an older, smaller congregation with a tumultuous past. Most pastors swear that calamities show up in threes. "When you experience a death in your congregation, you might as well clear your calendar because two more are around the corner."

A great Roanoke Valley flood delivered Saint Paul's first potential death punch in 1985.

The building had barely dried out before the next attempt on that congregation's life. An arsonist broke into the pastor's office at night, placed a stack of folders on the cleric's desk, and set it ablaze.

"There were twenty-eight of us meeting in a borrowed space in those days, and twenty-five of us were women," one of the members recalled. "We took a vote on whether to continue as a congregation. The vote passed, but only because of our sheer stubbornness."

A failed merger attempt with two small area congregations would have been Saint Paul's death knell had it not been for the miraculous procurement of a mortgage. The obstinate, faithful band of believers used the funds to construct a new building at the mouth of a large residential community. Most importantly, the building was on high ground. The facility served them well, but the mortgage immediately become a massive albatross around the congregation's neck.

"Saint Paul must grow, or it will die." That was the gist of my lunch conversation with the bishop, and precisely the challenge I was looking for.

According to the welcome signs and bumper stickers, "Virginia is for Lovers." It certainly offered Carrie and me a place to explore our passions. She spent mornings teaching at a nearby Lutheran preschool and evenings volunteering as a cardiac technician for the local First Responder unit. The Appalachian Trail, Blue Ridge Parkway, and the plethora of lakes and mountain biking venues made our new home a hiker and biker mecca. The southern Shenandoah Valley became our family's playground and wonderland.

Of all the places that I have called *home*, Roanoke fit our family most comfortably. Our *list of firsts* expanded with our first new home purchase and our first-time status as suburbanites. Grant and Lauren experienced their first school bus rides. They each had playmates who were actually within walking distance of our home.

Mention "Saint Paul Lutheran" in an exercise of free association, and I instantly will rattle off the names of twenty members before listing a single ministry or congregational trait. I remember the church as a collection of personalities.

Take John Stafford, for example. John was a young adult who had been attending Saint Paul for several years when he approached me about baptism.

"It would mean a lot to me, Pastor, if we could do this service a little differently. I'd really like the baptism to take place outside."

"Like in the parking lot, John?"

"Like in a mountain creek," he said.

"You do realize it's winter?"

"Not a problem. I made a commitment to read the entire Bible before being baptized and it will be spring before I'm ready."

It was obvious that getting John to take his faith seriously was going to be an issue!

A few months later, just after Easter, the choir led the congregation out of worship one Sunday and just kept going. We gathered again on the backside of the mountain and at the far end of a flowery meadow where John and I waded into the icy waters of Catawba Creek. The choir sang, and I delivered God's promises through a shivery liturgy as John courageously knelt and received his inheritance.

Saint Paul presented its share of challenges. For the first time in my ministry, I heard members of the same congregational family refer to one another as "they" and "them." I was their pastor one moment and a referee the next.

Given enough time, the sheep inevitably tussle. A little righteous sparring over a gospel issue can be healthy. I welcome congregational free-for-alls over matters of social injustice or theological interpretation. But congregational wrangling is much more apt to take place over the color of the walls in the women's restroom or the version of the Lord's Prayer that was used the previous Sunday.

Yet the little congregation persevered through their trials, kept pace with the mortgage, became self-supporting, and divorced themselves of all financial assistance from the wider Lutheran church. The worship attendance doubled over five years, and the little church became *not quite so little*.

In January of 1996, during one of our regular phone visits, Mom mentioned, "I heard from an old friend today. Ruth called from the beach and said that their church was having a tough time finding the right pastor. She asked me, 'Isn't your son a preacher?' I told her that you were, but that you were very happy where you were."

"Mom!"

That was all the encouragement the phone chain needed. The following day, Dick, the chairman of the call committee from King of Glory, North Myrtle Beach, South Carolina, called to invite me into a courtship. Several weeks later, Carrie and I stole away to the shore for our first date. The experience was underwhelming.

At breakfast the following week, I shared with my colleagues a litany of reasons for not pursuing the call. "There was little energy in worship. I saw almost no one under the age of sixty. The congregation was…"

True friends know when to interrupt a pointless rant session.

"Joe! You set yourself up. If your experience had been positive, the church wouldn't need you."

We pulled into King of Glory's parking lot in the summer of 1996 and unloaded our suitcases at a parsonage we agreed to live in sight unseen. This was the first move that Grant and Lauren made under protest. Not even the prospect of living next to the ocean was enough to entice our children away from their friends. But the sea has its way. The separation wounds that appeared fatal in July healed by August. If you ask Grant and Lauren today, "Where is 'home?'" they will respond, "We are from the beach."

The beach they refer to is the Grand Strand, a sixty-mile arc of especially expansive shoreline along the northern South Carolina coast. Myrtle Beach, the heart and commercial center of the Strand, is the annual destination for over fifteen million sunbathers, surfers, and golfers.

But it took more than sun and sand to lure me away from my beloved Shenandoah Valley. King of Glory was poised for explosive growth, and to ignite the evangelical fuse, all the congregation needed to do was leverage its three greatest ministry assets: location, location, and location.

With a sand wedge and a smooth swing, I could loft a golf ball from the church yard onto the playground of North Myrtle Beach's only elementary school. For nine months beginning each Labor Day, the building was occupied by over three hundred students who, like all children, wanted nothing more than to be fussed over and loved. Within earshot of the school bell, God planted a congregation of retirees, many of whom spent their days searching for something to do and longing for their grandchildren back home. It didn't take a prophet to imagine the possibilities.

When the bell rang at the end of each school day, a group of rowdy, rambunctious children found Carrie waiting at the end of the sidewalk, ready to shepherd them across the street to the church fellowship hall where, for the next several hours, they played games and worked on their school assignments with rotating teams of surrogate grandparents.

"You have no idea how wonderful it is not to fight over homework at night," parents reported. "This program has allowed us to just be family."

Location.

Turning south away from the school, I could cup my hands behind my ears and pick up the roar of the ocean waves. Six blocks down Eleventh Avenue was one of the widest and most beautiful beaches in South Carolina, a shoreline which was still lined by sea oats and sand dunes, unmarred by high-rise condominiums and the commercial sprawl of the Strand. It didn't take an innovator to imagine the possibilities.

The plan for King of Glory's first-ever Easter sunrise service on the beach was simple. Worshipers were to meet at church forty-five minutes before dawn to form a procession to the beach where a table was waiting with bread and wine. I printed sixty bulletins and ordered a box of small penlight keychains to be inscribed with the church name. When the keychains arrived, "Luthurn" was missing several vowels and the lights shone a useless red; otherwise, they were perfect. I handed out the final bulletin and began reading Psalms as our march set out toward the sea.

Ten minutes later, we crested the dunes and experienced our first Easter surprise. Through the waving sea oats and the early morning darkness, I made out the silhouettes of several hundred people encircling the makeshift altar. In my planning notes for the following year, I wrote "Print more bulletins. Prepare more bread. Nix the procession."

Location.

For nearly six years, King of Glory was the fastest-growing Lutheran congregation in South Carolina. The Easter sunrise service swelled to over six hundred. Weekly worship attendance and preschool enrollment maxed out the facilities' capacities. The choir overflowed the loft and spilled out into the congregation. The church called its first associate pastor, started a third-weekend worship service on Saturday evening, and commandeered the vacated parsonage for a makeshift preschool classroom. We spent much of our time resolving all the best kinds of problems and looking for ways to relieve our growing pains.

The leadership considered launching a satellite congregation, but the land was too costly. We gladly would have purchased adjacent land for expansion, but none of the neighbors were selling. As the prophets and innovators scratched their heads trying to imagine a way forward, the phone began to ring with courtship invitations from other congregations around the country. Eventually, I began to listen.

Jeff Hutchinson was a consummate high school distance runner in my day. He set North Carolina state track records that have remained unbroken for over forty years. I would describe Jeff in more detail, but I rarely saw him from the front.

There were two occasions at each meet that Jeff and I shared the same space. The first was at the start line of the 3200-meter races. There, in the *moment of truth*, he offered advice to racer wannabes, like me.

"Watch," he said. "The entire field will bolt off the line like the end of the race is at the first turn. Don't do that! Pace yourselves."

None of us listened.

At the sound of the gun, I left the ministry start line as if shot from a cannon. For a quarter-century after becoming a pastor, I ran an impressive, successful race and had no intention of restraining my pace.

But there are inevitable consequences for such hyper-focused, undisciplined running. Racers *hit the wall*. Ministers *burn out*. Regardless of how well we have trained, there is danger in running so fast for so long; we eventually forget why we started running in the first place.

"Hutch" and I were together again briefly in what I called the *second moment of truth*, that blurred instant late in the race when Jeff lapped me on his way to yet another victory.

6

THE GIFT OF SUFFERING

To be grateful for an unanswered prayer, to give thanks in
a state of interior desolation, to trust in the love of God in the face of
the marvels, cruel circumstances, obscenities, and commonplaces of life
is to whisper a doxology in darkness.

~ Brennan Manning, *Ruthless Trust*

…happiness is itself poisoned if the measure of suffering has not been fulfilled.

~ Carl Jung

I awoke in the wee hours of the morning curled in the fetal position and writhing in pain. Ninety minutes later, I was tethered to an IV bag as the emergency room nurse administered an injection of narcotics to a patient who does not take narcotics.

"On a scale of one to ten, how would you currently rate your discomfort?" she asked.

"Somewhere between 'intolerable' and 'excruciating,'" I responded and then asked for a bullet to bite.

I had experienced on-again, off-again discomfort in my lower abdomen and back for several days. But earlier that evening, as I sat down at my desk to begin assembling notes for a chapter I planned to title "The Gift of Suffering," the discomfort exploded into full-blown pain. After thirty minutes, my back was on fire, and I was giving serious consideration to renaming this chapter or nixing it altogether.

"Congratulations, Mr. Crowther!" the attending radiologist said as he flung back the privacy curtain and delivered the news. "You're in labor with four kidney stones. One of them is really quite impressive."

"Thank you. I've always been an overachiever."

The pain was also impressive. It came in agonizing, unrelenting, irrepressible waves as if someone had clamped my midsection in a large bench vice and was ratcheting it tighter and tighter. Eradicating the pain would require more pain — two surgeries, two urinary stents, and two weeks of recovery.

Pain is the great equalizer. It makes its rounds indiscriminately, without regard for ethnicity, socio-economic class, gender, or age. No one is immune. And when pain inevitably comes, we inevitably will attempt to avoid it.

Western culture is characterized by rational thinking, individualism, democracy, human rights, and the ceaseless pursuit of comfort. We have established institutions (including some religious) and entire industries that help anesthetize and insulate our lives from all things unpleasant. The discovery of analgesics equipped us with the power to alleviate pain, and Americans spend hundreds of billions of dollars annually accessing that power. To make life more convenient, yesterday's technological luxuries have become today's necessities. On the way to the electronics store, we are apt to stop at one of 300,000 fast-food establishments or 150,000 convenience stores. Were we to dissolve these industries, the American economy would likely collapse.

The Gift of Suffering

Richard Rohr writes, "By trying to handle all suffering through willpower, denial, medication, or even therapy, we have forgotten something that should be obvious: We do not handle suffering; *suffering handles us* — in deep and mysterious ways that become the very matrix of life and especially new life."[1]

A culture with such unquestioned and unchallenged disdain for suffering will surely push back at my next suggestion: Not all suffering is to be avoided.

At a fundamental level, pain is an essential part of a warning system the Creator hardwired into our bodies and spirits. That which hurts us also can alert us to that which is about to harm us. If the alarm is insufficient to demand a response, the child may not remove her finger from the surface of the hot stove.

"It is a good thing that the stones caused you so much pain," the urologist told me before surgery. "Had they not chased you in here, the larger stone was prepared to do some permanent damage to your kidney." I appreciated the message; I only wished the system would have sounded the alarm a little more tenderly.

At a higher level, pain can be an invaluable instructor and spiritual guide. If we release our pain or anesthetize it before we have learned all it has to teach us — if we acquiesce to the quick fix — we may jettison an opportunity for transformation. Carl Jung calls this suffering "meaningful," and Rohr refers to it as "necessary."

Author Sue Monk Kidd writes, "Where is our willingness to incubate pain and let it birth something new? What has happened to patient unfolding, to endurance? These things are…the seedbed of creativity and growth — what allow us to do the daring and to break through to newness."[2]

To see how the relationship between faith and suffering has played out in your life, try this simple exercise: Take two sheets of paper and draw two identically sized line graphs (xy), one on each page. Title the first

---

1 Richard Rohr, "Life is Hard," Center for Action and Contemplation, May 23, 2016, https://cac.org/life-is-hard-2016-05-23/.

2 Sue Monk Kidd, When the Heart Waits: Spiritual Direction for Life's Sacred Questions (San Francisco: Harper, 1990), 25.

graph, "Life Events," and the second, "My Journey of Faith." Next, label the horizontal axis (x) of each graph, "Age: (in years)." Use the same scale for each graph.

Plot ten to fifteen significant life events on the first graph. Place positive events toward the top (e.g., marriage, graduation, the birth of your children) and negative events toward the bottom (e.g., a job loss or the death of a loved one). On the second graph, place ten to fifteen dots representing the strength of your faith at various points in your life, then connect those dots with a line. When you finish plotting, lay one graph over the other and hold them up to the light. What relationships do you notice?

When I lead groups through this exercise, participants are often surprised to discover that their faith grew most notably during and immediately after times of crisis and disruption. Our wounds are our spiritual instructors.

One of the most significant life disruptors is Jesus. Contrary to the claims of prosperity theology, life gets considerably harder *after* Jesus shows up.

Consider the "Faith and Life Graphs" of Simon Peter, Andrew, James, and John. As far back as their families' stories reached, the men made their living on the sea. Jesus disrupted that order. "From now on, you will be catching people,"[3] he told them, and they left everything — the catch of a lifetime (symbolic of the best their ordered lives had to offer), family, home, and all that was familiar — and followed Jesus to fish for people in deep water.

Nicodemus was a leader of the Jews whose life changed trajectory after meeting Jesus.[4] The notation at the top of his "Journey of Faith" reports, "Born from above." Some people claim the note reads, "Born again." Regardless of where it comes from or how it takes place, it is difficult to imagine a more significant disruption to one's life than spiritual rebirth.

But before interrupting the lives of others, Jesus allowed his own life to be completely reordered. "Though he was in the form of God, Jesus did

---

3 Luke 5:1-11
4 John 3:1-10

not regard equality with God as something to be exploited, but emptied himself, taking the form of a slave, being born in human likeness. And being found in human form, he humbled himself and became obedient to the point of death — even death on a cross."[5]

In Jesus, God experienced human birth, winced when he struck his thumb with a hammer, and felt disappointment after being abandoned by his friends. In his humanity, Jesus found solidarity with anyone who has ever suffered or felt neglected, forgotten, frightened, passed over, or disenfranchised. God not only understands a mother's anguish as she sits helplessly at the bedside of a suffering child, but God also experienced it.

The universal symbol of the Christian faith is also a symbol of suffering. But the cross has become so ubiquitous that we easily forget it was once an instrument of torture. Dangling at the ends of our necklaces is a device for capital punishment. Could we reintroduce some of the ignominies of Jesus' sacrifice by imagining him strapped to an electric chair or lashed to a gurney while receiving an injection of lethal chemicals? How might wearing empty syringes around our necks reawaken us to the central, necessary role of suffering for our faith?

When we contemplate Jesus' suffering, several important truths emerge.

First, the Lord becomes the perfect model of the biblical lessons about pain. Since the One who was without sin also suffered, no longer can we assume that our pain is a result of sinfulness. I am no more deserving of pain than I am of receiving God's grace. Tragedy does not strike my family because of our sin, nor does it spare your family because of your righteousness. God suffered. All correlations between sin and suffering are off the table.

Second, the solidarity that Jesus establishes with us on the cross increases his approachability. Cornelius Plantinga Jr. claimed, "We do not refer each other to the cross of Christ to explain evil. It is not as if in pondering Calvary we will at last understand throat cancer. We rather lift our

---

5   Philippians 2:5-8

eyes to the cross, whence comes our help, to see that God shares our lot and can therefore be trusted."[6]

But regardless of our level of trust in Jesus, we crave order and shun disruption. As part of a culture of pain avoiders, we are reluctant to follow Jesus into deep water and are even less inclined to tote crosses. The church is much more likely to remake Jesus in the image of the *Divine Painkiller*, whose mission is to take the discomfort of the faithful and exchange it for a blessing.

We are no different from Jesus' first followers in this regard. Some of his disciples traipsed after him in hopes of being physically healed. Others were stirred by his teaching. Still others just wanted a free meal. No one, however, signed on for the suffering and self-denial.

Before Jesus reached the cross, not only did his followers peel away from the procession, but some also joined the opposition and shouted for Jesus' death. Peter and the rest of Jesus' closest friends watched him from a distance.[7] Following too closely might be painful. "Were you there when they crucified my Lord?" Of the twelve, only John could respond, "Here!" when the roll was called at the foot of the cross.

Forgive me if this feels a bit heavy or burdensome so early in our journey together, but it is important to lay a few more theological cards face up. I appreciate Philip Yancey, who writes, "There are two general errors in Christians' thinking about suffering: The first error comes when we attribute all suffering to God, seeing it as his punishment for human mistakes; the second error does just the opposite, assuming that life with God will never include suffering."[8]

Our faith does not inoculate us from suffering; instead, it invites us into a deeper, purposeful relationship with it. When understood in the context of faith, suffering becomes part of God's larger plan to transform all

---

6 Cornelius Plantinga Jr., "A Love So Fierce," The Reformed Journal (November 1986): 6.

7 Luke 22:54; Luke 23:49

8 Philip Yancey, Where Is God When It Hurts? (Grand Rapids: Zondervan, 1990), 96.

things. Our woundedness becomes holy. This theme is consistent and clear throughout Scripture: It is out of death that God brings life.[9]

We must be cautious at this point, however. While Jesus intends to invade our comfort zones and extend an invitation to self-sacrifice, he does not administer suffering. God can redeem our pain, but God does not inflict it. My luggage is not lying in the ditch because *God* loosened the knot. (We will take this up in greater detail later.)

Peter's life and faith changed drastically because of one impulsive, seemingly rash and reckless decision to follow Jesus. He left his boat, gear, and a net-breaking career catch of fish to pursue a radical rabbi that he barely knew.

That story used to trouble me. Peter's impetuousness made no sense until I realized that the decision to follow likely did not belong to Peter alone. "Follow me and I will make you fish for people" sounds a lot like Jesus' words to the paralytic, "Pick up your mat, and go home." Jesus delivers his disruption with miracle language.

Peter's life changed again just before the end of the Gospel. John reports that, shortly after the resurrection, Peter and six of his companions returned to fishing…for fish. Not only did the disciples abandon the call to fish for people, but they also ignored Jesus' directive to "let down their nets in deep water." According to John, the expedition was "only a hundred yards from shore."[10] Peter had circled back to a life that was safe, usual, and ordered — our typical default position in times of trial.

So, Jesus reissued the call. "When you were young, you used to dress yourself and go where you wished. But when you grow older, you will stretch out your hands so that someone else will dress you and take you where you do not wish to go."

In this rather bizarre passage, I imagine the mature Peter raising his arms like a toddler so God could clothe him and lead him into adventures he otherwise would not have taken. The Gospel ends for Peter the same way it began, with Jesus disrupting the apostle's plans.

---

9 Romans 4:17, among many others
10 John 21:8-19

As long as *my* plan was working — or at least appeared to be working — why would I have ever changed course? Remember, my journey was charted and resolute; straight, smooth, and ever upward. I was proud of everything I had packed. I spent years putting my wardrobe together and liked dressing myself, thank you very much. I would never willingly abandon my plan or leave my luggage lying on the beach to strike out in any direction other than my own.

Enter Sir Isaac Newton's first law of motion: "An object will remain at rest or in uniform motion in a straight line unless acted upon by an external force." Like Peter, I would have continued upon my ordered, familiar, shallow course for as long as life allowed. Apart from some falling or failing — the gift of suffering — I never would have explored deeper waters.

We do not choose to suffer. We do not have to; suffering inevitably chooses us. But what would happen if, instead of anesthetizing ourselves from it, we sat with our suffering long enough to learn its lessons? Could we be transformed by life's daily disruptions and trials so that we experience and appreciate the deepening of our faith in the moment instead of recognizing it years later when it appears on a Life Graph?

Jesus held on to his pain until it transformed him into the resurrection. Our suffering can become a gift when we find the grace to do the same. "For if we have been united with him in a death like Christ's, we will certainly be united with him in a resurrection like his."[11]

---

11 Romans 6:5

7

So, Ask

The Parable of the Man Who Sowed Good Seed — Part I

> Jesus put before them another parable: "The kingdom of heaven may be compared to someone who sowed good seed in his field; but while everybody was asleep, an enemy came and sowed weeds among the wheat, and then went away. So when the plants came up and bore grain, then the weeds appeared as well. And the slaves of the householder came and said to him, 'Master, did you not sow good seed in your field? Where, then, did these weeds come from?" (Matthew 13:24-27)

Every Easter, I sit in front of the same empty tomb and comb through the same resurrection story. I pray over it, study it, pray over it some more, examine the differences and similarities between the four accounts, compare the various translations of those accounts, consult with colleagues who have written about the story, read over the notes I recorded the last dozen or so times I went through this routine, and then pray over the story again. I mine out the lesson in every conceivable way short of leading an archaeological expedition to Jerusalem.

The tomb could not hold Jesus, but perhaps its story still conceals some biblical truth or secret that has evaded the rest of Christendom for the last two thousand years. If so, I will find it.

I am still searching.

My inner engineer is determined to solve Easter's mysteries by deciphering the story's single faithful interpretation. But this is where Scripture pushes back. The Word is much too lively and elusive to be pinned down in that way.

The tomb will eventually surrender new secrets, not because the story changes, but because *I* change, and my interpretive contexts change. I am not the same person who sat before the tomb last Easter, nor are the worshipers the same people who sat before my preaching. I could cue up a previous year's sermon verbatim, and it would speak to each person anew. Moreover, I could preach a new sermon to two thousand listeners, and it would be interpreted in two thousand unique but legitimate ways.

Ultimately, we do not excavate Scripture; Scripture excavates us.

Years ago, I led a Sunday morning adult forum in a study of Jesus' parables. Several weeks into our work, we dissected the parable commonly known as the parable of the weeds among the wheat, one of only two parables that Jesus tells and then circles back to explain. In the parable, a householder sows good seed in his field, but the enemy sneaks in and sows weeds.

Like Jacob wrestling with God, the class latched onto the parable and refused to release it until it supplied a blessing. As is the case with any text, each of the participants took hold of different handles within the parable. No two interpretations were the same…then, neither were we.

When the class met the following Sunday, everyone's understanding of the parable had shifted. The two studies took place on September 9 and 16, 2001. On the intervening Tuesday morning, the *enemy* slipped into our field, sowed his evil, and changed our context. Because of 9/11, evil now had a face.

The broad array of interpretations that any text can possess is pure grace for preachers, of course, but will frustrate anyone whose goal is to solve Scripture. How are we to understand God amid our experiences with the absurd, the catastrophic, the unnecessary, and the unjust? How can such a tragic world be ruled by a God that is powerful and loving? How do we make sense of evil? Where can we place our pain?

These are slippery, defiant matters that do not give up blessings easily. Wrangling with them is like wrestling a balloon; just when you think you have the opponent secured in a chokehold and ready to cry, "Mercy!" he pops out somewhere else or bursts.

When I traded my scientific calculator for theological journals, I swapped a profession of precision for one of theory. Engineers are problem-solvers. Hand your mechanical dilemma to an engineer and, voila! The issue is resolved. The design flaw is fixed, and the once-crippled machine roars to life again.

Theologians function differently. We spend our lives contemplating unsolvable matters. Hand your spiritual dilemma to a theologian, and you will be lucky to get it back at all. If you do, the problem will be unchanged, though it will likely be accompanied by several thick volumes of treatises suggesting a myriad of ways to think about the problem differently.

Ever since the serpent skulked into the Garden of Eden, philosophies and world religions have labored unsuccessfully to understand suffering and the presence of evil. The efforts have produced one theory after another, but little consensus. Ask twenty theologians to explain the 2012 Sandy Hook Elementary School massacre, the 2004 Indonesian tsunami, or a global pandemic, and you will receive twenty thoughtful but disparate responses. We have no unifying theology or common language for talking about unjust suffering.

As we turn now to consider what Scripture can contribute to our conversation, let me summarize our challenge: The problem of evil is as old as time, defies explanation, escapes our understanding, refuses to be captured, or even discussed with one common language, and is unsolvable. In other words, when it comes to evil and unjust suffering, my inner engineer can expect to remain frustrated until Jesus returns with a solution.

Early in the biblical narrative, the serpent tempted Adam and Eve with the promise of understanding the incomprehensible. Not all questions are intended to be answered. Just as the tree of knowledge and the empty tomb continue to conceal their mysteries, so, too, will the problem of evil.

But before we call off the expedition, what if we adjusted our destination? Instead of solving the problem, what if we searched for ways to coexist with evil and suffering? How might we wrestle with evil until it surrenders its blessing? What does our pain have to teach us? For these questions, we may indeed find answers.

The best study guide that the New Testament offers for the problem of unjust suffering is Jesus' parable most commonly known as the weeds among the wheat, or the wheat and the tares. I refer to this parable by a different name. A sidebar about the naming and interpretation of parables may be helpful as we get started.

I find that the central characters of Jesus' parables are the first people or acts that the parable mentions. Jesus did not name his parables; we did. And in many cases, we misnamed them. For example, the parable we commonly refer to as the parable of the prodigal son begins, "There was a man who had two sons." The younger son and his sinful exploits are important in the parable only because they point to the primary subject — the reckless and prodigal grace of the father (who, by the way, had two sons).

We turn now to a parable that begins, "The kingdom of heaven may be compared to someone who sowed good seed in his field." It is primarily the sower (and secondarily, the act of sowing) that represents the kingdom. The weeds certainly do not deserve top billing. So, during our time with the story, I will refer to this text as *the parable of the man who sowed good seed*.

A householder planted seed in his field and then went away. During the night, an enemy crept into that field and sowed weeds. When all the plants sprang up, the slaves were astonished to discover weeds among the wheat. They went straightaway to the householder to report the matter and ask for an explanation. The householder fingered the enemy.

The slaves then quickly turned their attention to rectifying the problem before it became a much larger crisis.

"Shall we gather the weeds?" they asked.

But the householder responded, "No. In your zeal to cleanse the field, you will damage some of the wheat as well. Allow them to grow together (coexist), and I will have the reapers deal with this issue at harvest time."

Consider first the slaves' question: "Master, did you not sow good seed in your field? Where, then, did these weeds come from?" Or presented more colloquially, "What the hell?" or "What gives?" These are all iterations of theodicy's first question, *Why*?

"The world was good when you finished creating it, Lord. Why is it no longer good?" "Where did cancer come from?" "Of all the cars that the drunk driver could have hit, why was the victim someone I loved?" "Why, if you love me, has my life turned out this way?" "Why are there weeds among the wheat?"

Of the 183 questions asked of Jesus in the four accounts of the gospel, he directly answered three. In good rabbinic fashion, Jesus much preferred to respond to questions by volleying back questions of his own. He then dismissed his inquirers to work out answers by themselves.

There are a few conclusions we can draw about the slaves from their questions. First, they assumed the goodness of the householder. Surprisingly, the central character (later interpreted as the Son of Man, or Jesus) did not subcontract the sowing to other laborers but tended to it himself. There is something about the householder and his planting that resembles the kingdom of heaven.

If you listen carefully, you may hear sarcasm and frustration in the slaves' questions. After all, they are the ones who must deal with this weed infestation now or suffer the burden of a bumper crop later. But the slaves were conflicted. The presence of weeds in the field did not sync with their understanding or experience of the householder's heart, nature, or character. Perhaps he used faulty sowing techniques or bad seed. The responsibility for this mess belonged to the householder, but the task of rectifying it belonged to the slaves.

The most important insight that the first part of the parable surrenders lies not in what the slaves asked but in the asking itself. That is, the householder willingly accepted the slaves' questions and displeasure. He did not rebuff their protest.

Remember that theodicy means a defense of God regarding the presence of evil. I earlier wrote that I was uncomfortable placing God on trial. However, this parable suggests that God is remarkably comfortable taking the witness stand and does not mind being cross-examined.

"So, Lord, where were you when the tsunami struck? When the house went up in flames? When the toddler fell into the pool? How do you account for the plane crash? Were you not on air traffic control watch that night?"

The Lord can handle a vigorous interrogation.

When Israel turned to other gods, Yahweh (the name which God revealed to Moses) decided to consume them. But Moses questioned God and essentially asked, "What will the neighbors think? How will this look to the Egyptians? They might consider that you brought Israel out to the wilderness just to smite them." God's plans did not jive with Moses' understanding of God's heart. Not only did Yahweh allow the protest, but God also honored it and "changed his mind."[1]

Again and again, the Psalmist questioned and cried out passionately to God. Job challenged God. "How long, O Lord? Will you forget me forever? Consider and answer me!"[2] "Why have you forgotten me? Why must I walk mournfully because the enemy oppresses me?"[3] Even Jesus agonized from the cross, "My God, my God, why have you forsaken me?"[4]

Have you ever shouted to the Lord? Shouted *at* the Lord? "Where were you?" "Where *are* you?" "How could you allow this to happen?"

Our wrangling with suffering begins in the heart, not the head. Passionately, perhaps even angrily, we call upon God to be accountable for the

---

1 Exodus 32:11-14
2 Psalm 13:1-3
3 Psalm 42:9
4 John 19:28

presence of evil. In the opening verses of the parable of the man who sowed good seed, Jesus confirms that God is up to the inquisition.

So, ask.

8

THE INCUBATOR LESSONS

To put it another way, pain is God's megaphone to rouse a deaf world. Why must it be pain? Why can't he rouse us more gently, with violins or laughter? Because the dream from which we must be wakened, is the dream that all is well.

~ William Nicholson, *Shadowlands*

Pray and let God worry.

~ Martin Luther

According to Southern standards, I grew up on a *farm*. The way we figured it in North Carolina, anyone who cobbled together a few acres and attempted to grow or raise something on them had earned the right to call themselves a *farmer*.

However, after moving to Kansas — the land of combine harvesters and rolling irrigation systems — I quickly discovered a loftier set of standards. No self-respecting Midwestern agrarian would consider my family's two hundred fifty acres anything more than a medium-sized backyard. Well, you can take the boy off the farm, but you can't take the farm — or the notion that he grew up on a farm — out of the boy.

My father made a living tooling around a laboratory, mixing test tubes and scribbling indecipherable notes. At all other times, he was a gentleman farmer. Much to my mom's chagrin, *other times* included Sundays.

"Milton, you can't work in the garden on the Lord's Day!"

"If the Lord stops growing weeds on Sunday, then I'll stop pulling them on Sunday," Dad would call back, his voice trailing off as the back screen door slammed behind him.

Our gentleman's farm was mostly comprised of woods and swamps. The only tillable land was a twenty-acre field immediately adjacent to our house and a fifteen-acre parcel at the top of the property. We leased both plots to a *real* farmer who planted soybeans, corn, and wheat, according to some seasonal formula I never quite figured out. Unless I wanted a shortcut to the creek or needed to retrieve a home run ball, I had no reason for ever entering the field.

My father gave most of his time to the birds and the bees, and his garden. By *birds*, I mean game birds. We raised wild turkey, geese, ducks, peacocks, quail, and at least five varieties of pheasants. Dad was initially drawn to these exotic creatures because of their plumage. The feathers supported his fly-tying hobby, which, in turn, supported his trout fishing passion. When the family showed up and commandeered Dad's discretionary time, the trout heaved a sigh of relief, but the birds had managed to capture my father's heart. My childhood was covered in feathers.

From the stocky gray-legged and bareheaded wild turkeys to the magnificent golden pheasants and peacocks with their intricately patterned iridescent plumes, every bird on the farm had one thing in common — they all entered life through the incubator.

For most of the year, the dusty, cobweb-covered room in the lower level of the barn served as storage for all the antique garden and tractor tools that we never used. But as soon as the hens began laying each spring,

Dad resuscitated the vintage wooden Montgomery Ward incubator and transformed the room into an avian neonatal ward.

You would find Pete and me there on many spring evenings just before dark, huddled close around our father as he led us through the same liturgy.

"Peter, I believe it's your turn to open tonight. What comes first?"

"Cut the power switch and wait for the fan to stop blowing." (We had the service committed to memory.)

"That's right. Slowly open the door. Slide out each tray, one at a time."

The eggs rolled as we pulled the metal levers at the edge of each shelf.

"The chicks will warm more evenly this way. They like that," Dad said. "Do you see this chick, boys…the way it's struggling to peck through the egg's shell? The chicks that are too weak to break out of the shell on their own power won't survive."

"You mean it'll die?!" we protested. "You have to help it, Dad!"

"It will probably die soon anyway," he explained. "It's nature's way."

Then he would peel away a piece or two of the shell, a little demonstration of grace. That was *his* way.

We learned early on that life and death are necessary partners. Where we discovered one, the other was always close at hand.

On most summer mornings, Dad phoned from the lab with a list of chores for Pete and me to complete before playing. If he got preoccupied mixing his potions, and Pete and I got unusually ambitious, we could wolf down breakfast and be on our way to the pool or the park or the woods before the phone rang. Otherwise, we got saddled with a list of responsibilities that kept us busy most of the day.

At least once a week, we had dead bird detail.

"Dig the hole deep, boys," Dad would say. "I don't want to see them again."

We were also responsible for the compost pile. Vegetable peelings, fruit waste, and grass clippings — all dead matter — were deposited in an area beneath the barn steps. Then, at spring planting, this compost was used as fertilizer to encourage new growth.

Each autumn, we marveled as God colored two hundred acres of trees.

The leaves which were not raked for compost were left to nourish the soil wherever God's breath chose to distribute them. Neither the leaves nor the winters were ever so deep that God did not call forth spring from beneath them. The cycle of life and death was daily evident and a natural part of the farm's rhythm.

There was nothing natural, however, about what happened in 1961.

My folks married a little later in life. Mom and my brother, Mike, who was six years old at the time, came as a package deal, an instant family. Several years later, Kristen Louise was born.

I know precious little about my older sister. Kristen entered the world with a hole in one of the chamber walls of her heart. She lived for twenty-eight days in an incubator. Children born with that condition today most often survive. And the fact that Kristen did not survive rocked my parents' world.

Sometimes, nature's way feels unjust. Parents do not outlive their children in a just world, nor are infants baptized through an incubator in a neonatal intensive care unit.

"As this child grows in years, you should place in her hands the Holy Scriptures and provide for her instruction in the Christian faith, that living in communion with the church and in the covenant of her baptism, Kristen may live a godly life until the day of Jesus Christ. Do you promise to fulfill these obligations?"

In a just world, parents would never have to answer such a question for a child they cannot hold or ever bring home.

Even as a young boy, I sensed that tending to the incubator was sacred for my father. He did not liberate the weaker chicks just to appease his sons; he defied nature's way to champion his daughter and settle his spirit.

I suppose we all search for peace in our own ways.

"Carrie, I know it's a little unsettling to have us working on you like this, Sweetheart. You can't see or feel what we're doing. But you just try and relax. I promise you're doing just fine. I'll talk you through the next few moments, and in just a jiffy, you'll be holding the next little Crowther."

Our second child was born on a bright December morning in 1988 at the North Texas Medical Center in McKinney, just north of Dallas. Dr. Parker, the attending obstetrician, provided the play-by-play.

"I am making the first incision, now. Next, I'll be removing the scar from your first C-section."

Two and a half years earlier, Grant entered the world amid considerably more drama. After hours of intense but ultimately unproductive labor, Carrie was rushed into emergency surgery. I was allowed to gown up and join the commotion just in time to see the delivering doctor hoist our firstborn into the air.

"These are the ovaries," Dr. Parker continued as he invited me to inspect his work a little more closely.

The two births could not have been more different. For the second go-round, we chose the birthdate. It was scheduled in my planner: *6:30 a.m., December ninth, 1988 — Check-in at the North Texas Medical Center.* I was gowned and waiting for Carrie when the nurses wheeled her into delivery. The medical team was collected and calm, even jovial. There were no labor pains. No pushing. The only decision I had to make was what background music played during the procedure. The anesthesiologist administered a spinal block, and Dr. Parker began his narration. Less than ten minutes later, he announced, "It's a girl."

"A *big* girl," one of the nurses chimed in.

Dr. Parker, an avid fisherman, added his own color commentary.

"Big? Honey, if this young'un were a bass, you'd have to mount her."

One of the many advantages of a scheduled delivery is that the help knows exactly when to arrive. Before Rachael Lauren had been swaddled and labeled, my folks arrived from North Carolina to rock and tend to all nine pounds of her. My mom adoringly told her new granddaughter, "You look just like Kristen."

I learned something else about my sister that day — she was beautiful. Except for Grant's disappointment that she was a *she*, she was perfect. So was our world — at least for a few hours.

"What's the matter?" Carrie asked. Before I even noticed that Dr. Parker had entered the room, Carrie had read his expression and determined that something was wrong.

"I just finished examining Rachael and discovered a loud murmur in her heart. I believe it is caused by what we call a ventricular septal defect, which is essentially a hole in the wall of the heart's lower chambers. The sound we hear is caused by blood rushing through that hole. This is not my area of expertise, so I have contacted a pediatric heart specialist in Dallas."

The free fall from elation to panic was dizzying. One moment, the likenesses that Lauren and Kristen shared had seemed purposeful. Seconds later, they felt more like a curse.

The crowds in the medical plaza mezzanine stepped aside as we arrived for our appointment. Their gestures seemed like an odd courtesy until I realized that I had bundled Lauren in a blanket and was cradling her as if she were an explosive device that might detonate at the slightest vibration. I held her away from my body and flexed my knees to absorb the elevator's lurching as we started up the medical tower to the specialist's office. Each time Lauren stretched or cried or sneezed, I winced and then held my breath until she calmed.

"Shh," I whispered. "Shh."

First to greet us in the waiting room were the psalmists and the gospel writers. Their words had been transposed in needlepoint, framed, and mounted on each wall. I remember only one of the sayings — "Your faith has made you well." If the purpose of the hangings were to comfort the anxious folks who waited beneath them, this seemed like an odd choice for a surgeon's office.

Jesus spoke these words several times to those he healed, such as the ten lepers who approached him "somewhere between Samaria and Galilee."[1] Jesus called to the ten from a distance, "Go and show yourselves to the priest." The priest was the only person who could declare the lepers *clean*. But they *weren't* clean. Jesus had done nothing to heal the lepers. He spoke no miraculous words over them. He did not touch them or commend their

---

[1] Luke 17:11-19

faith. The only motivation the lepers had for following Jesus' direction — other than desperation — was trust. On the way to see the priest, all ten lepers were made clean. Only one of the lepers returned to praise Jesus for the healing. Jesus told him, "Your faith has made you well."

The nurse called out, "Rachael Lauren Crowther."

The priest was ready to see us.

As soon as Carrie lovingly laid Lauren on the examining table and rearranged the blanket around her, the nurse blew into the room, snatched Lauren up as if she were a fumbled football, unwrapped, weighed, and replaced her. I growled.

"So, you're a pastor?"

The priest had sneaked up on us.

"I'm sorry?" I said, uncertain whether he was asking a question or making a statement of fact.

"Hi. I'm Dr. Wakefield. I understand you are a pastor."

"Well…studying in that direction anyway," I said. "But how did you know I…"

The doctor removed the stethoscope from around his neck and all the activity and clamor in the room immediately stopped. The nurses watched reverently as he pressed the instrument to Lauren's tiny chest. Then her back. Then her chest again. Like church regulars, they knew the liturgy and were waiting for the priest's pronouncement.

"Folks, I call this a musical murmur. No worries. This young lady is going to be fine."

And with that, the priest was done. He needed all of sixty seconds to pronounce Lauren "clean."

"So, tell me about your studies. Are you in seminary in the Metroplex?"

Carrie and I looked at each other with a furrow-browed "do you believe this guy?" expression.

"That's it?" I asked incredulously. "How can you be so certain? Aren't there tests that we need to run?"

"I've heard these types of murmurs a thousand times. Trust God."

Trusting *God* was not the issue. It was the haphazard whirlwind sort of exam that I doubted.

Here was the process that I had in mind: First, attach a piece of expensive, precision medical equipment to Lauren, the kind specifically designed to evaluate heart murmurs. Second, replace the Scripture verses on the wall with charts displaying heart murmur data, whatever those look like. Finally, take the strip of paper generated by the expensive equipment, compare the results to the charts, and hopefully discover that Lauren's results match the area labeled *Normal*.

Was that too much to ask? I would have traded the priest's pronouncement for that strip of paper in a heartbeat.

"The obstetrician said the sound of the murmur was caused by blood moving through a hole between the chambers," I prodded, "and that he was concerned by the loudness of that sound?"

"He's right. The noise is very detectable. I don't even need the stethoscope to hear it."

Had the doctor diagnosed Lauren by laying his ear to her chest, I would have swooped up our three-day-old…carefully…and made for the exit.

"Think about it. Which is louder, water rushing through a large hole or a small hole? Trust God," he repeated. "I tell you, she'll be fine. You'll see. Hey! Good luck with the studies."

He shook Carrie's hand and gave me a *keep working on it and you'll eventually get it one day* pat on the back. Then he spun around and left as suddenly as he had arrived.

Lauren's heart not only healed, but it also grew into the healthiest, most enormous, most generous heart I know. I cannot tell you if I ever trusted the doctor-turned-priest-turned-prophet or if time just bore him out, but somewhere along the way, I stopped worrying. Perhaps that is a form of trust.

I am the priest now. Most weeks, somewhere between Samaria and Galilee, I invite folks to stand and present themselves so I can, on God's behalf, declare them healed.

"You are forgiven," I tell them. "Your faith has made you well."

Sometimes, when this news seems too good to be true, those who have been healed will ask, "How can you be so sure?"

"I see signs of the Lord's goodness every day," I tell them. "Trust God."

"But how can we be sure?" they continue.

Then, I share God's story.

Whenever God's good news has been proclaimed, there has always been someone at hand to question it. We are just the latest in a lineage of doubters that stretches back to the beginning of time.

Scripture is filled with stories of those who shared our foibles and uncertainties yet were used mightily by God. When the Lord informed Abraham that, at the age of one hundred, he would be the father of many nations, the patriarch rolled on the ground in disbelieving laughter. Locked away in prison, John the Baptist was racked with doubt and the fear that he had spent his entire prophetic career preparing for the wrong messiah. And when Mary delivered the news of the resurrection to the first disciples, they considered her tale to be nonsense.[2]

While stories of Abraham, John, and the disciples are interesting — perhaps even inspiring — it is not the desire to learn more about the lives of biblical figures that draw us into God's story. We go to Scripture in search of *our* names.

The apostle John realized this. He concluded his account of the Gospel in this way: "These things have been written so that *you* might come to believe...and by believing, have life."[3] There we are. We are the reason for Scripture. These are our stories.

I have seen it happen time and time again. Once someone reads their name and God's name in the same sentence or hears their name spoken in prayer, God's story comes to life. The shepherds outside Bethlehem were

---

2 Genesis 17:15; Matthew 11:2-3; Luke 24:11
3 John 20:31

filled with terror at the glory of the Lord. Then, the angels called their names. "The Savior who has been born is for *you*," they sang, and the shepherds' fear turned to joy.

God's story found me long before I knew to look for it. Thanks to the preachers and teachers in the simple country church of my youth, I cannot remember a time when I did not know Jesus. And thanks to my parents, my experience of God was never bound to church or Sunday morning.

Every evening, we bowed our heads around the dinner table and invited the Lord into our conversations. As we broke bread together, we turned the blessings and the challenges of our days into parables. Then, in the summer evenings, the men met for vespers around the incubator in the little cobwebbed chapel in the barn. Each day ended the same way. We knelt together by our beds and together prayed, "God bless Mom and Dad, Mike and Joe and Pete." My name and God's name, side by side.

By Midwestern standards, I suppose our gentleman's farm was a little underwhelming. But it holds an enormous place in my heart, for it was there that my faith was formed and fashioned by parents who were living examples of grace. They were challenged and tried by life yet clung tightly to their trust in God. They responded to life's injustices with patience and steadfastness and taught their children to do the same.

9

Resetting the Table

After years of being taught that the way to deal with painful emotions is to get rid of them, it can take a lot of reschooling to learn to sit with them instead, finding out from those who feel them what they have learned by sleeping in the wilderness that those who sleep in comfortable homes may never know.

~ Barbara Brown Taylor, *Learning to Walk in the Dark*

As busy, active, relevant ministers, we want to earn our bread by making a real contribution. This means first and foremost doing something to show that our presence makes a difference. And so we ignore our greatest gift, which is our ability to enter into solidarity with those who suffer.

~ Henri Nouwen

Required Experiential Assignment: Report to the front desk of the Gettysburg Lutheran Home by 4:30 p.m. on a date to be prearranged with the GLH administration. Please be sure to clear the rest of that evening's schedule.

(From the syllabus for the seminary course, "Ministry with the Elderly.")

"Welcome to the Gettysburg Lutheran Home, Mr. Crowther. We are so pleased to have you with us. Give me just a moment, and I will get you settled into your room."

"Uh…room? I wasn't aware that I would need a ro…"

"Well, my instructions are to keep you here tonight, so unless you plan on sleeping in the hallway, Mr. Crowther, you're gonna want a room."

Before I could object or question her, the nurse began rattling off her instructions with the cadence of a drill sergeant.

"As I was about to say, your room is two hallways down and on the left. I have no key for you, so if you brought anything of value, now would be the time to leave it with me. On your bed is a gown. I need you to strip down to your skivvies and slip it on. It's all the clothing you will need until eight o'clock in the morning.

"You will also find a wheelchair in your room with your name taped to the back. That chair is your only way of getting around our facility during your stay. You may not stand unassisted for any reason. If you need to relieve yourself — and I assume you will — then you must call one of the nursing staff for help. If you are impatient or feel you cannot wait for us, then I have a specialized undergarment that I can give you.

"Dinner is in an hour in the dining hall. I trust that you will enjoy tonight's menu of various pureed dishes. At six-thirty, someone will take you to our evening arts and crafts workshop where you *will* be expected to participate. After class, the rest of your evening is free. You may do as you wish, but we hope that you will interact with other residents. Any questions?"

What I wanted to ask was, "Which military academy did you attend?" and "Did you memorize your lines or were they ad-libbed?" but all I managed to get out was, "So…which way is my room again?"

I had no issue with the "various pureed dishes." As a backpacker, I had learned to eat food that would sour a billy goat's stomach. Liquidized chicken would be a cinch. And regarding the evening attire, it is surprising how comfortable one can feel in a standard-issue hospital gown when surrounded by eighty-something-year-olds who are wearing the same. The wheelchair, however, was a different story.

I consider myself a mechanically minded and dexterous guy, but the chair and I locked horns in an evening-long battle of wills, with most rounds scored in my opponent's favor. Of course, the residents delighted in watching this skirmish. Several merciful souls pulled me aside and offered a few helpful pointers. The group had just begun schooling me in the finer points of "hallway right-of-way rules" when one of the orderlies appeared.

"*There* you are. Time for lights-out."

He whisked me away to my room and forced…I mean, helped me to bed.

After darkness falls in the wilderness, when the campfire burns down to embers, I lie awake in my tent for hours uploading all the day's events and listening to katydids and great horned owls. The sounds of this wilderness were strange and unsettling.

Across the hallway, Roger wailed pitifully and called for his wife. This set several other residents to howling, "We tell you every night that your wife's not here. Go to sleep!" Every few moments, the resident next door let out a most lonesome moan. I understood. I had been surrounded by people the entire evening, yet I, too, was lonely.

I was empathetic, but I could not truly be compassionate. I was not a co-sufferer for I was free to leave whenever I wished. If I became too flustered with the wheelchair, I could toss in the towel, stand, and walk away. If I became too impatient waiting for the nurse, I could easily slip to the bathroom unnoticed. I had options; my new friends did not.

I survived the restless night and, at 8:01 the following morning, stood unassisted and went to the bathroom without an audience for the first time in sixteen hours. After collecting my belongings from the morning charge nurse, I returned to my life, though not as usual.

In class later that day, our professor explained the obvious. "The purpose of the assignment was to teach you empathy for the elderly."

We all responded in harmony, "Well, it worked."

Years ago, when my mind was nimbler, I did not write my sermons; I sketched them. I walked among the people and preached from a memorized outline of simple images. These images helped me visualize where I wanted to take the congregation and how my message intended to get them there. When worshipers commented, "I had never *seen* that story that way before," I knew the visualization had worked. Listeners became spectators and the lesson captured their imagination.

Transformation begins with reimagination.

I approached this memoir in much the same way, by stringing together a series of images and stories. A vivid childhood memory became the on-ramp image for our journey. Watching luggage take flight from the roof of our Chrysler station wagon helped me reimagine the crises in my life. Recalling the explosion at my father's laboratory personalized the theodicy problem and made it more accessible.

But preaching from a memorized string of images can be risky. When the moves within the sermon are linear, then each point, thought, or story relies upon the preceding point, thought, or story. When I misplace one image and stray from my intended path, finding the way back without a manuscript to guide me can be a sweaty, frantic adventure, especially when a thousand worshipers are watching.

To help safeguard against this nightmare, I eventually learned to assign a theme to my sermon gallery. Instead of connecting images in sequence, like beads in a necklace, I relate each image to a larger, organizing image — my *North Star* image. When my memory misfires (and it regularly does), I simply circle back in my mind to my star and recollect my bearings.

The organizing image I chose for this book was a long banquet table. On it, I placed dozens of settings, each with an erasable placard for listing a chapter title.

The table was expansive, but not limitless. There wasn't room for all the stories I wanted to invite, so I had to be selective with my seating assignments. Several stories I did not think to invite just appeared last-minute, and that was fine. As it turned out, some of the stories I expected to seat showed up, looked around, decided this party wasn't for them, and left. Several chapters worked exceptionally well next to one another, while others had absolutely nothing in common and needed to be reseated.

One part of the table image was clear from the outset: My marriage to Carrie would serve as the centerpiece. There was no other place for it. I would work on the centerpiece first. After it was complete and in place, I would organize the other chapters around it. That was my plan.

The final years of our marriage were the source of my life's most intense and unyielding pain. When I began this project, the wounds were deep and still healing. Whether I peeled back the bandages slowly or braced myself and ripped them off, revisiting these memories was going to be unpleasant. But at least it would be short-lived. Only heaven knew for sure how much heart I had already given over to processing our struggles. For over a decade, it seemed as if I thought of little else. These chapters would virtually jump up and write themselves.

As soon as I began, however, something unexpected happened. The stories pushed back. Images became stubborn and sentences refused to cooperate with one another. I arranged the centerpiece in one way, then placed it on the table and stepped back to have a look.

"Nope. That doesn't work."

I have little experience arranging tables, but even I know that a centerpiece can't overwhelm the rest of the settings. The results of the first efforts were too harsh. Softening the presentation and tempering the language only made matters worse. For over a week, I filled the computer's trash bin with one draft after another. Each of them either dishonored the marriage and disparaged Carrie or failed to communicate the anguish that defined those years.

Dispirited and emotionally exhausted — and staring at a long, empty table — I rebandaged my wounds while I decided whether to look for a new image or a different project…or a therapist.

Sermon texts can also behave obstinately at times, but preachers don't have the luxury of laying a sermon aside. Ready or not, when the music stops, listeners expect I will have something to say.

Over the years, I developed a nearly fail-safe strategy for kickstarting last-minute inspiration. I go to an empty sanctuary, sit in an empty pew, focus upon an empty chancel, and ask a simple question: "What will the person who will soon sit here most need to receive from the person who will speak from up there?" This *turns the table* on my usual process, which amounts to sitting in my office and asking, "What do I want to say?"

The *empty pew strategy* is an exercise in reimagination that does for preaching what stripping down to my skivvies and eating pureed food does for ministry with the elderly — it leads to empathy and understanding. It seemed worth a try.

I located a long, empty conference table in the boardroom of a local church, took a seat in the head chair and, for the better part of an hour, stared at the spot where the centerpiece would be placed. I reflected upon my marriage, prayed, and reflected some more. Then, I got up and moved to the opposite end of the table.

I asked myself, "What would happen if I worked on the centerpiece from here?" "How might I reimagine the marriage and understand it differently?" "I know the hell *I* experienced during those years. Surely, they were hellish for Carrie as well. What was her experience like?" "How had Grant and Lauren been impacted by our struggles?" "Am I really up for a few more rounds in the wheelchair?"

I removed the bandages again, slowly this time, and returned to the computer. First, I spent a week rummaging through a quarter century's worth of sermon and lesson files in search of all work I had done on the topic of *suffering*. Then, I pored over Scripture, ferreting out and studying relevant but less familiar passages.

From the other side of the table, Grant's and Lauren's opinions became essential, so I spent time with my children to see what lessons they had to share, something I had neglected for far too long. Lastly, I resumed a research project on mental illness that I had begun and set aside during the final days of the marriage.

Throughout this process, I prayed. And as I prayed and studied and listened and learned...I wrote.

In the biographical film *Shadowlands*, one of C.S. Lewis's colleagues expresses his pleasure that God answered Lewis's prayers. Lewis, played by Anthony Hopkins, responds, "That's not why I pray. I pray because I can't help myself. I pray because I'm helpless. I pray because the need flows out of me all the time, waking and sleeping. It doesn't change God. It changes *me*."

Working on this project changed none of the events about which I have written, but the writing significantly changed me. I have come to understand Carrie less as the cause of my pain and more as a fellow sufferer in our shared experience of pain. I set out in search of empathy, but what I discovered — or what discovered me — feels much more like compassion. Somewhere along the way, my wounds began to heal.

The table has finally been reset. Nine months after nearly abandoning this memoir, I have finished the other chapters. All that remains are the stories that I was certain would jump up and write themselves. The chapters that were to be last became first, and the first have become the last. And all the writing was done from the *other* side of the table. Otherwise, the process has gone exactly as planned.

"So, when did the two of you first realize you were in love?"

Of all the *get-to-know-you* questions that I ask premarital couples, this is by far my favorite. I have posed it hundreds of times through the years and have determined that those who intend to be husband and wife are incapable of answering this question without first looking at one another and smiling. Then, as often as not, at least one of the betrothed — usually the groom — will respond, "Oh, I knew I loved her the moment I saw her. No question about it."

Most therapists reject the notion of instantaneous love. "Falling in love is a misnomer," they say. "You may fall into *infatuation*, but love, especially the kind of love that sustains a relationship over time, is something we *grow* into gradually."

While I agree with this in theory, I have two reasons to push back.

First, I also ask my question to couples who are celebrating their fiftieth wedding anniversaries. "When did you first know you were in love?"

Their answers are the same.

"I knew she was the one as soon as I saw her. And half a century later, I look at her and feel the same way."

But more importantly, I am a member of the "love at first sight" club. I would answer my question in the same way. "I was at a high school party when I noticed this beautiful, entrancing, playful girl on the other side of the room. Our eyes locked for an instant. That's all it took. She smiled, and the world forever changed. I was smitten. It would be a week before I gave her my letter jacket and class ring, but my heart belonged to her the moment she smiled."

The early part of our relationship were the *one anothering years*. We spent every moment we could with one another, experienced and survived adolescence with one another, and shared our hopes and dreams with one another. Before most of our friends had packed away their high school graduation gowns, I had collected my undergraduate degree. Carrie and I were married to one another and off to set the world on fire with one another.

In the race for my heart, Carrie arrived before the Holy Spirit. (In fairness to God, I should say that Carrie's smile captured me years before I sensed God's summoning tap on the shoulder. Who knows how long God had been working to get my attention?) A life of ministry was not a part of our original playbook. So, like any good quarterback that steps under center and sees an unexpected defensive scheme, we called an audible and found a way to do ministry with one another.

During our seminary days, one of my professors prophesied, "Carrie will be one of your ministry's greatest gifts."

He was spot-on and, at the same time, remarkably unfair. Even then I was aware that the traditional mantle of "minister's spouse" could one day weigh heavily upon Carrie's spirit. She gave ministry spousehood the "ole seminary try," but there was something about the role that just didn't seem to fit.

During my call interview at King of Glory, one of the team members' questions betrayed the typical expectations that most congregations have of their shepherds' significant others.

"So, what does your wife plan to do in the congregation?"

My tendency in those days was to shelter Carrie.

"Listen!" I said. "If I receive this call, there will be three persons in the church who have no pastor. The question you *should* be asking yourselves is, 'What does the congregation plan to do to support my family?'"

As it turned out, Carrie managed quite well for herself and did not need my sheltering. She taught preschool, organized and directed an after-school tutorial ministry for elementary children, and was at the church every time the doors were unlocked. The congregations I served adored her. But what's not to adore?

Carrie is exceedingly beautiful, both inside and out. With a heart the size of Texas, she dotes on her family…and the elderly…and her preschool students…and every distressed animal that has the good fortune of being rescued by her. An olive-skinned brunette with a radiant smile, Carrie possesses a magnetism that attracts the spotlight at every social event she attends.

What spotlight operators fail to appreciate, however, is how much energy their attention demands from her. Like most extreme introverts, Carrie spends a considerable portion of her life rallying the wherewithal to function in the presence of other people and then recovering from her performances. And, unfortunately, as soon as pastors' families settle into a comfortable, private corner backstage, congregations find a way to drag them back into the limelight.

My greatest challenge in introducing Carrie to you is determining which verb tense to use. Slowly, over time, many of the adjectives that once best described her just stopped working. I cannot point to a moment when the transformation started. There was no ignitor event. But along the way, the images in the family photo albums began to change.

Carrie's countenance gradually hollowed and the luster faded from her sparkle. Her moods became unpredictable and occasionally volatile as she regularly slipped away into periods of unexplainable sadness. It was as if her spirit were connected to a dimmer switch that someone, or something, was mercilessly dialing down.

I knew little for certain about Carrie's demons in those days. I could not name them, nor did I understand what encouraged them to show up or how to chase them away once they did. To make matters even more puzzling, and the enemy more inscrutable, Carrie seemed unaware of the changes that were taking place.

When someone who is visually impaired misplaces their glasses, they are faced with a daunting dilemma. They need their glasses to find their glasses. It is the same with those who rely upon their medication to help them remember to take their medication. If they miss a dose, getting back on track requires help from someone else.

Those with mental illness can experience a similar challenge. Understanding the illness requires the very mental faculties that are impacted by the illness. The formal medical term for this lack of awareness is *anosognosia*. For a person with anosognosia, the inaccurate insight feels as real and convincing as anyone else's perception of themselves. Few persons will seek treatment for a disease they don't perceive.

While there was much mystery surrounding Carrie's condition, there were several contributing factors I *could* identify.

In the spring of 1998, Carrie suffered a significant back injury after being thrown from the saddle of an especially rambunctious horse. The narcotics prescribed to control her pain unfortunately also calmed her emotional demons. The treatment which started with a doctor's prescriptive care spiraled downward in an all-too-common pattern of self-medicating, dependency, and abuse.

As far too many people know, substance abuse is a tremendous adversary in and of itself. But Carrie's abuse had a formidable tag team partner — heredity.

Though the matter has been long debated, many researchers believe that addiction is a familial trait. If addictive tendencies are heritable, then Carrie came by her predispositions honestly. She recalls meeting her biological father only once. Though he remains largely a mystery, he reportedly died quietly and alone as a middle-aged adult inmate in a Midwestern prison suffering from many of the same illnesses and tendencies that he likely handed down to his daughter.

For the first fifteen years of our marriage, Carrie and I were problem-solvers. When we had trouble paying the bills, I rolled up my sleeves and went to work on the seminary grounds crew waxing floors and trimming hedges. When the children cried during the nights, we researched parenting manuals and sought the counsel of friends. We were resourceful.

But this challenge was different. Mental illness did not honor our determination. We could find no way to *one another* ourselves through this. There were no manuals for calming depression in the middle of the night. And since Carrie did not perceive a problem, consulting experts was off the table.

As the world braced for Y2K and the imagined chaos of the millennial bug, I faced a much more certain, but equally elusive, foe. My wife was slowly disappearing, and I seemed powerless to stop it.

"Systematic Theology." "The Christian Understanding of Redemption." "Life, Death, and Salvation in a Multi-Faith World." Among a sea of complex theological course offerings in the Gettysburg Lutheran Seminary academic catalog, "Ministry with the Elderly" seemed a particularly practical option for my final senior semester. After all, how many of my parishioners would ask me to help them reconcile the differences between the moral influence theory of salvation and the notion of propitiatory sacrifice? On the other hand, one out of four of my Sunday morning pew-sitters would be over the age of sixty-five.

If congregational culture reflects the wider culture, then the percentage of members who are elderly nearly matches the percentage of those who are living with mental illness. Yet you will not find "Ministry with the

Mentally Ill" among the seminary course offerings at Gettysburg. I cannot tell you why.

But suppose such a course existed. What sort of experiential assignment might the professor use to deepen students' empathy for depression? Confinement to a wheelchair can help teach us about immobility. Wearing a blindfold may allow us to relate to the visually impaired. But how do we mimic hopelessness or despair, reproduce untamable hyperactive brain function, or manufacture distorted reality?

According to the National Institute of Mental Health,[1] in any given year, one in five adults in the United States has a diagnosable mental health disorder. One in twenty-five has a severe mental illness. Of the adults with mental health disorders, half will develop a co-occurring substance use disorder. Half of all chronic mental illness begins by the age of fourteen. Suicide is the tenth leading cause of death for all ages and is more common than homicide. Almost forty-seven million people in the United States currently experience some form of mental illness. Exactly *none* of these individuals chose their condition.

Yet, despite its prevalence, mental illness remains elusive. Why? How does this condition enjoy such immunity from our scrutiny? We speak of the struggles of aging with candor and humor but resist broaching conversations about our mental or emotional well-being. Why? I could relate to the trials of aging strangers after one night in a wheelchair. After a decade of living alongside mental illness, I still struggled to understand it. We endured in secret.

Even now — even from the other side of the table — as I reach to pull back the curtain on our family's struggles, my hand has begun to quiver just a little. Why?

---

1 "Transforming the Understanding and Treatment of Mental Illnesses," National Institute of Mental Health, https://www.nimh.nih.gov/health/statistics/mental-illness (accessed November 19, 2021).

10

THE TREASURE CHEST

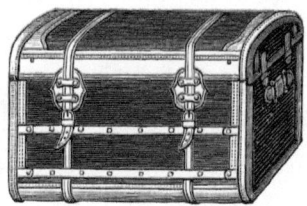

> We must learn to regard people less in the light of what they do
> or omit to do, and more in the light of what they suffer.
>
> ~ Dietrich Bonhoeffer, *Letters and Papers from Prison*

> I'm rightly tired of the pain I hear and feel, boss. I'm tired of bein on the road, lonely as a robin in the rain. Not never havin no buddy to go on with or tell me where we's comin from or goin to or why. I'm tired of people bein ugly to each other. It feels like pieces of glass in my head. I'm tired of all the times I've wanted to help and couldn't. I'm tired of bein in the dark. Mostly it's the pain. There's too much. If I could end it, I would. But I can't.
>
> ~ Stephen King, *The Green Mile*

I awoke yesterday morning to the sound of my phone vibrating across the bedside table. Beneath the image of Lauren's beautiful face, the time read *4:06 a.m.* I knew at once that this was the call I had been expecting at any moment for the past four years.

"Dad?" Lauren was weeping. "Mom died."

There is no way to soften the impact of those words. We can track every step of death's approach — even pray that it comes swiftly and gently for our loved ones who are suffering — yet somehow, the news still manages to ambush us.

"I'm so sorry, Sweetheart."

Carrie cheated death and defied medical odds for so long that the family began to wonder if she were invulnerable. On several occasions, her doctors sounded the alarm and urged the family home. Grant and Lauren made the hurried road trip across six states to North Carolina to find their mom had emerged from her coma and was sitting up in bed while the medical staff stood in the hallway scratching their heads.

Most of Carrie's health issues could be traced to either her failed liver or Vascular Ehlers Danlos syndrome. The liver disease was the unavoidable consequence of years of substance and alcohol use disorder. Vascular EDS is an inherited connective tissue condition caused by defects in the protein collagen. The vascular strain is the most severe form of the disorder. Its symptoms include increased fragility of arteries, muscles, and internal organs. The average life expectancy of those affected by the disease is forty-eight years.

On the evening before last, Carrie suffered yet another emergency. The only course of treatment riskier than operating was *not* operating, but when the surgeon began work shortly after midnight, the bleeding quickly became uncontrollable, and the procedure was halted.

Yesterday morning, Carrie's mother, Sandra, kept vigil by her daughter's bed. Fifty-four years and two months after giving birth to Carrie in the same hospital, she held her daughter again as she was reborn into everlasting life. Now, Carrie truly is invulnerable.

"It's like we lost mom twice," Lauren explained perfectly.

Although *loss* is a common euphemism for *death*, it is not a word I would typically use. But, for the moment, it works, not only because it helps cushion us from a reality that is still new and raw (which is, after all, the purpose of a euphemism), but also because it accurately describes what we experienced — twice.

I cannot tell you how or where or when we first lost Carrie. There was no phone call. No obituary. No funeral. She never left my sight, only my recognition. She slipped away slowly, a little at a time, until one day we could no longer find her.

We ultimately lost Carrie following another long-drawn-out illness. This time, there was a moment that marked our loss. It happened yesterday. A year from yesterday, the children and I will get together and remember what happened. Maybe then we will speak of *Mom's death*. Today, however, we are suffering from a *loss*.

It has now been three days since Carrie's passing (yet another euphemism). I spent last evening with Grant, Lauren, and her wife, Shelbi, sitting on the floor and sifting through four decades' worth of photos, mementos, and souvenirs. These dusty keepsakes have become our family's heirlooms. The ragged cardboard box which contains them is our treasure chest.

I imagine our family's treasure looks much like your own. There are pictures of holiday gatherings and vacations, awards and old report cards, and the trinkets that the children made "when they were little." Each gem has a story to tell. Last night, stories were exactly what we needed.

"These remind me that true love is possible," Lauren said as she pointed to pictures of Carrie and me posing on a beach, leaning against an Appalachian Mountain overlook, and crouching in front of a Christmas fireplace adorned with stockings and cedar. Each image was laced with memories that were at once painful and sweet.

Buried at the bottom of the chest was an old manila envelope stuffed full of cards and letters that I had written to Carrie during our teenage *going steady* years. There were tattered, yellowed newspaper clippings of my high school academic honors and results of all the two-mile races I didn't win. The stories which these treasures told were a little embarrassing. Knowing that Carrie had saved them all these years, however, was priceless.

One of the rarer gems in the chest was a uniquely posed picture that I took of Grant's great-great-grandmother standing behind her son, who was seated next to his daughter, who was standing over her daughter, Carrie, who was holding Grant. Five generations.

Lauren waved her hand over the albums lying between us. *Eeny, meeny, miny, moe.* Her finger came to rest over an unlabeled and faded cream-colored book. As she picked it up, two glossy black and white prints fell to the floor. They were stunning images of Carrie in her wedding dress taken just before our ceremony.

Like all good storytellers, the pictures did more than stir my memories; they awakened my senses and ushered the past powerfully into the present. Even after a quarter century, one glance into Carrie's expressive, chestnut eyes and I was hypnotized. My hand trembled as if Carrie were there with us, and I was fumbling to slip the ring onto her finger again. I heard her giggle softly, just as she had done at the wedding.

"Money was tight in those days," I said. "Mom and I couldn't afford a professional photographer, so all of these pictures were taken by family members."

Turning pages of underexposed, grainy pictures of motley-clad groomsmen, my atrocious tuxedo, and the simple reception table in the church fellowship hall, I realized that my explanation was probably unnecessary.

Lauren was the curator of the treasure chest, but she was not its creator. Carrie and I separated the images and assembled the albums years ago. Like the art and diplomas that now hang on my office walls, the items in the treasure chest were chosen for a purpose. They showcased the *us* we wanted others to see. The images are beautiful and the stories they tell are genuine. They are also incomplete.

People who live with mental illness live with the constant fear that their conditions will be disclosed. Inappropriate and stigmatizing labels, such as *mad*, *disturbed*, or *unhinged*, generate feelings of shame and fear. Family systems turn to euphemisms to disguise their conditions. Just as *death* can become a *loss*, *depression* is softened to *sadness*, and *addiction* is diminished to a *habit*. In sheltering their struggles from the world, people with mental illness can also separate themselves from those who can provide treatment and support.

Our family was a classic example. When it came to our struggles with mental illness, our family drew the curtains tight. No one was permitted to peek. But our secrecy came with a price.

Grant's middle teenage years were consumed by depression and substance abuse issues. Feeling our way through this awful dark maze was trying enough; camouflaging our experience from the rest of the world made our struggles unbearable.

"How is your family, Pastor?"

"We are fine, thank you. And you?"

Maintaining the daily façade was exhausting. The secrecy not only robbed us of energy that we could have given to our son, but it also deprived Grant of the support and the prayers from a community that loved him.

Just before his sixteenth birthday, Grant was admitted to a six-month out-of-state residential treatment program. We could have managed a week or two of secrecy, but we had no half-year containment plan. I carefully pulled back the curtains and invited the congregation into our struggle. The people of Atonement honored our vulnerability.

Grant's residential treatment proved unsuccessful, and his health continued to decline. In 2010, Grant reached the low point of his valley where he attempted to take his own life.

When I reached the hospital, I discovered that our congregational support system was still very much in place. A kind, older woman from the congregation had somehow gained access to Grant's ICU room. She was sitting next to his bed, gently rubbing the back of his hand, and assuring him, "Everything is going to be fine, Grant."

A second woman was helping the attending nurse clean the dried blood from Grant's face. She turned and assured me, "He's going to be alright, Pastor. Everything will be fine."

Those dear compassionate prophets echoed for me the same assurance that I gave them each weekend. "We know how the larger story ends," I told them. "It doesn't." Our lives will ultimately be redeemed, and our present trials will come to an end. Then, God will "wipe every tear from our eyes. Mourning and crying and pain will be no more."[1]

But until the never-ending part of our lives begins, things will not be fine. Here, in the middle chapters of life, people continue to live with mental illness. Parents lose their children, and children lose their parents far too soon. And much too much of the struggle takes place unnecessarily in the dark.

I will forever wonder whether Carrie's life might have taken a different course had she lived less secretly. By sharing more of our story with you now, I hope to encourage others to do the same. If we can destigmatize mental illness and remove its secrecy and shame — if we can dispel the myths while increasing public awareness and sensitivity — then more people who live with the conditions may discover the greatest treasure of all, a path out of the darkness.

In the early days of our relationship, Carrie's bouts of sadness were mild and fleeting. I never understood what caused them. I didn't need to, really. A little boyfriend affection was enough to chase the gloom away.

Over time, however, the sadness became a more frequent and unwelcome visitor. The longer it stayed, the more disruptive it became. Winter's melancholy became spring's agitation, and then summer's anger. And with each season, Carrie became less and less consolable.

Early one fall, while living at the beach, Carrie and I decided that a weekend away to see the Appalachian Mountain foliage would be good medicine. We slipped off to Asheville to join a handful of other couples for a three-day Marriage Encounter led by the therapist who conducted our premarital counseling. Barely one day into the event, Carrie became unexplainably agitated and angry and refused to stay. I fabricated an excuse — a skill that I had necessarily refined to an art — and we headed home early.

Such was life for us in those days. Carrie's behavior became more and more predictably unpredictable. I knew that the anxiety would surface but was clueless about what triggered it or what "it" even was.

---

1 Revelation 21:4

King of Glory was a high-profile congregation and a popular worship destination for vacationing Lutherans, many of whom belonged to churches that were searching for pastors. As a result, I received regular invitations to visit with call committees. For several years, I politely declined those invitations out of hand, but shortly after the turn of the new millennium, I began to listen.

In hindsight, it seems ill-advised — perhaps even reckless — to have considered relocating again when Carrie was so emotionally fragile. If we could not make a couples' weekend getaway work, what made us believe we could move halfway across the country and reestablish our lives? Maybe we hoped that a change would help us reclaim the magic we experienced during the early adventurous days of our marriage. Or perhaps we naively thought that a new start would bring new health. The truth is, I was desperate to discover any formula that would arrest whatever was happening to our family.

For a litany of reasons, after a little more than five years at the beach, we packed our lives once again and headed for Kansas City. You may recall my list of "ministry regrets." The entry for July 2001: "Leaving for Kansas, unprepared."

I slipped Kansas's *Point of Know Return* into the CD player and led the family caravan westward toward Overland Park, an affluent suburb just south of Kansas City. The life before us could not have been more disparate from the life reflected in the rearview mirror.

Grant and Lauren had been big, respected, important fish in little ponds. In their new reality, they would be average-sized fish swimming mostly unnoticed in large, unfamiliar waters. We left behind a resort area of beach shops, golf courses, and fishing piers where folks went to work in shorts and returned home with suntans, and we landed in prototypical, upper-middle-class suburbia where professionals wore ties and dresses and carried briefcases.

To be sure, we were drawn to Kansas precisely *because* of the differences. The Blue Valley schools afforded opportunities that the South

Carolina system could barely imagine, much less offer. Regardless, the transition awaiting us would be far more challenging than we anticipated.

Life had a new smell to it. We dropped our luggage in a newly constructed house down the street from the newly constructed Blue Valley West High School campus. We targeted this district hoping that Lauren and Grant would adjust more smoothly if *all* the students were new. New home. New school. New life. But amid this newness awaited the same old challenges.

Barely one month into the first semester, Grant already had fallen hopelessly behind in his work. It was safer for him to surrender without effort than to try and fail. Because it was too late to salvage the semester, we withdrew him from public school and enrolled him in a small private school in town.

Carrie's non-adjustment followed an unfortunately similar path. Overwhelmed and lacking the emotional wherewithal to find her way through the usual routine of settling into a new community, it was easier for her to remain cloistered at home for the first several years. She spent her days watching television, thumb-twiddling, and waiting for the kids and me to come home.

Meanwhile, I was absorbed by the new challenges of managing a large staff and a professional, high-expectation congregation over twice the size of the parish we left at the beach. I reneged on my promise to spend more time at home, and when I *was* at home, there was less of Carrie to spend time with. She was slowly, but steadily, slipping away.

Carrie eventually summoned the courage to take a job as an activities director at a nursing home. Still grappling with back issues, however, she quickly decided the work was too physically demanding and assumed a subsequent teaching position at a Montessori school on the far side of the county.

Carrie enjoyed the work and loved the children. As soon as she was in place in front of the classroom, she did a spectacular job, but prying herself away from home in the mornings became increasingly more difficult. Some days, the only way to ensure she made it to class was to drive her myself. As we sat in the car together in front of the school and waved to parents as they dropped off Carrie's students, I looked for the right combination of words to inspire her to follow her class into the building.

"You can do this. It will be fine. I am only a phone call away."

One evening Carrie announced, "There's a set of triplets in my class. Their parents asked today if I would be willing to watch them in our home. I told them I would."

She quit her teaching position at the next convenient opportunity and set up class in our basement. The arrangement worked out wonderfully for the children, but it further insulated Carrie from the world. Apart from a quarterly appearance at church and an occasional trip to the store or the doctor's office, she fashioned a life that rarely required her to stray beyond our front door.

Her mood swings became more unpredictable and volcanic. To avoid the confrontations and steer clear of the line of fire, I manufactured reasons to remain at the office longer. This, of course, only compounded the issues.

I came to refer to Carrie's expressions of rage as "episodes." There was much that I did not understand about the episodes. What caused them? Was there any way to preempt them, avoid them, or short-circuit them once they started? How could Carrie be so angelic one moment and completely transformed the next?

I moved about our days together carefully, praying that I would avoid Carrie's trip wires. In the evenings, her triggers were especially hypersensitive. Nights were unbearable. If I drifted off to sleep first, I was regularly awakened by an episode that persisted into the early morning hours or ended with Carrie's passing out, or both. Each successive bout of unconsciousness lasted a little longer. The first time that she was unrevivable for more than a few minutes, I phoned 911. By the time the paramedics arrived, however, she had come to and refused transport.

There is no safe place to lose consciousness, but Carrie's episodes tended to end on the stairs or next to especially hard, sharp objects. After striking her head on the elliptical trainer, the paramedics saw indications of a more severe injury and prevailed upon her to be examined. She was concussed.

The next episode did not wait for her injury to heal. The following evening Carrie's anger resumed where the previous episode left off. She threatened, "The nurses at the hospital asked me last night if there was anything I wanted to tell them about how I fell. I almost told them that you were responsible. Next time, I will."

From that point, whenever Carrie passed out, I checked for injury, monitored her breathing, placed a pillow under her head, covered her with a blanket, and just let her sleep. When morning arrived, she would greet me with a kiss and ask, "How did I fall asleep in the hallway (or the living room, or the den) last night? And where did this bruise come from?" That became our new routine.

I avoided the fray any way I could. Some nights, the downstairs bathroom became my storm shelter. Other evenings, I chose to leave home and walk the neighborhood for a few hours, though by doing so, I risked being locked out of the house when I returned.

My name appeared on the weekend preaching docket most weeks, so I retreated more quickly from Saturday evening episodes. I turned off the phone to silence the repeated calls and messages and slept on the couch at the church office. As soon as Carrie discovered my car hidden behind the sanctuary, however, she stood in the alley, throwing pebbles against the window.

Among all the mysteries connected with Carrie's disappearance, there were two things about which I was certain. First, Carrie did not choose her demon; it selected her. The first victim in this story was Carrie.

Second, Carrie exercised no more authority over her demons than I did. Our therapist gave her strategies to help short-circuit the episodes. I watched her desperately call upon them, but when she reached her "point," the strategies were simply no longer available to her.

It was one o'clock on a Sunday morning. I looked out my second-floor office window and saw Carrie standing in the alleyway below. In one hand, she held her phone, still glowing from the sixteenth message just left on my voicemail. In her other hand were the small landscape pebbles she had been tossing against the panes.

Her last words to me when I left home were, "Don't come back. Don't you ever come back!" Now, a little more than an hour later, she was pleading for me to return home. This was one moment when I knew exactly how she felt. I wanted nothing in the world more than for my wife to come home.

As last evening came to an end and the treasure chest lay bare, I asked Lauren, "Wouldn't it be nice to have a replay button? We could go back and do things differently?"

"Maybe," she said, "or maybe we all did the best that we could."

11

CALLING OUT THE ENEMY

The Parable of the Man Who Sowed Good Seed — Part II

"An enemy has done this." (Matthew 13:28)

When Mary came where Jesus was and saw him, she knelt at his feet and said to him, "Lord, if you had been here, my brother would not have died." When Jesus saw her weeping, and the Jews who came with her also weeping, he was greatly disturbed in spirit and deeply moved. He said, "Where have you laid him?" They said to him, "Lord, come and see." Jesus began to weep. So the Jews said, "See how he loved him!" But some said, "Could not he who opened the eyes of the blind man have kept this man from dying?" (John 11:32-37)

Before pressing *PLAY* again on the parable of the man who sowed good seed, let's revisit the frame where we paused the story in chapter 8.

The slaves are standing before the householder, puzzled and a little perturbed. In the background, the sun rises over a beautiful wheat field that, from a distance, looks healthy and well-tended. However, lying on the ground in front of the slaves are small bundles of weeds that suggest otherwise. The slaves enter the weeds into evidence as *Exhibit A* in their inquisition of the householder. I will rewind a few frames and replay their questions: "Master, did you not sow good seed in your field? Where, then, did these weeds come from?"

Our next segment won't last long, so be prepared. Ready? *PLAY.*

"An enemy has done this." *PAUSE.*

That was the householder's entire response to the slaves' complex question. He called out the enemy as the perpetrator of the infestation — but offered nothing more.

The householder (Son of Man) may not have sidestepped the slaves' question entirely, but his response certainly leaves us wanting more. The disciples also were dissatisfied. After Jesus told the parable, the Twelve circled back to Jesus to ask for an explanation. Only then do we learn that the enemy is *diabolos*, the devil.

I have a list of my own cross-examination questions for the householder: "This was a valuable field. Why did you not exercise better control of it or make provisions for it to be guarded?" "Who was responsible for the enemy, and where did he come from?" "How did you know the enemy had done this damage? Did you see him in the field? If so, why did you not stop him? Or do you just recognize his work?" "What recourse do we have against the enemy now? Can he be held accountable? Punished?" "What is to prevent the enemy from causing the same damage again next planting season?"

I do not belittle what the householder *did* provide. Not at all. There is a wealth of gospel in those five words. By straightforwardly declaring that no evil came from his own hands, the householder provided an undemanding corrective for some common misconceptions about God's role in evil and the suffering that results from it.

For example, "God never gives us more than we can handle." True, but not true enough. According to the parable, when it comes to our suffering, God gives *none* of it. God had no hand in your mother's Alzheimer's, your job loss, or the arthritis that is developing in the one good knee you have left. This suffering is not goodness in disguise or part of a larger divine plan that God will reveal in due time. Suffering originates elsewhere. It is not of God.

"God gives me suffering to strengthen my character." Or "God sent this cancer as a wake-up call." Again, no! God may commandeer the suffering that already exists in our lives and repurpose it, but the Lord does not order up an illness to make better people of us. The parable is clear; your lymphoma did not come from God. However, once you have lymphoma, the patience, deepened faith, and healthier lifestyle that you acquire as a result of the disease have God's fingerprints all over them. The Lord rarely allows a good crisis (of someone else's making) to go to waste.

A very similar scene played out in Bethany, around Lazarus' tomb.[1] Mary and Martha, the dead man's sisters, were puzzled and perturbed when Jesus finally showed up in Bethany.

"Lord, if you had been here, my brother would not have died."

The sisters' frustration is understandable. After receiving their plea for help, Jesus dallied for two days before setting out for Bethany. "Why the delay? What gives? Do you not care?"

Mary and Martha are questioning Jesus' compassion.

Anyone who has ever waited on the Lord knows the sisters' disappointment. Why are we left to languish in our despair for so long? When God possesses the cure we need, and the authority and power to administer it, but chooses not to make the house call, how can we *not* question God's compassion?

Sure, we take comfort in knowing that suffering does not come from the hand of God, but Mary and Martha were not writhing in remorse over causality; their cry was for healing. They sought comfort and mercy. A wife does not phone 911 to learn *why* her husband's breathing is labored. She calls because she is looking for a savior.

The sisters never actually asked a question of Jesus. The Jews who were spectating from the mourners' gallery asked on their behalf — and on ours.

"Could not he who opened the eyes of the blind man have kept this man from dying?"

---

1   John 11:1-44

There! That is the question we want Jesus to answer. "I understand that you didn't sow the weeds in the field, Master, but didn't you have the power to stop the one who did?"

But as usual, Jesus did not finally show up on the scene of the crisis for question-and-answer time or to deal with the sisters' discontent. According to his sidebar conversation with the Father, he had come so that those in Bethany would believe that God sent him. Raising Lazarus was a sign of God's power and Jesus' identity.

But what if the Lord had stopped short of performing the miracle? How would the scene have played out differently for Mary and Martha had Jesus proclaimed himself as the resurrection and then immediately resumed his march to the cross, leaving Lazarus in the tomb? Is this not *our* challenge? Are we not envious of the demonstration that Mary and Martha received? "Raise one of *our* loved ones from the dead, and we, too, will be satisfied. We will also believe!"

Or would we? Time for a theological sidebar.

The raising of Lazarus achieved Jesus' intended purpose, but only partially. Many of the Jews believed in Jesus…but not all of them. Why? How is it possible to witness a four-day-old corpse walk forth from its tomb and then not fall in line behind the One who made it happen? I suppose we would have to ask the witnesses who, instead of recommitting their lives to Jesus, essentially sealed Jesus' fate on the cross by going directly to the religious authorities to report what had taken place.

Or we could fast forward a few weeks to Jerusalem where Jesus leads a frenzied, palm-waving procession of peasants into the holy city. Some of those who race after Jesus used to be lame. Others who shout, "Hosanna!" were once mute. And before they encountered Jesus, many of those who watch the spectacle had been blind.

But as soon as the procession is over and the trial begins, these witnesses will become silent. Jesus' followers will look and run the other way. Jesus' miracles will no longer be enough for them. At the first sign of suffering, they abdicate their faith in their Healer.

John tells us, "Although Jesus had performed so many signs in their presence, the people did not believe in him."[2]

But the most egregious deserters were the disciples themselves. No one witnessed more of Jesus' miracles than the Twelve. For three years, they had round-the-clock front-row seats to the ushering in of God's kingdom. Yet when the women returned from the empty Easter tomb to report that the Lord had been raised (in precisely the manner he had predicted), the disciples refused to believe.[3]

The point is this: While it is easy to claim, "Had I been there, I would have believed," history says, "Not so much."

But even if we managed somehow to defy human history and remain faithful to Jesus because of his miracles, we still will have missed the point. God established *faith* as the foundation of our relationship together. Faith believes what it cannot see. The more proof God provides — the more answers the householder offers up during his cross-examination — the less faith we need. Jesus told the disciples, "Blessed are those who have not seen and yet have come to believe."[4]

That may be little consolation for those who stand before the householder with their long lists of unanswered questions. Like the slaves, we would have arranged things differently. Yet it is not our field. The householder has been willing to entertain our questions. But in the end, the most he will offer in response is his own question: "Do you trust me?"

As we prepare to press *PAUSE* again on our study, allow me to oversimplify my takeaway from our parable so far. When God rested on the seventh day, the entirety of creation was good. Given my experience of God — and the admittedly limited testimony of Scripture on the topic — I find the prospect that God would later introduce evil into the world to be irreconcilable with the heart and nature and character of the Creator.

---

2 John 12:27
3 Luke 24:11
4 John 20:29

So, we have come full circle to the slaves' original question: Who sowed the evil seed?

Until Christ returns to take the witness stand, many of our cross-examination questions will remain unanswered. But for now, let us agree upon this: Regardless of who bears responsibility for the presence of evil, God is not the delivery person.

12

What Might Have Been

The only things I regret, and the only things I'll ever regret are things I didn't do. In the end, that's what we mourn. The paths we didn't take. The people we didn't touch."

~ Scott Spencer, *Endless Love*

Of all the words of mice and men, the saddest are, "It might have been."

~ Kurt Vonnegut, *Cat's Cradle*

Nothing existed beyond the wings of our 747. No cities. No neighborhoods. No buildings or streetlights. Only the starry Tanzanian night. For over an hour, the only visible artificial light emanated from the jet's strobing beacon. This was not the same world I left in Amsterdam.

"Ladies and Gentlemen, we have just begun our final descent into Kilimanjaro International Airport."

Had the pilot not narrated our approach, I would have sworn he was undertaking an emergency maneuver to turn a desolate moonlit field into a makeshift runway. Fortunately, ahead of the jet and in full view of the cockpit were the lights of a lone airstrip.

I leaned back in my seat and exhaled. I had been waiting to hear those words for months, but now that I had finally reached Africa, all I wanted to do was turn around and head home. It had been a long night.

I went to Tanzania in July of 2009, one week ahead of a team of my parishioners from Atonement. Our ultimate destination was Mwanza, a town on Lake Victoria's southern shore, another short flight from Kilimanjaro. The team's objective was to help Paula and Denny, our dear missionary friends, construct a medical clinic.

But before I started pouring cement and slinging hammers, my brother Pete and I intended to share an adventure together.

Mount Kilimanjaro has all the characteristics we admire in a mountain. At 19,340 feet, it is the tallest peak on the African continent and the highest point on the planet reachable without technical gear. The week-long climb to Kili's summit begins in the rainforest and traverses five distinct climate zones before reaching arctic conditions at Uhuru Peak.

Tanzanian law requires climbers to secure a licensed expedition team. As soon as the climb begins, the hired Swahili guides cry out, "Polepole!" ("Slowly!") The secret to a successful summit is maintaining a moderate, steady pace while making strategic, incremental altitude adjustments. Nearly half of the expeditions that strike out for Uhuru — even those with healthy and well-conditioned climbers — turn back short of the summit. All along the route, ascending groups greet the sobering sight of unsuccessful colleagues being helped or carried down the mountain on stretchers or in body bags. Kili claims an average of ten lives annually.

The human body is likely to experience altitude sickness at 8,000 feet. At 19,000 feet, unless wrapped in an airplane, you can count on it. When the blood is starved of oxygen, fatigue sets in, the brain swells, and breathing becomes shallow. Confusion, nausea, and rapid heart rates are usual.

To combat these symptoms, many climbers start a regimen of acetazolamide several days before the trip. This medication makes the blood more acidic and efficient at drawing oxygen into the cells.

"Not much call for that stuff around here," my primary care physician said. Kansas is one of the more altitude-challenged states.

The months of training were complete. The gear was collected and shoehorned into two brand-new bright yellow North Face duffle bags. Tent, bag, poles, backpacking mat. *Check.* Summer clothing for the first stages of the hike and Marmot parka, wool mittens, and balaclava for the arctic summit. *Check.* Vaccinations. *Check.* Antimalarial medications. *Check.* A small container of my father's ashes to spread once we reached the mountain's summit. *Check.*

The final item on the checklist was *take acetazolamide. Check.*

Barely fifteen minutes after swallowing the initial dose, my body sent a clear message that it was not pleased. My arms and face revolted with fiery pins and needles and prickly sensations. A field of angry crickets set to chirping in my ears. My lips, cheeks, and hands felt twice their normal size. Breathing became heavy and labored, and I began to sense that I might see the evening's dinner for a second time.

I raced to the computer to research the drug, something my flatland doctor had apparently neglected to do before prescribing twice the recommended maximum dosage. The pharmacist on call promised a miserable but survivable night. He was prophetic. By morning, all the side effects were gone, save the breathing issue.

It was go-no-go decision time, and my lungs were laboring as if I were already standing at Uhuru Peak. I weighed my options for all of thirty seconds, downplayed my concerns to Carrie, then grabbed the gear and headed for the airport as planned, hoping that the issue would resolve along the way.

A body takes a surprising number of breaths during an eighteen-hour flight. Each draw raised new questions. What if this as-yet-undiagnosed issue worsened and required medical attention? Or a surgical procedure? My purpose for going to Tanzania was to help improve medical care for others, not consume it myself. No one with options ever chooses to be anesthetized in this part of the world. But what if one has no other options?

Twenty-two hours after leaving home, the pilot welcomed us to

Tanzania. The only change in my aching chest was that it had been delivered halfway around the world.

I found Jeremy, my chauffeur, waiting on the other side of a ninety-minute immigration ordeal. He chucked my gear into the back of our limousine, an old chopped-off open-air Toyota 4Runner missing a door, a headlight, one seat, and a few other helpful but nonessential parts and we headed for Arusha.

Jeremy was an affable fellow. He wasted no time striking up a conversation. We were barely a mile out of the airport before he discovered that I was Lutheran.

"So am I!" he shouted excitedly above the wind and engine noise.

I was not surprised. The Evangelical Lutheran Church of Tanzania is one of the world's largest denominations. I fully expect that one day soon, the ELCT will send missionaries to the United States, especially if they all have Jeremy's zeal.

"You will like your motel. It is very nice," he promised as the lights of Arusha came into view.

After a 747 field landing and a ride in the back of an open-air, panting, one-eyed Toyota limousine, my expectations were not that high. Besides, at that moment, I was much more concerned with knowing why a city of greater than 400,000 inhabitants was so lifeless. The streets were deserted. I decided that it was probably better not to ask.

Jeremy pulled up to the side of the motel and sounded the horn. An attendant instantly appeared, unlocked a gate, and allowed us passage down a narrow alley that obviously had been designed with a considerably smaller limo in mind. Jeremy didn't seem to mind a few more scrapes along the concrete walls. They helped redistribute some of the Toyota's scars.

The long, odd journey made reuniting with Pete especially heartwarming, though discovering him sheltered in bed behind mosquito netting was a little disconcerting. Brothers can communicate with phrases and one-word sentences, so we caught up with one another in no time.

Then, I shared my news. "There's an issue," I said sheepishly. "I am having difficulty breathing."

"Well, that's not good," he replied.

Pete has an extraordinary gift for grasping the obvious.

Jet lag combined with respiratory issues made for a third straight miserable, fidgety night. Hyped up from caffeine and insomnia-induced jitters, I placed a call the following morning to Paula in Mwanza to inform her of my arrival and, more urgently, to collect medical counsel.

"Well, that's not good," she said, though with a little more empathy than my hiking partner.

Paula connected me with a doctor from Minnesota who was volunteering in Tanzania at the time. He was equally comforting.

"Understand that if this is a cardiac issue, over here, you're basically dead. They have no way to deal with it."

"Thank you. I cannot tell you how much better I feel."

I walked a few miles to a local doctor's office on the outskirts of Arusha, where I was directed into an open examining room. By *open*, I mean that three of the room's walls had large windows but no glass. We were essentially outside. Following a routine exam, the doctor reached into a wooden drawer and retrieved an unwrapped syringe to draw blood, then prepared the smear using a standard handheld hairdryer.

After an hour of speculating and head-scratching, the doctor appointed his nurse to shuttle me to the Arusha Lutheran Medical Centre for testing. She became my guide and lead blocker for the remainder of the day, cutting paths through a maze of busy, unmarked hallways packed with ailing, moaning, local patients who were obviously in much more distress than I. I understood nothing they said but read their expressions perfectly.

"Make way for the rich white guy!"

"We'll have a chest X-ray and one of *those*. And we should probably get one of *these* as well."

I don't recall the precise tests that the nurse ordered, only that the process felt like buying tickets for carnival rides. I paid cash, a small fraction of the cost I would have paid for the same tests in the states, and proceeded to the chest X-ray room where I exchanged my paperwork for a tie-in-the-back gown. I gladly put it on. It was the only part of the day that felt familiar.

The technician motioned for me to crawl inside a large white piece of equipment as the nurse prepared my IV. Uncertain whether the test would last five minutes or an hour, I asked, "May I use the restroom before we get started?" When hand gestures are the only means of communicating, this can be an incredibly awkward question. The tech pointed to a hole in the floor in the far corner of the uncomfortably small room. I smiled and shook my head in Swahili.

Yet one more needle went into my arm. At least this one had been wrapped. The nurse attached a plastic funnel to the other end of a long, thin, rubber IV tube through which she then poured a white liquid. My arm immediately started turning colder. I blurted out the only Swahili word I knew, "Polepole!" which actually sort of worked. It solicited a smile, but the nurse kept pouring. I tried again. "My…arm…is…cold," as if spacing out the words made them easier to translate. She smiled and adjusted the room thermostat.

At the end of the day, we were no closer to a diagnosis. Pete and I were scheduled to begin our adventure at sunrise the following morning. Vesna, the owner of the guide company, recommended that Pete begin the climb as expected.

"Making up a day's hike will be easy for you," she said. "If you feel better, you can start tomorrow and catch your brother."

I had traveled halfway around the world to wish Pete well and watch as he climbed into the van with the porters to be shuttled to the trailhead of *our* epic hike.

"Break a leg!" I called as they drove off.

The next order of business was to ensure that my broken heart was not also diseased.

I relocated to the more affordable Lutheran retreat center in Moshi, the spot where I was to rendezvous with the parishioners at the end of the week. For the next several days I stayed up into the wee hours of the morning and rose before the sun to consult with doctors back home (at $7.95 a minute). After several days of long-distance medical musing, Tom, an emergency room physician and member of Atonement, spoke the words I had been waiting to hear.

"Pastor, you have symptoms, but no diagnosis. You really should come home."

The following night, while flying west somewhere over the Atlantic Ocean, I passed the Atonement delegation headed east. I silently prayed blessings upon their journey, though with a twinge of envy. The U.S. doctors arranged for KLM to have a wheelchair waiting for me at the arrival gates in Dar es Salaam, Amsterdam, and Detroit. I thanked the agents but declined. I could not bring myself to be wheeled down the concourse as Pete was trudging down our mountain.

Just before departing Tanzania, Vesna had phoned to relay her team's report of a successful summit. I imagined Pete standing triumphantly on Africa's rooftop. As soon as the cameras were stowed and the congratulations were complete, I pictured him reaching into his parka zip pocket for the small vial I brought from home. For the first time in days, I smiled as I thought of Pete opening the vial and releasing some of Dad's ashes to the wind. I am sure Dad smiled, too.

Carrie retrieved me from the airport in Kansas City and delivered me straightaway to Saint Luke's South Emergency, where Dr. Tom was waiting. He took one look at the films that I had so carefully toted from the other side of the world, tossed them in the trash, and rebooted the entire process. No tickets were necessary this time around, and the restroom was well-marked and private.

It would take several days to identify the culprit responsible for this fiasco of an adventure — an inactive gallbladder ticked off by acetazolamide. After a brief outpatient arthroscopic surgery to remove the organ, the rest of my body immediately simmered down.

Mount Kilimanjaro is so massive that she claims entire weather systems for herself. She chooses to spend most of her time shrouded by the clouds. But on rare occasions, Kili will unmask herself and pose for the cameras, as was the case the afternoon before I left Moshi. I grabbed my camera and snapped several pictures of the mountain just about the time Pete's team was approaching the summit. Of course, he is a little difficult to make out from fifty miles away.

A much better, sharper picture of Pete was taken a few hours later by a member of his guide team. My brother is standing beneath the Uhuru Peak sign at the top of the continent, his arms spread in the *Victory V*.

Though both images will find their way into our respective treasure chests, they are vastly different. One image tells a story of success and accomplishment. The other will serve as a reminder of what *might have been*.

Luke's Easter story took place on the evening of the first day of the week, somewhere along the road to Emmaus.[1] The resurrected Jesus joined Cleopas and his unnamed companion, though neither of the disciples recognized him. When Jesus, the stranger, asked the travelers what they had been discussing with one another, the disciples "stood still, looking sad." Then Cleopas shared their story of what might have been.

"We had hoped that Jesus would be the one to redeem Israel," he said.

The most despairing sound that the human voice can make is the sound of hope in the past tense. Apart from hope, we cannot survive for long.

Jesus veritably exploded upon the disciples. "How foolish you are and slow of heart to believe!"

The redemption they longed for stood two feet away, but they were too consumed by regret to recognize it. The disciples nearly missed Easter because they would not release the pain of Good Friday.

Jesus completed his earthly ministry the same way he began, by calling his followers to turn around. Change your perspective. Your heart. Your mind. This is no simple turning. Releasing regret is hard work, to be sure. Restoring hope may require forgiving others or ourselves. It may be

---

[1] Luke 24:21

necessary to reframe our losses or failures or understand our disappointment differently.

Regret is an especially painful emotion. It is also remarkably instructive.

Henry David Thoreau said, "Make the most of your regrets; never smother your sorrow, but tend and cherish it till it comes to have a separate and integral interest. To regret is to live afresh."

Turning around does not ask, "Why?" or wallow in, "If only I had…" It merely inquires, "What now?"

Historians are uncertain as to the location of the ancient Judean town of Emmaus. I like that. I prefer to think of the road that Cleopas and his companion walked as the same path each of us takes during times of regret. It is the move to a lonely apartment following a failed marriage, the trip to the hospital for a first chemo treatment, or the ride home from the cemetery after the burial of a loved one. Most any journey that begins with "I had hoped" can lead to Emmaus.

I traveled nine thousand miles to conquer a mountain and the closest I got to Uhuru Peak was a Tanzanian emergency room. I could either harbor the pain of that disappointment forever or find a way to release it. As it turned out, walking the road to Emmaus likely demanded from me the same strategies and resolve I would have used to summit Kili.

The journey from "I had hoped" to "What now?" can be grueling, even for the most spiritually fit. We dare not travel it too quickly. "Pole-pole!" Nor should we undertake the journey alone. Completing this climb requires an experienced Guide who has walked our path before us, who has experienced our sorrow, brokenness, and pain, and overcome them — a Guide who knows every bend in the trail, the best places to rest, and the especially difficult sections where he will need to encourage us.

Look for this Guide if you wish. But in the end, he will find you. In fact, he has already helped lead you out of more than a few tight spots, but like the disciples, you just didn't recognize him at the time.

I flew halfway around the world to *not* climb a mountain. Instead, I spent the week with my Guide.

I am all the stronger for it.

13

14 Norman Street

Life must be understood backwards, but it can only be lived forward.

~ Soren Kierkegaard

Home isn't where you're from, it's where you find light when all grows dark.

~ Pierce Brown, *Golden Sun*

Early on a December morning in 2009, I stood alone on a street corner in Jerusalem and watched as the Holy City awakened. Both She and I were as still in that moment as either of us would be for the rest of the day. Suddenly, the calm was interrupted by an adolescent boy who brushed past me hurriedly, playfully zigzagging through the empty market stalls. He called out in Arabic to his companion, and together they disappeared around the corner. I had traveled sixty-five hundred miles to see that boy, and in an instant, he was gone.

I pulled the phone from my jacket pocket and read from the second chapter of Luke's Gospel, "When the festival was ended, and Mary and Joseph started to return, the boy Jesus stayed behind in Jerusalem, but his parents did not know it."[1]

The following morning, our group climbed aboard a small vessel at Magdala and put out upon the Sea of Galilee. When we reached the middle of the lake, the captain cut the engines and, for the second time in as many days, my spirit was still. Without instruction, everyone honored the moment with silence.

We had come to the Holy Land for this purpose — so our senses could experience what before had only been available to our imaginations. As we swayed in cadence with the boat's rocking and listened to the sounds of the waves and the mewing calls of the gulls, I read from Matthew: "Early in the morning, Jesus came walking to them on the sea."[2]

There are as many reasons for taking pilgrimages as there are pilgrims who take them. We may be motivated by a desire to flee something, such as an encumbered or uninspired life, or we may be in search of something, such as spiritual discernment, forgiveness, a miracle, or the wisdom of those who have traveled before us. Regardless of our reasons for visiting sacred places, when the past speaks powerfully into the present, we rarely return home unchanged.

Samuel Crowther was fifteen years old when he left Blackburn, England. He somehow managed passage on a transatlantic ocean liner and traveled unattended to the United States where he went to work in the weaving mills of Providence, Rhode Island. As soon as he was settled, he sent word for his sweetheart, Emily, to join him. Together they started a life and family in the new world.

Following Emily's untimely death, Grandpa shared the remainder of his life equally with his five far-flung children. He navigated his annual

---

1 Luke 2:43
2 Matthew 14:25

circuit as any self-respecting Englishman would — clockwise. He called Massachusetts *home*. Each journey began and ended in the boroughs southwest of Boston. The first stop was Maryland's Eastern Shore, then to North Carolina, then to Southern California, then home.

Every three months, Grandpa tightly packed all his belongings into an enormous shiny, black trunk, and then wedged the trunk into the back seat of a shiny, black Volkswagen Beetle. When it was time to leave, he whistled his faithful Weimaraner, Ador, onto the front seat and set out for his next destination. Grandpa was eighty-five years young when his fender was bent by another driver. The children conducted an intervention and developed a new travel plan.

"Next trip, Pops, we're putting you on the bus."

This worked well for everyone, except Ador, I suppose.

My earliest childhood memories of Grandpa are of a seventy-something, jolly, balding, bow-legged, pipe-smoking, English gentleman who laughed loudly and worried never. My last memories of him are much the same. He died quietly at home just shy of his one-hundredth birthday.

In the fall of 2004, I shepherded a small group of sixteen travelers on a tour through the United Kingdom. Dad decided to join.

"It's high time I visit the mother country," he said.

By *mother country*, he intended more than Westminster Abbey, Stonehenge, the English countryside, or any of the other sites listed in our tour itinerary. The trip to the United Kingdom was my father's *pilgrimage*.

So, at the age of eighty-seven, one century after Grandpa made his teenage voyage across the Atlantic, Dad visited England for the first time. His primary destination was the place where his father's journey began — 14 Norman Street, Blackburn.

I made sure that our itinerary afforded the group a free day in London. While others conspired to visit Big Ben, Harrod's, Saint Paul's Cathedral, and as much of the rest of London as could be crammed into a ten-hour day, Dad and I struck out on a 220-mile jaunt north to Blackburn. We had only one destination in mind.

I fought our pint-sized, rented European Ford Fiesta through London's unfamiliar streets, trying desperately to avoid being swallowed up by the morning rush hour traffic. Overriding my preference for the right side of the road...circling roundabouts clockwise...shifting gears with my left hand...and turning my navigator's foldable map right-side-up so he would send us north instead of south — I felt as if we had landed in our own private episode of British comedy television.

When I reached to downshift, but instinctively used my right hand and opened the driver's door instead, Dad asked, "Are you sure we're up for this?" I just kept driving.

It took nearly four hours to travel from downtown London through the English countryside and around to Manchester's north side. Blackburn was considerably more extensive and industrialized than I had imagined. The chances of finding Norman Street by happenstance were nil. I spotted a post office and considered that if anyone had a good sense of the city, it would be the mail deliverers.

"Norman Street, you say?" The postmaster rubbed his chin, rechecked his maps, and in a puzzled Cockney accent replied, "Can't say me ever heard of it."

A female lorry driver was politely eavesdropping on our conversation. Demonstrating the hospitality Londoners are famous for, she said, "I know Norman Street. Follow me." She led us across the city and deposited us in the general vicinity of our destination, then pointed.

"It's in that direction," she said. "Just a block or two."

"Hey, Sonny!" Dad called to a teenager walking the sidewalk. "Can you help us? We're looking for Norman Street?"

The boy shrugged his shoulders and then called to his companion. They each dropped their skateboards to the pavement and disappeared together around the corner. It seemed curious to me that a young boy in the twenty-first century would be ignorant of the whereabouts of local streets when, more than a century earlier, and at nearly the same age, Grandpa had managed to navigate his way thirty-one hundred miles from Blackburn to Providence.

"I wonder if that is the Anglican church that Dad attended. It must be," Dad said. "It's the only one around. You know, I bet this tree was just a little sapling when your grandfather was a boy."

The past was beginning to show itself.

We discovered 14 smack-dab in the middle of Norman Street. It was a plain, austere, red-brick structure with unadorned windows. The only feature that distinguished 14 from 12, 16, or any other house on Norman Street was the door. It was off-white rather than pure white. There was no yard. No lawn. Only a brick sidewalk and a front doorstep. It hardly seemed the sort of place that anyone would travel across town, much less four thousand miles, to see. Yet the two of us stood on the edge of the street and stared as if we were beholding the *Mona Lisa*.

"Well? Aren't you going to ring the bell?" I finally asked.

"Do you think we should?"

"You've come a long way to see it. You'll never have a better chance."

A very British, middle-aged woman answered the door. The brief stoop visit was more of a presentation than a conversation.

"My name is Milt Crowther. My father, Samuel, was born in this house in 1890," Dad reported proudly, and then he chattered on for a few more minutes. The woman received us very graciously, and a little cautiously, as she probably should have. I took several pictures, and we were on our way. We accomplished our mission, but the pilgrimage was far from complete.

Dad had been his typical loquacious self throughout the tour, but on our return to London, he became downright garrulous. I reclined my bucket seat, set the cruise control to 140 kilometers per hour, and piloted our mini-machine southward down the wrong side of M6. Dad regaled me with a stream of consciousness reminiscing about his move from New England to North Carolina, the details of his purchasing the farm, his courtship with Mom, and a few dozen other topics.

"Your grandmother's hair was blonde and long and straight. When she let it down, it hung below her waist. Grandpa came home one day and discovered that she had cut it clear up to her shoulders. Oh, was he mad!" Dad chuckled. "Long blonde hair was in high demand during the war for making crosshairs for bombsights. She just sold it without asking him."

All he required from me was a nod or a "hmm," and he was off to the next tale.

"I don't know if I ever told you how I bought the farm."

"Hmm."

"I arranged to purchase the house and a few acres of land from the lady who owned it. But on the day of the closing, her son was involved in some sort of shenanigans. She was so upset that she decided to toss in the entire 250-acre plot instead of leaving it for his inheritance. I got 250 acres and the house for $13,000. Just good timing, I suppose."

Around Birmingham, the stories crossed over into an arena where Dad spent little time — romance. He shared how a mutual friend where he worked arranged for a blind date with Mom. Then, taking his first deep breath in over an hour, Dad cupped his hands behind his head, leaned back in his seat, and said, "Yep, I suppose your mom is the best thing that ever happened to me."

The comment was priceless and preciously out of character. It also expressed a truth with which the entire family would agree. Mom is the best thing that has happened to all of us.

The pace of our tour ramped up considerably the following morning. We took to the streets of London as if we were making up for lost time instead of free time. At several points during the afternoon, Dad reached out and pressed the back of his hand into my chest.

"Slow down," he said sharply, almost embarrassingly. "I'm not as fast as I used to be."

This was my father's second arresting comment in two days. He rarely confessed his heart or admitted his limitations. Just the week before, or so it seemed, I had been the one begging, "Hey, Pops! What's your hurry?" as we chased the Weimaraners through the marshes and climbed the hills around the farm in search of quail. His pace and reflexes were quick and sharp then. By the time I realized a covey had flushed, Dad could shoulder his shotgun and drop two birds. But that was yesterday.

Dad lived as a bachelor until his mid-forties, so he learned to keep himself company. In the rare moments that he was not reading (sometimes when he was) or visiting with someone (sometimes when he was), he hummed. No one considered his humming to be especially lyrical, more just noise. But the noise served a valuable purpose. Dad seldom volunteered how he felt. If he were ill, we typically learned several days *after* he visited the doctor. The humming was a type of indicator light that let the world know all was well with him.

Not long after returning from his Norman Street pilgrimage, Dad stopped humming.

I do not know what finally took Dad, only that his death followed long months of steady physical weakening and frustratingly frequent trips to the hospital for blood transfusions. He measured his worth by his capacity to invent or produce or fix something. Sitting for hours at the hospital each week, strapped to IVs and "just taking up space and time," his spirit began to atrophy. Once the highlight of his day became the afternoon walk to the mailbox, I knew that he would not be long for this world.

Several months before his death, Dad and I worked on a project in the front yard of the farmhouse; I planted roses underneath a row of split rail fences as he leaned against the post and supervised.

"I don't think I'll be around much longer," he said suddenly. Dad never was one for easing into a conversation. Then he paused. This was one time that "hmm" would not be enough.

Noticing the rose bush in my hand, I said, "You know, Dad, someone once asked Luther, 'What would you do if you knew the world were ending tomorrow?' Luther said, 'I would plant a tree.' I thought it was a beautiful response even though I didn't understand what he meant at the time. Later, I learned that Luther was planting a tree when the question was asked. So, I think he was saying, 'I'll control what's in my hands at this moment, and trust God to take care of the rest.'"

I don't know if it helped, but as we turned our attention back to the roses, he began to hum.

Christians do not remember as the rest of the world remembers. Rather than thinking nostalgically about something that occurred long ago, our remembering ushers the past powerfully into the present.

Jesus commanded his disciples at the last supper, "Do this to remember me." His words were not an invitation for us to sit around a table today, eat bread, drink wine, and think about a time when Jesus was *really* in the world. Instead, Jesus commanded us to put him together again in our presence. In our remembering, we *re-member* Jesus. That is, we member him again.

"Remember me when you come into your kingdom." The thief hanging on the cross next to Jesus did not intend a worldly sort of remembering.

"Today, you will be with me in paradise," the Lord promised. You will be re-membered there.

In the table prayer before communion, the church declares a mystery. "Unite our prayers with those of your servants of every time and every place." This meal transcends time and space. All the faithful — past and present, near and far — come together at one table.

We don't need to travel halfway around the world to experience spiritual transformation. Sometimes, the most powerful pilgrimages occur in familiar, ordinary places. For me, one such place is a simple table of grace where each week I remember, among others, a sister and a grandmother I never knew, a jolly bow-legged English gentleman, and my garrulous father.

The past and the future merge into a present moment, and together, we share a foretaste of the glorious feast yet to come.

14

Deus Loquens

This would be my consolation; I would even exult in relentless pain;
for I have not denied the words of the Holy One.

~ Job 6:10

And those who were seen dancing were thought to be insane
by those who could not hear the music.

~ Author unknown

I am a procrastinator. I would tell you more about my condition now, but I prefer to put it off as long as possible.

Parish ministry will tolerate many pastoral character deficiencies; procrastination is not one of them. Amid the weekly grind of preaching and teaching, there are consequences to putting off sermon preparation and lesson planning to the last minute.

In 1998, an especially late Lenten season lulled me into weeks of dawdling. I awoke suddenly on a Monday morning in early February, much closer to Ash Wednesday than I care to confess, and discovered myself in a bind. The first item of business on that night's council agenda at King of Glory was *Approve Pastor's Plan for Lent*. So, I made an extra-large pot of coffee, rolled up my creative sleeves, and began what would become one of the more memorable days of my ministry.

Several hours and three mugs of coffee into the morning, all I had to show for my brainstorming was an impressive case of caffeine jitters. Each time I began tracking a promising Lenten theme, my attention was hijacked by the same bizarre, irrepressible vision of a mission congregation on a tropical island. I recognized neither the church nor its location. All I knew for sure about the vision was it didn't come from me.

Daydreaming about palm trees and deep blue ocean waters might seem natural enough during mid-winter, but I am much more of a snow-capped mountains kind of guy. Had someone offered me a free trip to Tahiti or the Florida Keys, I would have gladly traded it for a compelling Lenten program. As it turned out, I got both.

I was pouring coffee mug number four when Len, one of King of Glory's more spirited members, burst into the office with a mystery-solving announcement: "Pastor, Eileen and I have just returned from Maui. We worshiped with a mission congregation there that needs our help!"

I turned my eyes toward heaven and whispered, "Now cut that out."

Albert Einstein said, "Coincidence is God's way of staying anonymous." That may be true, but I have never considered that God desired anonymity. I think the Lord just enjoys being recognized more than showing off. Believing is seeing. Faith is the dust that reveals the Holy Spirit's fingerprints.

It took considerable restraint, even for a procrastinator, to wait until three p.m. (nine a.m. in the Hawaii-Aleutian Time Zone) to phone the office of Kihei Lutheran Church. I introduced myself to Rev. Dave Krueger and asked if he might consider a mission partnership with a sister congregation that was a mere forty-eight hundred miles away. Before I could finish the question, he responded, "Absolutely!"

So, as it turned out, I had quite a story to share with the council that evening after all. The proposal to send half of our Lenten offering to KLC was met with a unanimous "aye," and our mission partnership was off and running. The next few years were marked by pulpit exchanges, shared ministry ventures, and a steady flow of financial support westward across the Pacific.

In 2006, after years of worshiping in a public school cafeteria, KLC completed construction on the congregation's first building. Dave phoned me in Kansas to extend an invitation to the Service of Dedication.

"I don't believe that I ever told you how much your contact meant to me," he said. "The very morning you called I had decided to hang it up. Ministry had stalled. The Hawaiian economy was tanking. Kathy and I were ready to move back to the mainland and start over. But your call helped encourage us to stay."

Coincidence?

It has always been God's nature to speak. In the beginning, the Lord fashioned the universe using words, not labor. The Creator said, "Let there be light and water and creatures," and it was so. God spoke creation into being.

For as long as we have pondered God, theologians have described the Creator as loquacious, garrulous, chatty, voluble, and verbose. The Protestant Reformers wrote about *Deus loquens* — *God's speaking*. *Loquens* is the Latin root of the English word for *eloquent*.

Martin Luther considered faithful preaching to be nothing less than God's own voice. He even suggested that we can hear God with our eyes. "Let the man who would hear God read Holy Scripture," he wrote. Our dreams can be arenas for God's speaking, as can our consciences, or the voices of those we consider to be less than ourselves.

Most people of faith are comfortable with the notion of God speaking, as long as *Deus loquens* is mediated in some way. We listen for God in sermons, dreams, or a passage of Scripture. No one bats an eye during Bible studies when I ask, "What is God saying to you through this verse or story?"

In the post-worship receiving line, folks may comment, "The Lord certainly spoke through you today, Pastor." And since you are still reading, I assume that you are willing to entertain the possibility that God could forge a relationship between two congregations by speaking through visions.

However, when it comes to experiencing God's unmediated voice, our spiritual sensibilities become a little more skittish. Begin a sentence with the phrase, "The Lord told me...," and you will see foreheads furrow and eyes roll upwards. We believe that God delights in our prayers, but when God answers us audibly — when our communication *to* God becomes a conversation *with* God — the faithful quickly become skeptical. Samuel, Moses, David, and Mary may have experienced *Deus loquens*, but we do not fathom God speaking to us in the same way.

So, I share with some trepidation that I have experienced the Lord's audible voice twice — once in the summer of 2009 and again three years later. Both instances changed my life.

Christmas is typically not the most wonderful time of the year for families living with mental or emotional illness. Any occasion that took my family out of our routine had a way of dialing up the intensity of Carrie's episodes. At home, I had an escape plan. The office became my storm shelter and decompression chamber. But traveling through Kentucky in the middle of a twenty-hour Christmas Day road trip, a rented SUV offers little refuge.

Carrie's health continued to spiral downward in 2009. That summer, our family made the annual retreat to my folks' beach cottage in Ocean Isle Beach, North Carolina. Carrie loved the beach. She was at home there. That may explain why the week went so well. It may also explain why everything disintegrated on our final day.

When it came time to head west again, Carrie disappeared.

We planned to make the two-hundred-mile drive to my folks' farm in time for dinner and an evening visit before striking out for Kansas the following morning. We packed the suitcases and souvenirs into the van, swept a week's worth of sand from the cottage, and blew the whistle to load up. Everything was ready, except Carrie and Samson, her little Yorkshire Terrier. They were nowhere to be found.

We phoned her repeatedly, but no answer. I scampered down to the beach, suspecting that she was saying her goodbyes for another year, but there was no sign of her. The kids split up and searched the beach shops and convenience stores. No luck.

So, we settled in and began our vigil. We had little choice.

Late afternoon came and went, as did any hopes of making it to the farm in time for dinner, and still, there was no word. I phoned Mom to apologize for the usual change in plans. At least with family, there was no need to manufacture excuses.

On the front deck of the cottage was an old weathered wooden swing that was seldom used. It became my lookout where, for the rest of the evening, I waited and prayed.

There was nothing unusual about this disappearance. I had long since learned that life with Carrie was scheduled in pencil. We regularly canceled dinners with friends, trips, and family plans due to last-minute episodes or emergencies. We had come to expect the *something unexpected*. What made this day so remarkable was how unremarkable the day had been — how abnormal our normal had become.

I knew how the rest of the day would play out. Carrie became uneasy after dark, so I trusted that dusk would accomplish what we could not; it would coax her back. The kids would not demand to know where she had been or complain, "We looked all over for you!" There would be no explanations or apologies for having kept us waiting and worried, and no one would dare to question Carrie for fear of the reprisal we might unleash.

None of us would be angry or upset, just numb. As I sat on that old, weathered swing, I opened the prayer spigot, and years of anguish came pouring out.

God and I visit every day, but only a handful of our conversations can I recall a decade later. What marked this prayer was the most profound sense of déjà vu that I have ever experienced. I flashed back to a mirrored moment during the previous summer's trip: I was sitting in the same spot, offering the same lament, and suffering through the same feelings of hopelessness.

"How can I break this pattern? I don't know that I can survive another year like this. If we are having this same conversation next summer, Lord, there will be nothing left of me."

As soon as the sun touched the horizon, Carrie materialized with Samson in her arms. She had been gone nine hours.

"I'll let you know when and if I'm ready to leave," she said sharply and went directly inside.

It was at that moment that God spoke. With a voice so clear and resolute that I hear it still, God said, "It is enough."

Three simple, tender words.

The voice did not startle me; it was familiar. It was the same voice that I experienced in Scripture, in my imagination, and through the voices of others. But on this occasion — and for the first time in forty-six years — God's voice was direct and audible. I heard it.

I whispered the words several times to myself. "It is enough. It is enough."

I did not question what *it* meant, for I knew. The Lord and I had been speaking for hours about *it*. *It* was the disappearances, tripwires, episodes, and sleepless nights. *It* was my relentless pushing back against the harsh truth that the marriage was essentially over and had been for some time.

It was time to bring *it* to an end.

It had all been enough.

On an unusually hot Saturday afternoon in the spring of 1976, Dad decided it was high time he passed along his passion for fly-fishing to Pete and me. We were preparing the garden for planting when he switched off the tiller, wiped his brow with the handkerchief he always kept in his pocket, and announced, "Boys, go grab your fly rods." Dad was impetuous like that.

For the next several hours, we attended our father's first backyard fly-fishing workshop where we learned the four-count rhythm of casting. Twelve- and thirteen-year-old boys have only so much patience for fishing the fescue. Two lessons were our limit before we began campaigning to try our hands at *real fishing*.

Dad relented. The following Saturday, we moved our instruction to the water.

The Linville River is much like any other river in western North Carolina until it enters the Linville Gorge Wilderness. Above the falls, the current becomes swift and treacherous. Choosing that spot to test our novice casting skills was a bit like strapping on skis for the first time and heading straight for the black diamond slopes.

Today, Linville attracts large crowds. Barriers and trails have been erected to discourage the weekend warriors from wandering too close to the river's edge. However, the Linville Wilderness of my youth remained mostly undiscovered. The authorities trusted that the few hikers who ventured to the falls would use their God-given common sense to steer clear of danger.

It must have appeared to the park ranger that I lacked in that department as he made a point of approaching and informing me, "Son, two weeks ago, we dragged the body of a thirteen-year-old boy out of the river downstream. Looked to be about your age. One wrong step and you could be next. You watch yourself. Hear?"

"Yes, sir," I said.

I was taught to be respectful, but like most preadolescent boys, I was also hopelessly self-consumed. A few moments later, daydreaming about my picture on the cover of *American Fly Fishing* magazine, holding all the trout I had not yet caught, I ventured off on my own.

"Joseph!"

I was suddenly startled by a shout that came from behind me. The voice was familiar; the sound it made was not. My father rarely raised his voice or called me by my given name. It was not his volume that startled me, however. It was his expression. Dad was not angry; he was frightened. This was the first time I had heard the sound of my father's fear.

Dad's vision was locked on the river below me. I was perched precariously on a ledge directly above one of the swiftest, fiercest sections of the river. Below, the raging current cut through the boulders, spilled over the falls, and plunged deep into the gorge.

I froze.

Dad tried talking me off the ledge.

"Place your left foot there," he said, motioning to a rock on the edge of the precipice between us.

Nothing doing! I thought of the Ranger's earlier warning and imagined my body plummeting over the falls and being dragged ashore downriver, limp and lifeless. My first misplaced step could be my last.

I just shook my head.

"Can you edge your way toward me?" he asked. "Small steps. Just slide your feet along. Don't worry about your equipment. Drop it if you need to."

But it was no use. Like a cat in a tree, I was petrified. So, my father laid aside his gear, removed his jacket and vest, and lowered himself to his knees.

"Alright...look at me," he said intently.

Slowly, he crawled toward me, inching himself along the inside of the ledge.

"Look at *me*!" he shouted again above the roar of the river. "Now give me your hand."

Before I could summon the courage to reach for my father, my father reached for me. He locked his grip around my wrist, and ever so cautiously backed both of us to safety.

On the night of Jesus' betrayal, Simon Peter was called out as a follower of Jesus. "I know you!" the servant girl said to Peter as he warmed himself by the fire in the courtyard of the high priest. "You are a Galilean. Your accent gives you away. You were with the Nazarene!"

Three times, Peter was identified. Three times, he denied his Lord. "I do not know the man," he lied.

Then, as Jesus had predicted, the cock crowed. The Gospel writers chose the Greek word, *phoneo*, to describe the rooster's crow. It means *shout*. Peter, all full of himself, had wandered into a most dangerous place. God used the *shout* of a rooster to rouse him and call him back to safety.

On a chaotic summer evening in 2009, the Lord told me, "It is enough." There is much that I do not know about those three words. For example, I cannot tell you how loudly they were spoken or if you would have heard them had you been sitting next to me on the swing. I cannot explain what distinguished that prayer from the tens of thousands of other prayers I have offered through the years. What made it deserving of a response? Or had God always responded in this way, and I just missed it?

In Scripture, those who hear God tend to be in lonely places, away from the world's clamor and noise. Jesus routinely separated himself from the rest of the world to be with the Father. Moses and God entered a tent where they spoke face-to-face, and Samuel was lying down in the temple when God called his name. Was that the key? Had the old, wooden swing become my lonely place apart?

Suffering can also attune our ears to God's frequencies. C.S. Lewis wrote, "Pain insists upon being attended to. God whispers to us in our pleasures, speaks in our conscience, but shouts in our pains: it is His megaphone to rouse a deaf world."[1]

Perhaps we must reach the floor of our spiritual valley before our ears are opened.

Ever since God first spoke us into being, we have searched for ways to influence the Speaker. What is the formula? Will three hours of prayer in my lonely place plus two parts of extreme misery result in a response from God? The engineer in me wants to know. Or is it the Adam in me still longing for the one fruit that is not mine to pick?

I suspect that you and I have no more influence over *Deus loquens* than we do over any other expression of God's grace. There is no formula

---

1 C.S. Lewis, The Problem of Pain (San Francisco: HarperSanFrancisco, 2001. First published 1940), 91.

for God's speaking. We cannot order up visions that connect us to unfamiliar congregations six time zones away. Our options are clear and straightforward when it comes to grace: we can either accept it or refuse it.

In the end, I believe that God heard my pleas from that old, weathered swing and, for reasons that I will likely never know, decided it was time for a conversation.

Yet even after that moment of grace, it took five more months for me to act. On an evening in early November, I shared with Carrie the only options I saw for our marriage moving forward.

"We can look into residential treatment for you."

"I'm not going anywhere," she interrupted.

"Then, we could spend some intentional time apart while we work with counselors."

"We are not separating," she said.

Only one viable option remained. I filed for divorce the following day.

15

The Limoncello Revelation

If pain doesn't lead to humility, you have wasted your suffering.

~ Katerina Stoykova Klemer

For by the grace given to me I say to everyone among you not to think of yourself more highly than you ought to think...

~ Romans 12:3

I knew Eleanor would be a challenge the moment she greeted our group outside London's Heathrow Airport. She was edgy, loud, and abrasive. A rather large woman, both she and her personality consumed more than their share of space on the coach. For eleven days in Great Britain, Eleanor was our guide.

As tour leader, my job was to keep group members happy and spiritually fed. I hired regional and local guides to do most of the heavy lifting. Their job was to keep the group informed and Pastor Joe happy.

Guides are veritable troves of knowledge and are essential for a successful tour. They can make or break a group's experience. I worked with almost thirty guides over the course of fourteen international tours. All were exceedingly affable and managed their way into the hearts of the group members…save one.

Eleanor was one of the most self-absorbed people I ever had the displeasure of meeting. Between short, cryptic lessons about Churchill, Shakespeare, or Hadrian's Wall, she treated our group to an interminable litany of *Eleanor's Adventures*. And when the microphone was not available, she hijacked a nearby conversation and redirected it to herself. She told far too many jokes and then laughed far too loudly at herself afterward. (I suppose someone needed to.)

I tried to make allowances for her. Most tour companies required a minimum group size of sixteen travelers before assigning a guide. Our group barely made the cut. The math worked out well for us, of course — more room on the coach, greater mobility, shorter lines — but was much less favorable for Eleanor. Half the average group size translated into half the tip-take for the guide. Factor in another twenty percent deduction for the poor jokes, and you understand her eagerness to get our group in the rearview mirror and on to a more profitable payday.

But when Eleanor had the moxie to approach me with an open palm on the final morning of the tour and ask, "Do you have something for me?" she managed to sour what little empathy I had for her.

Fortunately, there were enough colorful characters in the group (including my father) to balance out Eleanor's personality, and Great Britain does a fine job of presenting herself. Even so, when the evaluation survey arrived from the travel company, I responded honestly.

"Two, four, six, eight…sixty-three."

Seven years and seven tours after Great Britain, I shepherded a much more sizeable group through Italy. With a flock that large, not only did I serve as host and chaplain, I was also tour sheepdog. I had never counted so many so often.

Twice during the week, I had to leave sixty-two sheep on the bus and go in search of the one that was lost. No pastor wants to be remembered as the shepherd who lost a perfectly healthy sheep, especially that close to the Vatican. It was simpler and safer to count.

Occasionally, the itineraries of different tour groups synced up with one another, and we found ourselves sharing meals or standing in lines next to the same folks each day. That was the case in Italy, and you will never guess who emerged from one of the adjacent groups in Florence.

Not surprisingly, I heard Eleanor before I saw her. I was busy counting when that familiar sharp voice cut through me. I slowly turned, as if trying not to attract the attention of a wild animal on the path behind me. Then she laughed. I no longer needed to look. "Don't worry," I assured myself. "It has been seven years. She has probably led upwards of fifty tours since our time together in London. There was no way she would remember me or my review. Nothing to be concerned ab…"

"Pastor Joe!" came a shout from across the Piazza del Duomo.

It felt as if the entire city of Florence stopped and turned to witness our reunion. The crowd parted like the Red Sea as Eleanor abandoned her group and pushed her way toward me. Thankfully, our guide, Fiona, knew Eleanor and intercepted her just as she started to throw her arms around me (thereby doubling her tip).

"È bello vederti di nuovo." The two colleagues exchanged kisses and an Italian, "Good to see you again," before Eleanor returned her attention to me. Instantly, the excitement drained from her expression.

"Pastor Joe! You have changed," she sang, with an apparent concern that I didn't expect would be part of her emotional repertoire.

"What do you mean, Eleanor?"

"You have changed," she repeated. "I remember that you were a pastor of a large church…had a beautiful wife and family. You were 'all that,' and kind of full of yourself."

("Tell me what you *really* think, Eleanor. Don't hold back.")

"But you've changed. Something has happened to you. You have been through something, I can tell."

I was flabbergasted. "Eleanor, we should talk."

When our long day was complete, and all the sheep turned in, Eleanor, Fiona, and I settled into the corner table at our hotel bar where the ladies introduced me to limoncello. My companions drank and reordered, and drank and reordered. I sipped. Together, we shared conversation into the wee hours of the morning.

We did not talk about current events or Italy. They didn't bellyache about the recent tour groups they had been assigned. We spent hours discussing matters of faith. We spoke of God's grace and the surprising ways it had manifested in our lives. I rattled on about my divorce with the sort of candor I reserve for closest confidants, and they listened as such.

"I just don't believe that we can grow in our faith without going through some sort of suffering," Eleanor preached. Then she prophesied, "God has some large plans for you, Pastor Joe."

Four hours before we were all due back on the morning coach to start the new day, we reluctantly broke away from one another, and more hesitantly from our conversation. "*Buona notte.*"

I lay awake, imagining how the previous day might have played out in heaven. I pictured God whispering to the angels, "Pssst. Watch! I'm about to get especially creative with this one." Of course, it was just like God to deliver a prophetic word using a messenger I would have walked across hot coals to avoid. I eventually fell asleep that morning strangely renewed, because of Eleanor. Because of Eleanor!

My new friend was astonishingly spry at breakfast. She obviously did not miss many meals and, as a result, managed her alcohol well.

Fiona, on the other hand, was much slighter and moved cautiously when she finally stepped onto the morning coach. The large coffee she carried was fitting for the hour, but the sunglasses she wore were not. I took the microphone and led the group in a half-hour of off-the-cuff devotions to give our guide a few moments to compose herself — perhaps a small expression of the enormous grace we spent the night discussing.

Eleanor never explained herself. She read my grief as if it were tattooed across my forehead, yet not once during our limoncello-fueled theological marathon did I think to ask, "How?" Maybe some moments are meant to be experienced rather than explained. As I say, I didn't ask, and she didn't volunteer. Unless I learn otherwise (and I won't), I will assume that clairvoyance is just one of her spiritual gifts.

Regardless of how she knew — and as unsettling as it was to admit — Eleanor was spot-on. At the time of the London tour (and long before), I *had* been a little self-inflated (alright, *considerably* self-inflated and full of myself). I was too busy evaluating Eleanor's deficiencies to notice my own shortcomings, too concerned about the speck in my neighbor's eye to see the log in mine.

The Lord refers to such behavior as *hypocrisy*.[1] Webster defines hypocrisy as "the practice of claiming to have moral standards or beliefs to which one's behavior does not conform." In my line of work, we refer to this as "failing to practice what you preach."

I wish that I had known Eleanor, the prophet and teacher, sooner. Who knows? Had I not been so busy judging Eleanor, the tour guide, maybe I would have.

Of all God's holy eccentricities, I may be most grateful for the way the Spirit speaks through those we consider to be less than ourselves: children; the neighbor we don't especially like; the hungry, homeless, or lonely person we seek to bless but who, instead, blesses us; the least, the last, the little, and the lost. These are the people we must humble ourselves to hear.

My greatest lesson on humility came during an impromptu workshop on grace, held at midnight in the corner of a Florentine bar, and taught by the Holy Spirit masquerading as a limoncello-guzzling, slightly haughty British tour guide. Go figure.

---

1 Matthew 7:5

16

I Have a Feeling We're Not in South Carolina Anymore

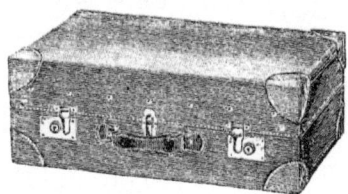

Never has a pastor thrown in the towel from being fed up with Jesus, despite Jesus' demands being notoriously excessive. What kills clergy is the church.

~ Will Willimon, *Accidental Preacher*

God uses chronic pain and weakness, along with other afflictions, as his chisel for sculpting our lives.

J.I. Packer, *God's Plans for You*

One Sunday morning, late in the winter of 2001, as I was taking my regular pre-service stroll along the back of the sanctuary, Gert, one of King of Glory's snowbirds, reached across her pew and whacked me on the arm with some sort of rolled up booklet.

"I brought you something," she said excitedly above the sound of the organ prelude. Realizing she had also captured the attention of the worshipers around us, Gert smiled, winked, and mouthed, "It's a newsletter from the congregation I was telling you about."

Her *telling* had taken place in the previous Sunday's post-worship receiving line and went something like this: "You know, Pastor Joe, my home congregation in Kansas is looking for a senior pastor. I think that you would love it there." That was all Gert managed to get out before the parishioner in line behind her shooed her away.

Members have good cause to stifle such conversations; few events disrupt the life of a congregation more than a pastor's departure.

Congregations that are seeking a pastor can connect with candidates in a variety of ways. A pre-service snowbird newsletter thrashing may show off the Spirit's creativity, but it is not the bishop-sanctioned method. The task of pastoral headhunting or talent scouting officially belongs to congregational call committees.

My first surprise experience with a call committee took place barely a year after ordination. A group of four obviously unrelated visitors slinked into worship last-minute and took seats in the back pew. In a congregation such as Saint Luke, they might as well have been carrying a flashing neon sign: "Don't mind us. We're here to check out your pastor."

Weeks later, I learned that one of the strangers had sidled up to Carl, a long-standing member and noted prankster, and asked, "So, what do you think about your minister?"

Carl pondered for a moment and said, "You know, ole Pastor Crowther is one of the best…as long as we can keep him off the bottle."

The call process is disruptive for the pastor as well. There are interviews, clandestine trips to size up the potential new bride, and the inevitable inquisitions of members who become suspicious when they cannot account for their shepherd's whereabouts for a few days: "You wouldn't be thinking about leaving us now, would you, Pastor?" The entire process feels adulterous.

The process inevitably ends with someone being disappointed. As with any potential relationship, if expectations are high and the first date goes poorly, everyone around the table is discouraged. The call committee must cross a name off the list and begin the process anew while the candidate is left to wonder how they might have handled the date differently.

If the stars and planets align and the courtship promises a match, then the *new* congregation may raise the stakes and extend a call. The next move belongs to me. Saying "yes" means that life for our family will once again be uprooted, packed into boxes, and replanted in another part of the vineyard. The congregation I am serving is (hopefully) disappointed as they must bid farewell to yet another shepherd and then begin the long and arduous process of discerning the sort of leader they wish to woo away from another congregation.

Saying "no" also has its consequences. Shortly before Gert's newsletter ambush, I had been invited into conversations with two tremendous congregations in Ohio and Maryland. They whisked Carrie and me off our feet, and we quickly fell in love with both. The problem was, while there was plenty of mutual attraction, as with many whirlwind romances, I did not sense the compatibility that makes for a lasting relationship. There was no spiritual nudge to pursue either. When the churches extended calls, I was left to deliver the awkward *thanks but no thanks* response.

On our flight home from Maryland, Carrie and I decided to call a moratorium on church dating. It was simply too stressful. As the plane banked over the Atlantic and prepared to land home in Myrtle Beach, I said, "The Spirit will have to tug hard to pull me back into the call process anytime soon."

This, of course, is precisely what happened a few weeks later when I rediscovered beneath the clutter on my desk Gert's newsletter from Atonement Lutheran Church in Overland Park, Kansas.

As I read it, something inside of me stirred. I turned to the computer and pulled up Atonement's website. The feeling intensified. The more I read, the faster my heart raced. The Spirit's nudge that I had been waiting for all winter decided to show up as soon as I turned my head.

"So, tell me about Atonement," I said to Gert when she answered the phone.

"I'm so glad you're interested, Pastor Joe. I'll let them know!"

"That's not what I said, Gert. I'd just like to hear a little more."

A little more led to a little more, and a few days later, Gail, the chair of Atonement's call committee, phoned to survey my level of interest. After I agreed to toss my hat into the conversation ring, she responded, "Good. You're number forty-six."

That seemed safe enough.

After reviewing candidates' mobility information, the committee whittled the list down to eleven. A round of phone interviews left three standing. Then the traveling commenced. Members of the committee visited North Myrtle Beach; Carrie and I flew to Kansas. Three months after the Spirit's first stirring, Atonement extended a call offer.

The distance between King of Glory and Atonement was far greater than the thirteen hundred miles that separated the congregations geographically. Life is laid back and simple in South Carolina. The expectations that folks have of one another are gentle. For example, when a Southerner says, "I will see you on Thursday," she might mean this Thursday or two weeks from Thursday. She is merely inviting you to further conversation.

The professional world of Johnson County, Kansas, spoke a new and strange language. Members of Atonement's ministry teams talked of *deltas* and *deliverables* and refused to attend meetings if a detailed agenda was not distributed at least one day in advance. A colleague described Overland Park as "the toughest place in the country to do ministry. Members expect church excellence, and if you don't deliver, there are a dozen churches down the street that will." I think he was spot-on.

Ministry in this new setting was faster, larger, better-resourced, and deeper in debt. The cumulative facility square footage of my first three congregations would fit comfortably inside Atonement's footprint with room to spare. Six months into the call, I was still stumbling upon rooms I hadn't realized existed. With a seating capacity of nearly one thousand, the newly completed asymmetrical five-aisled worship space was filled with art and natural light. It was spectacular, as was the $46,000 per month mortgage that came with it.

More impressive than the sanctuary were the people who sang and prayed and worshiped in it. Thanks to the nearby Hallmark headquarters and the stellar arts programs in the Johnson County Public Schools, the talent pool seemed bottomless. If Rick, our Director of Worship, and I could imagine it, there was someone within earshot who could make it happen.

Steve was an artist with a passion for worship projects. One Sunday morning during my first January at Atonement, I said to Steve, "When John saw the graveclothes in the empty tomb, it was enough for him to believe. I'm imagining graveclothes around the Easter altar area that somehow swoop out over the congregation. See what you can do with graveclothes."

Throughout worship, I watched Steve as he sketched, mused, erased, and sketched some more. By the benediction, he had the art plan for Holy Week and Easter conceptualized. Hundreds of feet of white cloth would wrap around a chancel rock garden, rise upward through the cross and ceiling rafters, stretch over the sanctuary, and tie off in four places along the balcony. It worked.

The cloths were reset for Pentecost Sunday; youth filled each strand with thousands of torn pieces of red paper. As the reader presented the second chapter of Acts, choir members in the balcony flapped the cloths as if shaking out a bedsheet, and tongues of flame wafted down upon the worshipers. With each successive Lenten season, the art and engineering became more involved, sophisticated, and beautiful.

Rick was a master of curating worship that was creative and ever-changing. On any given weekend, worshipers might be treated to a glorious pipe organ, jazz quartets, brass ensembles, strings, flute choirs, bells, consummate vocalists, youth choirs, bluegrass groups, bagpipes, or even drumlines. Artists employed liturgical movement, hanging mobiles, creative readings, drama, banners, and choreographed processions. The congregation honored the preaching moments and trusted me to be imaginative and innovative.

Worship was one hallmark of Atonement's ministry. The second was outreach.

Five years into the call, I arranged for a sabbatical experience to begin a second doctoral program, in Missional Leadership. What finds its way into the pastor's heart eventually gets transferred to the congregation's heart. My reading and class experiences seeped and sometimes poured into my preaching and teaching. Consequently, there was a coalescence of energy and resources around outreach and the adoption of a new mission statement: *Grow Deep — Reach Wide*.

Members also dug deep to give widely. At one point, annual gifts beyond the congregation topped $400,000. We hired Brooke and Mary Ann, two Missional Life Directors who kept members' sleeves rolled up and hands at work in the community. A ministry culture that had concerned itself with internal growth made a vast, sweeping turn outward toward the world.

Like cruise ships, large congregations must change direction slowly, otherwise, folks just end up frustrated with their faces pressed against the portholes. But even intentional, carefully planned, missional change will stir the discontentment of some.

Reggie McNeal, my doctoral professor, shared with me, "Pastors of churches that go missional rarely last more than seven years following the shift. And they seldom leave their congregations by choice."

Atonement experienced its share of challenges long before the ship began making its cultural turn. My predecessor-once-removed failed to show for worship one Palm Sunday and was later discovered somewhere in Colorado. Ministry just became too overwhelming for him.

At the end of an unsettled pastorate, and amid circumstances that remained undisclosed, my immediate predecessor was asked by the leadership to resign after manning the helm for eight years. Atonement was a vibrant, dynamic ministry with a great deal to offer its members; it just seemed to be particularly rough on its shepherds.

My books were still in the moving boxes when two members of the local collegial Welcome Wagon stopped by the office to greet me. But as soon as we had been introduced, the conversation changed.

"Watch your back," my colleague whispered, then stopped mid-sentence to look both ways as if we were trading government secrets. "I know this congregation. Be careful."

But I was a fixer. I followed difficult pastorates and helped restore congregations to health. If Atonement suffered from a systemic failure that caused them to rub out the senior pastor every few years, I was just the guy to repair that system.

"Thanks for the concern, but I have no intention of becoming the next casualty," I said. "I'm good."

And with that, I shelved their counsel alongside my pastoral care books. That's where they remained for the next eleven years.

Fast-forward to a Sunday evening in May of 2012 and a cryptic phone call from John, president of the vision board, the congregation's leadership team. The purpose of the call was to request that I attend a special meeting of the board scheduled for the following night.

"Tomorrow night?" My "pastor-sense" — that tingling at the base of the skull that detects approaching danger — was firing off the charts. The board had never scheduled a meeting apart from me. "What is this about, John?"

"We'd rather wait and share tomorrow," he replied, well-rehearsed.

"Is there an agenda?"

"Again, we would rather talk tomorrow."

As soon as the non-conversation ended, I phoned Janice, Atonement member and assistant to the bishop.

"I am tempted not to go until I see an agenda. None of this feels right," I said.

"I think you should go. Just listen to what they say and try not to be defensive," she counseled.

"So, you knew about this?"

"Just try to listen to what they say," the third non-response in about as many minutes.

Any meeting that had been scheduled *without* me was most assuredly *about* me. And since no one in the know was willing to share the agenda, I could assume that the subject matter would not be positive.

At the time, ministry felt solid. Excitement and energy among members were high. Allegiance to the congregational mission was vital. Average worship attendance had increased by twenty-five percent during my tenure. While not explosive growth, it was considerably more robust than our denomination's trends, which were in decline. Teams were hard at work planning the congregation's upcoming fiftieth-anniversary celebration. Such a ministry backdrop made John's call even more mysterious.

The vision board was a unique, talented group of leaders. Collectively, they represented far less church leadership experience than any board that served during my pastorate. For most purposes, I considered their inexperience an asset. The more *churched* one becomes, the more difficult it can be to think outside the box or reimagine ministry from the perspectives of those who don't belong. At forty-nine, I was the group's senior member.

Board members seemed uncomfortable as they arrived, fidgety and nervous. I had preached in front of these folks for eleven years. I could read their body language and expressions. I knew their mannerisms. I had prayed with them and counseled them. I had been a guest in their homes, officiated their weddings, baptized their children, and taught them in class. That night, however, these friends felt like strangers.

Though no one said it as John invited everyone to take their seats, the unspoken message was, "Let's get this over with."

Instead of turning to me for the usual half-hour of prayer and devotions, John called the meeting to order by distributing a handout which, as I suspected, contained a list of formal concerns.

The concerns seemed random and unrelated. Some items on the list appeared valid and worthy of conversation. Other concerns were baseless and outright false. Still others seemed petty and trite.

For example, the board took issue with my housesitting for members during the months following my divorce. Additionally, I had not contributed financially to the ministry at the level they felt was appropriate. In their opinion, I hadn't kept a sufficient number of regular office hours and was often unavailable when the secretary needed me. I had micromanaged the process to select vision board members.

If offered a do-over, I would have simply said, "I'll study this more carefully and get back to you," and then dismissed myself. Instead, I clumsily tried to respond on the spot.

"Yes, I accepted invitations to stay with folks over the past year," I explained, "including one from the assistant to the bishop and her husband. As contributions to the ministry have been strong, I have directed my offering to other ministries. That's certainly something we could talk about. I have had one day off since February, so unless you are worried about burnout, my schedule should not be an issue." John marked through that concern on his copy.

"And if you're suggesting that I handpicked members of this group to benefit myself in some way, then it looks like I could've done a better job."

So much for not appearing defensive.

I was bitter, though not about the concerns. Most were products of rumors or misunderstandings, and the concerns that had merit were certainly not impeachable offenses. It was the process that I resented, and it was the process that worried me. I would write an official response, but if the board had been interested in a response, or reconciliation, they would have invited me into a conversation. Instead, they had ambushed me with accusations.

Everything that had taken place that night was about delivery. I had been served. Nothing else mattered.

The meeting ended as awkwardly as it began. John admonished the group to keep the document confidential, then adjourned. I retired to my office down the hall, just as I did after every board meeting. A handful of members typically dropped by just to talk about football or politics or life for a while. My only visitors that night were voices from the past.

"Watch your back."

The warnings of my colleagues that I had been so quick to dismiss a decade earlier now seemed eerily prophetic. Yet even if I had taken their words to heart, carried them with me daily, and used them as a survival mantra, the vision board would have been the last group to arouse my suspicion. These were the folks I trusted to circle the wagons and protect me, not surround and accuse me. I knew them, or so I believed.

So many of life's plans were scattered in the road behind me. But amid all the heartache and uncertainty, at least one suitcase remained secured.

Atonement had been a dependable sanctuary, the one place where I knew what to expect when I walked through the doors. Here, I still experienced a sense of call and purpose. When all else failed, this was the one place where I remained successful and appreciated.

But in a matter of moments, everything changed. I sat in my office, shell-shocked and numb, wondering how long it would take for the next shoe to drop…or, in this case, for the next knot to loosen.

17

EMPATHY FOR FATHER MCKENZIE

We bereaved are not alone. We belong to the largest company in all the world — the company of those who have known suffering.

~ Helen Keller, *We Bereaved*

Before the truth sets you free, it tends to make you miserable.

~ Richard Rohr, *Falling Upward*

Most preachers will confess to experiencing some version of the same, recurrent nightmare:

"I have just started my sermon, and everything is going well, when I look down to discover something is missing; it could be my manuscript, or my robe, or part of my clothing. In the kinder, gentler version, I am standing in a wraparound pulpit. But most often, I am standing in the center aisle, wearing nothing but my boxer shorts, and I have nothing to say."

In my dream, I arrive at church around nine o'clock on Saturday morning, as I do each week, and set to work memorizing the Scripture and working on the sermon for that evening. I am halfway through John's story of the Woman at the Well when there comes a knock at the open office door. I look up and see Ray, a member of the Saturday evening usher team. He is cradling an armful of bulletins and appears a little antsy.

"Pastor? Are you ready? Folks are waiting," he says as he taps his watch and motions toward the sanctuary.

"What folks, Ray? And what are they waiting for?"

"The worshipers are waiting for *you*! Rick finished the prelude ten minutes ago, and the crowd is getting concerned and a little restless."

"I don't understand. Why is there a crowd in the sanctuary at nine-thirty in the morning, Ray?"

"Pastor. It's Saturday evening, and the church is packed. But it won't stay that way long if you don't robe up and take your place."

Puzzled, I dash off toward the sacristy to throw a robe on over my jeans and t-shirt. I have about one hundred feet of hallway and two minutes of robing time to manufacture something to say.

After I step into the pulpit and survey an impatient congregation, my dream concludes in one of two ways: In the rarer version, the Holy Spirit shows up in full force and we knock the impromptu sermon out of the park. Most nights, however, I swallow deeply and begin to stammer and stutter as I search for words. Mercifully, that's when I wake up in a sweaty panic.

The previous several days had felt a lot like that nightmare, only I hadn't awakened. John summoned me to a board meeting that, by all indications, had been in session for weeks, maybe months. And nothing I experienced from leaders on Monday night suggested that they were even remotely interested in anything I had to say.

I spent Tuesday morning crafting a response, nonetheless, all the while humming the melody to the Beatles' "Eleanor Rigby." With a newfound empathy for Father McKenzie, I began writing words that I suspected no one would hear.

In the Gospel of Matthew, Jesus laid out a four-step process for Christians who take issue with one another. It begins, "If another member of the church sins against you, go and point out the fault when the two of you are alone."[1] Nowhere does the Lord counsel us to hold secret meetings or build cases with which to ambush one another.

I took a mid-morning break to contact the bishop and request a meeting.

"I can stop by Atonement on my way back from central Missouri tomorrow evening if that works," he offered.

"I'll be waiting in my office," I replied.

Initial Visit with the Bishop ....Wednesday, May 16, 2012

"Before we get started, I need to apologize for being so exhausted," the bishop confessed when he arrived on Wednesday evening. "It's been a day!"

"Same here," I said.

Bishop Gerald Mansholt was elected to his office late in June of 2001, the same month my family moved from South Carolina. While no one officially runs or campaigns for the position of bishop (and anyone who wants it deserves it), the prevalent opinion among pastors in the synod was that Jerry, as he preferred to be called, had ogled the office for years.

Close your eyes and imagine *bishop* and you likely have Jerry pegged. He is a tall, imposing man who wears his office typically, both in demeanor and dress. His words are measured and chosen with extreme care as if every syllable is being recorded, and he rarely appears without a fuchsia clerical shirt and hernia-sized pectoral cross.

We had surprisingly little history together. Two years earlier, I had informed Jerry of my impending divorce. He sounded the trumpet and gathered Atonement's leadership to help strategize a communication rollout to the congregation. His invitation to leaders was quite cryptic, including only a location (someone's home instead of our usual meeting room at church), time, and a note stating how imperative it was that each member attend. The reason for the meeting was rightly and intentionally withheld.

---

1   Matthew 18:15 ff.

The board managed its first perfect attendance in recent memory. I don't know what calamity or scandal the leaders expected, but when the bishop called the meeting to order by saying, "It's a delicate matter when a pastor goes through a divorce," the entire room heaved a collective sigh of relief.

Atonement was the largest and most financially supportive ship in the synod's fleet. Anything that threatened to rock this boat, such as a pastoral divorce or the developing and as-yet-unexplained drama, would naturally collect the admiral's attention. But when the admiral begins communicating with the ship's crew without the captain's knowledge, we have a fundamental breakdown in healthy order.

"I apologize for not informing you of my meeting with the vision board. I don't usually handle things that way, but the board was insistent that I keep it secret," he explained.

And when the admiral begins taking orders from the crew, we open the door for mutiny. Growing up on the farm, we referred to this as the tail wagging the dog.

Jerry confessed to being too tired to read my response that night but vowed to review it soon.

Executive Team's Meeting with Staff . . . . Tuesday, May 29

Before his phone call, I had a deep respect for John. Most folks do. He is charismatic, affable, and a master at rallying support for a project, all gifts which make him both a stellar congregational president and the person you do *not* want to see on the opposing side of an issue. Over time it would become abundantly clear that this was John's process. He turned the ignition switch and kept pressure on the accelerator.

Church members have a proclivity for wrangling over the pettiest matters. I have seen congregations nearly split over the color of the carpet in the fellowship hall or the ratio of red Christmas poinsettias to white. Before this drama unfolded, I had considered that a little righteous sparring over an issue of social injustice or theological interpretation could be healthy for a congregation. I may have been wrong.

Late in 2010, John and I locked horns over a theological issue. During the previous year, the ELCA[2] adopted a social statement on human sexuality that resulted in predictable upheaval throughout the denomination. In response, Atonement organized a team to study the statement and its implications for the way the congregation offered hospitality to the LGBT community. John insisted that the team be dissolved and that it was my responsibility to do the dissolving.

"I don't want to save the congregation from this issue," I told him. "The conversation is worthwhile, regardless of your position." My comment did not sit well with John; neither did several of my sermons.

Not long before the ambush, John opened an executive team meeting by asking, "So, what did everyone think about Pastor's message this weekend?" His demeanor and deeply flushed face suggested that he had clearly not been a fan.

"Does no one else think that a pro-homosexuality sermon is inappropriate?" The team refused to take the bait.

The homily had addressed the broader issue of hospitality, though John heard something more specific.

"I encourage you to go back and listen to it again, John," I said. "I think you'll see that…"

"I don't need to listen to it again," he interrupted. "I know what you said!"

I suspect John also knew that listing "Pastor Joe's openness to the gay and lesbian community" among the board's formal concerns would have elicited tremendous pushback. Yet I have little doubt that, were it not for this part of the backstory, I would not be writing this chapter.

I am still uncertain what the executive team hoped to accomplish by assembling the staff on the final Tuesday morning in May. If their goals were to further rile and frustrate us, they were remarkably successful.

The team stuck stridently to their vow *not* to reveal the issues raised by

---

2   Atonement belongs to the Evangelical Lutheran Church in America.

the board, so most of the staff's questions were simply deflected by appealing to the need for confidentiality. This tactic became a pattern. When members called upon the board to justify its actions, the typical non-response was, "We cannot disclose that information. But if we could, you would understand."

The most poignant and revealing moment during Tuesday's meeting took place when Rick asked, "Do you realize that, if Pastor Joe leaves, you run the risk of splitting this congregation in half?"

After several moments of awkward silence from the other end of the table, the answer came back. "Yes."

Phone Call from The Bishop .... Week of June 3

Jerry phoned early in the first full week in June. "Joe, there is a Catholic Consultation Center in St. Louis that the synod occasionally uses for psychological testing. Would you be willing to spend a few days there during the week of the seventeenth?"

"That's not a question, is it?" I replied.

Bishops are trained when to remain silent.

Bishop Meets with The Board and Me .... Monday, June 11

On the second Monday in June, two months after they began meeting *about* me, Jerry and the vision board finally decided to meet *with* me. But getting the appropriate parties together in the same room did not ensure that the appropriate conversation took place.

No engagement of issues was allowed. No explanations. No attempts at reconciliation. The only purpose for the gathering was to provide Jerry an opportunity to lay out his next steps.

"I am going to make no recommendations in this matter until I first interview members of the staff and have the results of Joe's psychological evaluation in hand."

The former would take place at Atonement by the week's end. I made the four-hour drive to St. Louis the following Sunday evening.

St. Louis Assessment .... June 17–21

The Saint Luke Consultation Center is a Catholic facility just west of downtown St. Louis. I arrived late on a stifling hot Sunday evening and dropped my bags on the floor of a former dorm room turned guest quarters. The Center had attempted to soften the space's institutional feel with a few pictures and appointments. It hadn't worked.

The echo was eerily familiar. I had been here before. Almost twenty-seven years to the day, my professional journey began in another dorm room in another life. As I had done then, I introduced myself to the room and wondered if those who occupied it before me shared my misgivings and doubts.

Throughout the four-day stay, I divided approximately four hours of contact time between a psychologist, a nun/life coach, and a social worker. Each took their turn rummaging through my psyche and delving into my family history. The team administered all the classic instruments: Rorschach inkblot tests, the Minnesota Multiphasic Personality Inventory, the Sixteen Personality Factors Questionnaire, and an IQ assessment. I had taken each half a dozen times through the years, either as part of my undergraduate work in Psychology or just for fun, but never when the results really mattered.

This work could have been easily accomplished in a morning and afternoon. I spent most of my time in the Gateway City thumb-twiddling, sightseeing, and pondering how in the world I could have landed in such a god-awful predicament.

To make matters more unpleasant, there had been an incessant, annoying drumroll crescendo building throughout the week in preparation for Jerry's arrival on Thursday morning. He planned to attend the evaluation team's readout of discoveries and recommendations. I could hardly wait.

I lay awake for hours early that Thursday morning in the most uncomfortable bed I had ever not slept in. I didn't mind the insomnia. Some of my most meaningful conversations with God take place at two in the morning. Besides, if I fell asleep, I might have to deal with Ray again and suffer the embarrassment of standing mute before an impatient congregation. More than sleep, I needed to process with the Lord all that had happened during the previous five weeks.

Had you asked me on May 12, the day before John's phone call, "Joe, what part of your life's plan gives you the greatest joy and confidence?" or "Of all your luggage, which suitcase is most secure?" I would have responded immediately, "My vocation. Absolutely!" I am a parish pastor. It was the only professional gig I had ever known. I had no reason to imagine a future apart from ministry, or ministry apart from Atonement.

Had you asked me the same questions on my wedding day, I would have answered with equal conviction, "My marriage. Absolutely!" I had no reason to imagine a future without Carrie.

And had anyone asked my father in the summer of 1969, "Which of the suitcases on the luggage rack are most secure?" he would no doubt have responded, "All of them! Absolutely!"

Yet, despite all our certainties, life continued to unravel. That's what the Lord and I discussed in the wee hours of Thursday morning.

When I finally drifted off to sleep, I didn't dream of ushers or extemporaneous sermons. I returned instead to the back of an old wood-paneled Chrysler station wagon motoring through the Sandhills of South Carolina and to Pete's innocent announcement: "There it goes."

I awoke from my dream with a new and unsettling awareness of just how foretelling my five-year-old brother's words had been. But even more disconcerting was the awful premonition that this day, I would likely hear those words once again.

18

The Report

> Ultimately, in the battle against lies and violence, truth and love have no other weapon than the witness of suffering.
>
> ~ Pope Benedict XVI

> On the last day, Jesus will look us over not for medals, diplomas, or honors, but for scars.
>
> ~ Brennan Manning, *Ruthless Trust*

The Psychological Readout .... **Thursday, June 21**

Had you said to me in early May, "A nun, a psychologist, a social worker, and a bishop walk into a conference room...," I would have waited for the punch line. But when just such a group sat down at table with me on the third Thursday of June, no one was joking.

Seated immediately to my left and at the table's head was the lead psychologist. Close your eyes and imagine *psychologist,* and you likely have this guy pegged — middle-aged, smartly dressed, though exclusively in earth tones. His countenance was kind but quietly demanding, which served him well as our convener.

To his left and directly across from me sat the nun. She was a delightful and affable soul who, at least for our meeting, traded her habit for street clothes to appear more in her role as a life coach than a religious figure.

The social worker sat quietly at the far corner of the table, so emotionally and physically detached that I am not sure she could legitimately be counted present. But when the convener prodded her, she woke and responded on cue.

Jerry sat to my right, dressed in his usual bishop garb.

I have described the other participants around the table, so it is only fair they have the opportunity to introduce me as well. According to my copy of the report, "Pastor Crowther was neatly dressed and groomed and appeared his stated age. He was cooperative throughout the evaluation and maintained appropriate levels of eye contact. He shared information about himself and his history with apparent candor and completed all the tasks involved in the assessment procedure. As a result, the evaluating team felt it was able to ascertain significant information pertinent to his functional capacities."

So there.

What followed during the hour-long readout, however, was considerably less flattering. The written report summarized, "It is the view of the evaluating team that Pastor Crowther seriously underestimates the emotional impact of distressing events in his life. He exhibits a tendency towards denial and minimization which reduces the ability of this intelligent and well-intentioned man to bring the full weight of his resources to bear on himself and his personal well-being."

The team further listed evidence of depression and possibly post-traumatic stress.

"A talented, hard-working, and high-achieving man, his ability to gauge the impact of highly distressing events on his own emotional state is notably underdeveloped for a person of his age, intelligence, and level of education."

In short, the team considered me a gifted but troubled individual.

The psychologist tapped the report on the table, stowed it back in the folder, and set it aside. "So, Joe...we are interested to know what you think?"

If your goal is to evaluate someone and then handicap that person's ability to respond to that evaluation, then cast that person as defensive. Suggest a state of self-denial. Then, any protest inherently affirms the evaluation. Right? Any pushback by my talented, intelligent, and well-intentioned self would prop up their professional judgment that I was highly stressed and emotionally immature.

Had I said what I *wanted* to say, I imagined the psychologist standing and calmly declaring, "Folks, I think we are done here," and then recessing the team from the room, leaving me alone with the bishop to explore the list of available three-point parishes in western Kansas.

How about asking this over-intellectualizing pastor, "How do you *feel*?" That question I could answer. Baited. Cornered. I felt that no one could possibly arrive at such conclusions from a handful of inkblots, personality inventories, and a few hours of conversation. Try shaping all of *that* into a response that does not sound defensive!

Impatient with my silence, the psychologist volleyed the question *I* wanted to the other end of the table. "How do you feel about the report, Bishop? Anything to add?"

Jerry collected himself in his usual cautious, contemplative manner. Then, ignoring the question altogether, he took a grenade, pulled the pin, and lobbed it in my direction.

"Joe, there have been accusations of your sexual misconduct at Atonement." He then paused so we could experience the full impact of the blast wind. "I have investigated the accusations," Jerry continued, "and have determined that there is nothing to them."

My underdeveloped ability to gauge the impact of highly distressing events was being put to the test. First, how were these claims even remotely relevant to the discussion at hand? Second, if the accusations were disproven, why mention them at all? My answer came more quickly than I wanted. The purpose of the first announcement was to prepare me for the primary detonation.

"Joe, I am meeting with your vision board next week to recommend your resignation. You've had a good run at Atonement, but I think it's time to move on."

Volley back to the psychologist.

"Joe, we recommend that you enroll in a program of therapy to address these concerns, such as the program we offer here at the Consultation Center. You would be in residence with us for six months at a cost of...."

"Time out!"

I interrupted before he could deliver the invoice. I still had no response, but my life had entered a sudden tailspin, and I desperately needed to get at least one of *my* hands on the controls.

I knew the symptoms of depression all too well — the persistent sadness, emptiness, restlessness, and thoughts of suicide. I didn't have the disease, but I lived with it. Depression threatened the very lives of those I loved most. My B.A. in Psychology may not have prepared me for an academic sparring match with this group, but I *had* been credentialed by experience.

Moreover, I slept well, ate well, and exercised daily. I shepherded my flock with grace. No. I could not accept this report, at least not entirely. And there was absolutely no way I would spend six months in any residence other than my own.

"I know I have been through a great deal," I said, breaking the awkward silence. "No one appreciates that more than I do. And I am glad to do the necessary work to figure out what sort of toll all of this has taken. But surely there is a way to accomplish that without residential treatment. Maybe I could...."

"We recommend a residential program," the psychologist interjected. "You can't give this the sort of attention it deserves while running a parish full-time."

That actually made some sense to me.

"Fine," I continued. "I still have several months of sabbatical left and would be glad to…"

"In our opinion," he stopped me again, "proper treatment will require more time than that."

"So, I can undergo a period of treatment here and then secure ongoing treatment afterward back home…maybe even work part-time for a while," I suggested.

No response. Apparently, when it comes to remaining silent, psychologists and bishops receive the same training.

So that was it. I had nothing left to leverage at that moment. No authority. My goal now was to make it out of the room before I lost anything else. I hung my head.

"I know you'd like to think you're okay, Pastor," the psychologist concluded as he placed the folder in his briefcase and pushed back his chair. "But no one can go through what you've experienced and not have significant issues to work on."

As soon as the meeting was completed, I asked Jerry for some processing time. He checked his watch, hesitated, then reluctantly agreed. We discovered an empty lounge at the end of the hallway.

Once again, this time without the Catholic gallery present, I proposed repurposing a portion of my sabbatical to do the required work for returning to Atonement. Jerry was having none of it. That matter was closed.

"So, what's next?" I asked.

Jerry pulled out his calendar.

"Doesn't the vision board meet next Tuesday?"

I wanted to say, "You've met with them more than I have recently. You tell me." I just nodded.

"I will be there to make the recommendation. But right now, I have to get back to Kansas City." And with that, we were done.

"Will you at least promise me this?" I asked on the way out the door. "If you have any communication with my leadership over the next week, will you include me?"

He agreed, then made a quick, awkward exit.

During the interminable ride home, I replayed the morning's events over and over, inserting all the comments I wished I had said but could not conjure up at the moment. No matter where I sliced it, the process smelled rancid.

First, a bishop paid a counseling service to evaluate one of his pastors. That bishop would subsequently use the results of that evaluation to justify a resignation recommendation. Second, this evaluation was necessarily confidential, so it would be tossed atop the "if you only knew what *we* know but can't tell you about Pastor Joe" stack of noninformation. Finally, the Consultation Center delivered an evaluation, then sought to profit from that evaluation by selling me a six-month residential treatment plan to remedy a condition only they felt I had.

This was a new world for me, but the ethics seemed suspect at best. However, if I wanted to challenge the system, I first had to survive it.

Jerry was going to recommend my resignation. What if I decided not to comply with that recommendation? What if the vision board could be persuaded not to accept it? There were plenty of entry points for the Holy Spirit to show up and redeem this miserable process. I laid the worries aside, at least for a few miles, and prayed.

Late on a Thursday morning in June, a nun, a psychologist, a social worker, a bishop, and a gainfully employed, well-intentioned, talented, intelligent, defensive, and possibly slightly depressed and emotionally traumatized Lutheran pastor walked into a conference room. What took place in that room changed that pastor's life forever.

Yet Another Surprise................................**Monday, June 25**

I wrapped up a premarital counseling session on Monday evening, stepped out of my office, glanced down the long, dark hallway, and unexpectedly spied Jerry ambling around in the lobby outside the sanctuary. It was obvious from his expression that he neither expected nor wanted to be discovered. He immediately changed direction and headed my way.

"A few of us are meeting in the chapel," he said. "We would like you to join us in a few moments. I'll come to get you."

And with that, he whirled around and was gone.

Us? Who was *us?* I was willing to wager June's salary that it was not the pastoral appreciation team. All I knew for sure was that *us* didn't include me…yet.

A month previously, Jerry apologized for meeting with the board without informing me. On the prior Thursday, he promised there would be no communication with my leadership that didn't include me, yet the pattern continued. I returned to my office, closed the door, stared at the wall, and waited to be retrieved.

19

WAITING FOR THE SPIRIT'S HAIL MARY

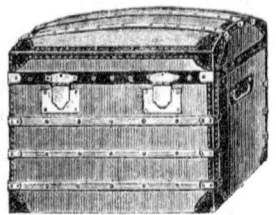

For there to be betrayal, there would have to have been trust first.

~ Suzanne Collins, *The Hunger Games*

I think it is very good when people suffer. To me that is like the kiss of Jesus.

~ Mother Teresa

YET ANOTHER SURPRISE *(continued)*.................. **Monday, June 25**

The chapel is one of my favorite spaces at Atonement. A small, intimate room connected to the sanctuary by a two-ton, sliding wooden door, the chapel serves well as a prayer room, a holding area for groomsmen before a wedding, and overflow space for Christmas and Easter worshipers. The designing architects pitched the concept of an ancillary chapel by promoting its versatility as a sacred multipurpose room. But I doubt that *ambushing the senior pastor* would have been a strong selling point for the building committee.

A handful of chairs were arranged in a circle in the center of the space. Seated in them were Janice (assistant to the bishop), John (vision board president), several vision board members, and two extraordinary pastoral colleagues who were also members of the congregation.

Rev. John Frey had been my part-time associate pastor for the previous eight years and a very dear friend from the moment we met. A man of consummate compassion, John invested his heart in caring for the parish's sick and shut-in.

Pastor Richard was a retired member of Atonement and senior pastor supporter extraordinaire. He regularly stopped by the office or took me to lunch. Every visit we shared ended with a tearful attempt to convince me that I was too busy.

"You need more staff to help you," he pleaded.

"Thank you, friend," I always said, heartened by the genuine concern of someone who had "been there."

"The vision board met last evening," Jerry began.

I made yet one more notch next to the lists of illicit gatherings and broken promises.

"They voted to request your resignation. There was unanimous expression of appreciation for your ministry, but the board felt that this was in your best interest."

I had been ambushed and taken off guard so often over the past month that I honestly thought I was insusceptible to surprise. I was wrong.

All heads in the circle turned toward me as if we were spectating at a tennis match and Jerry had just served up a soft lob. Once again, I found myself positioned across the room from my usual seat. On far more occasions than I care to recall, I delivered the dismissal notification to a staff member. I despised it. Perhaps Jerry did as well. "Dispense the unwelcome news quickly," we tell ourselves. "It will be less painful." That may be true on *that* side of the room, but I can now attest that those who receive the news appreciate compassion. I deferred the next words to someone else.

Jerry passed the ball around the circle and invited everyone to share what they had appreciated about my ministry. It was a nice gesture, though a bit hollow given the context.

Pastor John expressed beautifully what our shared ministry meant to him. "Working with you has given me the best years of my career. I was very reluctant to support this, but when I heard that it was best for *you*, Joe, then I decided to go along."

Richard followed suit. "Friend, when my wife Connie died, it took years for me to mourn and recover. A divorce is like a death. You must take care of yourself, so you will be able to do ministry again soon." Jerry had obviously already leveraged the St. Louis report even more zealously than I expected.

After the circuit was complete, Jerry outlined the specifics.

"The leadership has agreed to offer six months of severance pay for you and benefits and medical insurance for you and Lauren for the same period."

Janice chimed in to make sure I realized how unprecedented the offer was and how appreciative I should be. Once again, all eyes returned to my side of the court.

The weeks leading to this moment had taught me many hard lessons, one of which was to never *react* in a situation like this, but to *respond* only after considerable thought and prayer.

"Well," I said slowly, "I guess I have a lot to pray about."

John, Jerry, and Janice immediately cut their eyes at one another concerningly.

Jerry replied, "You don't understand, Joe. This offer is good only if you tender your resignation this evening."

"Unbelievable," I whispered to myself. "And if I decide not to resign?"

"First off, you would forfeit the opportunity for severance. Secondly, we would hold congregational forums during which you and the board would share your positions. The matter would ultimately be determined by a vote of the membership. But no one wins in a process like that."

It was clear to me that I stood to gain a great deal from a process like that. I would have gladly opened the chapel's wooden door and invited the entire congregation to join our deliberations. I considered the way the process had been handled — the covert meetings, the admonishment to keep vision board concerns confidential, the insistence upon an immediate resignation. It all veritably shouted that the board wanted this handled quickly and quietly. If the cards they held benefited them, they would not have hesitated to lay their hand faceup for the congregation to see.

The only question was whether I should call their bluff.

"You cannot possibly expect me to make a decision like this without praying over it. Even Luther got a day to respond before the emperor at Worms,[1] and he had known what was coming for weeks. I have had all of five minutes to consider this."

Jerry didn't appreciate my answer...or my comparison of his group to the Holy Roman emperor's tribunal. He looked at John — again, the driver of this process — and received the not-so-secret affirmative nod.

"You have one day."

STAFF MEETING SURPRISE .... Tuesday, June 26

The balcony was my favorite space in my tiny, single-bedroom, second-floor apartment. It was a small, sacred space connected to the living room by a sliding glass door. Every night I went to this chapel to pace and pray and process my day.

My first petitions on Monday evening were laced with bitterness. I thought of St. Teresa of Avila's fist-shaking declaration to God. After slipping down an embankment during a fierce rainstorm, the irrepressible nun cried out to heaven, "If this is how you treat your friends, it is no wonder you have so few of them!"

---

1   The Diet of Worms was a meeting of the Holy Roman emperor Charles V's imperial diet (or assembly) at Worms in 1521. Martin Luther was summoned to appear. In the Edict of Worms, Luther's teachings were condemned as heretical.

I flashed back to words spoken by another bishop amid a different storm: "Joseph, it is an amazing thing to me that God calls people like you to the ministry."

Could Bishop Michael have been onto something at my ordination? Maybe he recognized signs the Holy Spirit had missed. Maybe God discovered that my original letter of call ended up in my box due to an angel's clerical error and had finally gotten it rerouted to an appropriately-gifted woman who had spent the last quarter-century working as a Ford engineer outside Detroit. I suppose it could happen.

That evening, as usual, God's patience outlasted my resentment.

Was this a time for righteous anger? Should I grab a slingshot and stand opposed? What were the consequences of publicly calling out this injustice?

There was a reason that John reacted so indignantly the previous week when he learned that I had shared the vision board's concerns with the staff; he was well aware of the mutual respect the congregation and I had for one another. If members felt that I needed forgiveness, they would share the Lord's peace freely.

With that confidence, I wondered, should I call the vision board's bluff? If so, would the board back down? I was certain that a vote would result in my favor, but what effect would the drama of such a process have upon the congregation? Would it strengthen the church? Dispirit it? Divide it? Monday was one of God's more silent nights.

I had one card yet to play before folding the deck. The staff met first thing each Tuesday. In the morning, I would share the bombshell news of Monday's ambush and ask that we pray together for the Spirit's direction. Perhaps together, we would discover an option I had not considered. Perhaps.

But as soon as I pulled into the parking lot Tuesday morning, I discovered a fundamental flaw in my plan. I assumed that "You have a day" meant that I had been granted twenty-four hours to respond. The fact that Jerry and Janice were waiting for me outside the front door indicated that he had intended to say, "You have until dawn's early light."

The thumbscrews were about to be tightened.

We cloistered in my office where, for the next hour, our conversation did little more than replay what had been shared the prior evening. I intentionally dawdled and delayed, partly to frustrate the process, but mostly in hopes that the Holy Spirit had a last-minute revelation or Hail Mary play up His sleeve.

There came a knock at the door; it was Pastor John.

"Joe, the staff is together and waiting. Anything you want me to tell them?"

If I had to select a courier for the Holy Spirit, it would be John, but this was not the message I was hoping for.

"Thank you, John. Could you please let everyone know that I'll be there in a moment, and that we may have several guests this morning?"

John conveyed more compassion with his facial expressions than most people managed with their entire vocabularies.

"Sure," he said, and closed the door quietly.

"You both know that I will not have another call in six months. I would like severance to include benefits for Lauren and me for one year."

Jerry looked at Janice. She said, "I think the board will agree to that."

"And what sort of therapy will I have to complete before you consider me eligible for a call again?"

While Jerry did not have the authority to remove me from my current position, he was the sole gatekeeper for future opportunities. I needed assurance that he would not send me through a one-way professional turnstile with no option for return.

"I will require enough sessions with a counselor who can then assure me that you are ready for ministry."

"And those can be local? And outpatient?"

"I am fine with that," he confirmed.

"This entire process has reeked," I said.

"I know," Jerry responded as if he were not responsible.

"You get to tell the staff," I said. "They are all waiting in the narthex."

"Not yet. I still don't have the resignation letter."

I swiveled my chair to the computer.

"Fine. You dictate."

As the two-sentence letter printed, Jerry began choreographing the rest of the week.

"I will have an email announcement sent to the congregation today notifying them of the resignation and that I will be here tomorrow evening to address this issue and answer any questions."

"They will hear the news from their pastor first," I demanded. "*I* will send a letter today and address the matter at worship this weekend. Next week, you can do whatever you want."

Once again, Jerry was not pleased, but there was also little he could say other than, "I'll be here next Monday evening."

LETTER TO CONGREGATION...................... Wednesday, June 27

Dearest Friends in Christ,

"I give thanks to my God always for you because of the grace of God that has been given you in Christ Jesus...." (1 Cor. 1)

The last Congregational letter I wrote to you several years ago followed a particularly difficult event in my personal life. In that letter, I expressed my desire to "model grace in the midst of brokenness." I pray that I have been faithful in this regard. Where I have struggled to be equally faithful is in the extension of the grace to myself.

Recently, I was diagnosed with post-traumatic stress disorder, the product of a lengthy litany of personal life and family trials that have taken place over the past years. For the most part, I have managed to conceal the effects of this disorder from you. In some ways, I have kept them hidden from myself. But the time has come to heed the counsel of others and my own sense of the Holy Spirit's guidance and begin what will surely be an intensive season of both emotional and spiritual healing.

At the recommendation of our bishop, with the prayerful support and understanding of the vision board, and after considerable prayer, today I offered my pastoral resignation to the Congregational leadership.

Please know that Atonement is in no way responsible for the stress that I am experiencing. Ministry is hard work, to be sure. But this congregation has been a wellspring of blessing and joy for me ever since I first stepped into the office eleven years ago this week. My time among you will remain a treasure that I will always hold dear to my heart. I am exceedingly proud of all that we have accomplished together and how well-positioned this congregation is to grow into its second half-century of ministry. But my healing will come only with absolute commitment to the process in front of me…and then later, with a fresh pastoral start on the *other side* of that process. Atonement is far too precious to me — and its impact too significant in the Kingdom — for me to attempt to juggle both the work of healing *and* the responsibilities of my calling.

My final weekend with you will be July 14-15. The upcoming weeks will be filled with difficult, blessed days. But as I've said to you regularly, the Lord is not stumped by the challenges ahead. God will most surely bring redemption, both in my life and in the life of this extraordinary congregation.

In Thanksgiving for our ministry together and very finally in Christ,

Pastor Joe

Rev. Dr. Joseph G. Crowther

20

WHEN THE PREACHER DOESN'T KNOW

This sermon was preached the weekend following the announcement of my resignation at Atonement.

When Jesus had crossed again in the boat to the other side, a great crowd gathered around him; and he was by the sea. Then one of the leaders of the synagogue named Jairus came and, when he saw him, fell at his feet and begged him repeatedly, "My little daughter is at the point of death. Come and lay your hands on her, so that she may be made well, and live." So he went with him.

And a large crowd followed him and pressed in on him. Now there was a woman who had been suffering from hemorrhages for twelve years. She had endured much under many physicians, and had spent all that she had; and she was no better, but rather grew worse. She had heard about Jesus, and came up behind him in the crowd and touched his cloak, for she said, "If I but touch his clothes, I will be made well." Immediately her hemorrhage stopped; and she felt in her body that she was healed of her disease. (Mark 5:21-29)

"Do you know what I like most about your sermons?"

That's what my friend asked me on Tuesday afternoon as we sat together at Kauffman Stadium. It may seem like an odd question to ask between innings at a Royals game, but my friend is a member here at the church, and I had just shared with him the news that I would be stepping down as pastor in a few weeks.

"Do you know what I like about your sermons?" he asked. "I really like when you admit that you don't know something. I figure if there are important things that you don't know — someone who has spent an entire career studying the Scriptures — and if you still don't have life completely figured out and all together, then it's alright if I don't have life all together either."

I appreciated the comment, though I am still processing it. Truth is, it took me a little off guard.

I am wondering if others feel the same way. Would you agree with my friend? Don't worry, I won't ask for a show of hands. But does his opinion resonate with you? Do you like your pastors a little less-than-together? Rough around the edges? Maybe even slightly flawed?

What qualities do you most value in a pastor? Suppose there was a *Pastors' Quarterly* magazine. What sort of pastor would you imagine on the cover?

I recently read someone's tongue-in-cheek description of an ideal pastor.

1. Sermons are exactly twenty minutes. They inspire and convict everyone while upsetting no one.
2. Works from seven a.m. to ten p.m. in every type of work from counseling to custodial service.
3. Is twenty-seven years old with thirty years of ministry experience.
4. Tall and short.
5. Thin and heavy set.
6. Handsome or attractive, but not overpowering.
7. One brown eye and one blue eye.
8. Is always at the office.
9. Has perfect children.
10. Is talented, gifted, scholarly, practical, popular, compassionate, understanding, patient, levelheaded, dependable, loving, caring, neat, organized, cheerful, and above all, humble.

Through the years, I have interviewed with a dozen call committees. Not one of them has ever said, "Pastor, there is just one last matter we need to discuss before we decide to recommend you to the church. Please understand, this is something we ask all our candidates. You don't have your life all together, do you?"

What if I asked the same question about worship? My experience is that folks are rarely shy about sharing opinions regarding worship. Which parts of the worship service do you value the most? Music? Communion?

One of the benefits of sitting up front throughout the service is that I can watch your reactions to the music, the prayers, and the sermon. Judging from your expressions and levels of engagement, I know that many of you value "the music" or our "time with the children."

One part of the service that few would list as most meaningful is the Confession.

"As a called and ordained minister of the church of Christ, and by his authority, I declare to you the entire forgiveness of all your sins."

Have you listened to the way we typically respond to that stupendous news?

(Quietly) "Thanks be to God."

When you get home this afternoon, go to our web page and watch the beginning of any worship service. Listen to the confession. It sounds as if we are whispering our appreciation.

Your response has an exclamation point. "Thanks be to God!"

Your relationship with God has been resynced. You are pardoned and restored. This is stellar news! Yet as I look around, I see worshipers still meandering into worship. Others are greeting their neighbors or sneak-texting on their phones. I see you wiping sleep from your eyes.

If we realized what God is doing for us at that moment, we would be wiping *tears* from our eyes.

Those who are new to liturgical worship often ask, "Why do we have confession? And why put it first in the service? It seems a little awkward and depressing."

I understand the questions. To be sure, publicly declaring our shortcomings is difficult. It feels a little odd to stand next to those who know us and admit that we don't have our lives fully together, worked out, or squared away.

Even now you may be thinking, "I can't act too interested in what Pastor is saying, or someone will think I *need* this message." Paying attention to a sermon like this, or appearing too remorseful during confession, might become grist for the rumor mill.

So, we whisper the responses and pretend the confession isn't really for us.

Yet if you have not come for forgiveness this morning, what brings you here? If you are in search of something other than grace, then you can probably get a better deal somewhere else.

Maybe you've come for the music. Many do. But while our worship arts program is top-notch, there are institutions, theaters, and clubs that offer music exclusively. You might get a better show somewhere else.

Is it the food and coffee that draw you here? We have a tremendous café. Just down the street, however, you'll find a shop that specializes in coffee. You can find anything you want there.

But if you've come this morning to confess that you don't have life all together, that you have fallen short of God's glory…

If you want to renew a right relationship with God…

If you are looking for a community in which you can safely say, "There are some things I did this week that I should have left undone, and some things I should have done, but didn't"…

If you want a clean slate and a new start…

…then you are in precisely the right place. Forgiveness is the Lord's specialty, and we excel in serving it up.

But understand that I am not talking about a cerebral, intellectual confession. It is one thing to *know* that life is not as it should be. The confession is altogether different when it comes from deep in the soul instead of the head.

And I am not talking about admitting that *others* don't have life together or that, collectively, *we* have erred as a nation or a culture or a denomination. We are gifted at speaking for others or being part of a group. What I am talking about is a personal confession. I am referring to *you*.

I know so much about the coffee shop I mentioned a moment ago because it is my office away from the office. You will find me there as many mornings as not, sitting in the corner and working. I overhear groups railing about others. This week I have learned that family values have disintegrated, the schools in our country are failing, both major political parties are corrupt, and the healthcare system is diseased. And that was just Monday!

I am not talking about others. This conversation is about you and me.

Admitting our shortcomings and the need for forgiveness can be difficult, but unless we engage confession boldly, we rob ourselves of a fuller experience of God's mercy.

There are three characters in this morning's lesson. None of them have life all together.

I know our first character well. His name is Jairus, a leader of the synagogue. As the community's spiritual director, he is the person others approach with questions about faith. But Jairus pays a price for his esteem. His life is constantly on display and under scrutiny, which is a challenge because, like everyone else, Jairus' life is not always together. In fact, in today's lesson, Jairus' world is not only disordered, but it is also upside down.

I know this because a man in Jairus' position would never consult with an itinerant, upstart rabbi like Jesus unless he were desperate. And if he did, he would send a messenger. He would certainly not approach Jesus personally.

But Jairus' world has become so dismantled that, not only does he address Jesus publicly, but he also throws himself at Jesus' feet. He does not inquire of Jesus, or politely or formally ask Jesus, or even petition Jesus. Instead, he repeatedly *begs* Jesus for help. His daughter is dying.

Nothing afflicts a parent's heart more than a hurting child. I have watched the strongest men brought to their knees when the health of their child is compromised. Jairus is such a man.

Jairus is utterly vulnerable. He will tell you at this moment, "I do not have life all together."

In many ways, the second character in our story is Jairus' exact opposite. This woman is not a leader. She has no social standing. As far as we know, she has no name. And if her lot in life were not miserable enough, she is also ill. For twelve years, the woman has been bleeding, which also means that she is unclean, ostracized, and living in isolation. She is unable to bear children or have friends. In short, she is desperate.

"If only I can touch his cloak," she says.

She will brave the crowds. She will brave anything at this point if, by doing so, there is the slightest possibility she will be healed. I think we can safely say that she does not have her life together.

So, who is our third character? Do not forget the little girl. Jairus' daughter is twelve years of age, nearly old enough to bear life. In Jesus' day, she is also approaching the age at which she can marry. But she may not live long enough to realize either. She most certainly does not have her life together.

Each of the characters in today's lesson boldly presents their pain and fear to God. Each of them is healed and restored.

For eleven years, I have sat beside your hospital beds, shared late evening visits around your kitchen tables, and stood with you as we commended your loved ones to their resting places. I have refereed fights, seen your dirty laundry, and witnessed your failures and disappointments.

And you have witnessed mine.

You shared in the trials of my family as we struggled to hold it all together, sometimes successfully, and other times, not so much. You supported us through Grant's illness and a marital divorce.

I do not know (there is that phrase again) what this community of faith needs to do to become a safer place for those who are less than perfect. Perhaps that transformation begins with a pastor who leads by example.

But I know this: becoming such a community is vitally important because the only way to trust God's great "I love you" is first to hear God's gracious "I know you." And as long as we think we are fooling someone — a loved one, coworker, neighbor, or ourselves, we can never really trust that God loves us just as we are.

If you hear nothing else this day, hear that again.

God loves you just as you are.

The Gospel is clear. It is our imperfections that bring us to God, not our good deeds. Jesus has always gotten along famously with sinners and the unrighteous. It was the unrepentant who gave Jesus fits.

To receive the gift of abundant life, you do not have to be smart, attractive, popular, wise, or worthy. You need not be accomplished. In fact, the world may not even know your name.

Even now, Jesus' mercy is searching out the messy, disordered, unattractive parts of our lives. He said as much.

"I came to heal the sick and raise the dead."

It's Jesus' specialty.

That is what I have thought about since Tuesday afternoon at Kauffman Stadium when a friend's comment reminded me of the heart of God.

"Do you know what I like most about our conversations?" God asks. "I like it when you admit that you don't have life all together."

21

At the Base of "The Trough"

Human life is far more important than getting to the top of the mountain.

~ Edmund Hillary

Today is your day! Your mountain is waiting, so…get on your way!

~ Dr. Seuss, *Oh, the Places You'll Go!*

"So, Joe, tell me what happened at Atonement."

I fully expected to field that question at some point during our visit. After all, no bishop worth his or her salt would give me another crack at ministry without a satisfactory explanation for my current professional predicament. I had hoped, however, that we might at least get to know each other for a few minutes first.

"Do you want the hour-long version or the five-minute version?" I asked.

"Do you have a ten-minute version?"

Truth was, I had no persuasive version of any length.

The initial stop on my late August 2012 *Bishops of the Southeast Tour* was in the office of Bishop Herman Yoos in Columbia, South Carolina. Anticipating that a return to the parish would be complicated at best, it seemed wise to circle back to a synod in which I might have less to explain. Although my pastorate in North Myrtle Beach predated Herman's administration, I had been the senior pastor of his synod's fastest-growing congregation for nearly six years. Surely that counted for something.

I communicate for a living. For a quarter-century, I had delivered the good news of Jesus Christ in ways that were accessible, compelling, and persuasive. I have a doctorate of homiletics. Yet I could not craft an honest, credible narrative to explain what happened at Atonement. Nothing worked, including the ten-minute impromptu version of the ordeal that I pitched Bishop Herman. Nevertheless, his response was like salve for my wounded soul.

"That must have been very difficult for you," he said.

There! I heard it. Finally, the sound of pastoral compassion. I just needed to wait three and a half months and travel twelve hundred miles to receive it from some other pastor's pastor.

He offered me a book.

"This has meant a great deal to me," he said. "Call me after you read it and we can discuss it together."

"I would like to pray for you if that's alright," he continued. "And there are some issues that I am dealing with. I would appreciate it if you would pray for me as well?"

We took each other's hands, and for the better part of ten minutes, I prayed with a true shepherd. Whether our time together resulted in interview possibilities or not, the trip had been worthwhile.

But the question remained. What happened?

Ironically, my search for a next call would have been considerably easier if only I were more blameworthy. Had I become apathetic toward my call or my flock, failed to show up for funerals, mistreated staff, allowed the demons from home to sneak up the backstairs of my psyche and impact my work at church, then the outcome at Atonement *still* would not have been justifiable, but at least it would have been more explainable.

"I made a mistake, Bishop, but I have done the hard work of repentance and am ready to shepherd again." That is honorable and credible. There was no honor, however, in accepting blame that did not belong to me, nor was anything to be gained by villainizing my former leadership.

The final and most truthful option was to confess, "I don't know what happened, Bishop." Saying "I don't know" may have played well from the pulpit, but no prelate will take a chance on a pastor who simply shrugs their shoulders.

When a pastor unexpectedly leaves a congregation, bishops are not the only people asking questions. Any congregation worth its salt will also want to know what happened.

During the last week of June, after eleven years together, and with no forewarning, Atonement members received a letter notifying them that our marriage was ending. Ninety-eight percent of the membership had no inkling that our relationship was even in trouble. The few who *were* aware could offer no satisfactory explanation of the concerns. But then, neither could I.

About half of the current members had been at Atonement when I arrived. They remembered our courtship and the months of premarital work together to determine if we were an appropriate match for one another. They had a voice in the marriage. They voted privately, then stood publicly at the service of installation and said, "I do."

When it came to the dissolution of the marriage, members had no such privileges. There was no opportunity to participate in crisis counseling. No one even asked their opinion. Members just returned home one day to find that I had my bags packed and one foot out the door.

Some were in shock. Others were seething. Long-time members were chanting, "Here we go again." I was now the third in a parade of pastors to leave Atonement under duress and without a call in hand. Folks had experienced enough.

On the first Monday in July, Atonement's demand for an explanation was squared off against a bishop who had no intention of divulging details.

Ray, one of the ushers, had asked on Sunday morning, "Do you need anything for the meeting tomorrow night, Pastor?"

"You may want to pass out some tissues, flak jackets, and helmets," I said.

I was only half kidding.

PUBLIC FORUM WITH BISHOP......................... **Monday, July 2**

As folks began to file into the pews on Monday evening, I turned to Ray and said, "It looks as if we'll not be operating on Standard Lutheran Time tonight."

Atonemenites tended to straggle into worship five to ten minutes late. I could never explain SLT, nor could I find a way to change it. But on this night, the pews were filling unusually early.

I sensed from Jerry's backstage expression that the attendance was considerably larger than he had expected. He was more robotic and guarded than usual as he stepped to the microphone and read verbatim from a script. The words we received came across like the remnants of a former speech that had survived the legal team's tweaking.

Right out of the gate Jerry attempted to manage expectations.

"For those looking for answers tonight, much of what I have to say will be inadequate."

He then helped fulfill his prophecy by delivering a ten-minute report filled with innuendo and insinuation, but void of details.

Jerry spoke of presenting issues but refused to name them. He mentioned my psychological evaluation and his interviews with staff, but, understandably, shared no specifics. The only precise charge he surfaced was the allegation that had been disproven — sexual misconduct. While I appreciated his admonishment of the rumormongering, raising the issue only served to unnecessarily introduce sordid images to a room full of folks who had not, at least until that point, entertained the possibility.

There was a palpable, unsettling frustration stirring throughout the pews. As Jerry closed and stepped away from the lectern to entertain questions, I worried that the spark from one edgy comment might transform this sacred space into the set of a weekday afternoon talk show.

I imagined the headlines in the *Kansas City Star*: "Pastor's Resignation Leads to Congregational Melee." Those fears were not calmed when the first questioner angrily asked, "How dare a handful of persons decide for the entire congregation? Where is *your* resignation?" Again, bishops are trained when not to respond.

Melanie, a successful, thoughtful businessperson, rose next to speak. During the prelude to her question, she casually mentioned, "Joe has done a tremendous job for this congregation…" At that point, Melanie was interrupted by a long round of applause, a moment of grace in an evening filled with vitriol and pain.

Those around me forgave. Even without complete knowledge of the offenses, and likely assuming the worst, they demonstrated the kind of support and forgiveness that many of their leaders had not. Perhaps there was no more persuasive testimony to the depth of our relationship as shepherd and flock.

After the applause ceased, Melanie said, "Joe, I know you're here. I hope you felt the love in that response." Indeed.

The words which were most helpful in quelling members' doubts came from Pastor John:

> "Often, as we were in the back of the sanctuary preparing to come out for worship, I would say, 'Joe, how are things going?' And he would tell me some unbelievable, awful things. And I would say, 'Joe, how can you go out there and preach?' And he would come out here and preach the best sermons and conduct himself admirably and greet people and smile. And that would go on week after week after week. I don't think a person in this room could tell what he was wrestling with. The issues. The constant pain.

"I was fearful that, if he went against the powers that be, it might hurt his standing in the church. But primarily, it was for his healing that I supported this. I would never want anything for Joe that wasn't for Joe's good."

Maybe the evening forum provided me with the best possible response for prospective bishops' questions. When they would ask, "What happened?" I could share the video of Pastor John's remarks and the congregation's expression of forgiveness, along with a copy of the hundreds of "your ministry meant so much to me" letters that members shared, and say, "Here are a few things that have meant a great deal to me. I think you will find them helpful. Have a look and give me a call. We can discuss them."

FINAL WORSHIP SERVICES . . . . Saturday & Sunday, July 14-15

For three services, the sanctuary was as full as it had ever been in the middle of summer. The Kansas City Brassworks, Atonement's brass sextet in residence, performed. The Chancel Choir was in exquisite form. Rick pulled a few stops on the organ that I was not aware the instrument even possessed. To visitors, worship looked and sounded like Easter in July, but for those in the know, the stench of Good Friday's betrayal still lingered.

The background image for my message was The Trough, a treacherous section of loose boulders near the approach to the summit of Longs Peak in Rocky Mountain National Park, Colorado. The success rate for serious climbers looking to summit Longs is less than fifty percent. It is often standing at the base of The Trough that climbers, dehydrated, exhausted, and suffering from altitude sickness, elect to turn back.

"Here's the secret to a successful summit," a fellow climber shared. "Instead of looking ahead to what lies in front of you, look down the mountain at how far you've come. Sometimes, this gives a climber just enough encouragement to reach the top."

My friend's advice seemed a little Pollyannaish to me, but when I stood weary and desperate before the last push to the summit, I was willing to try almost any strategy. Instead of turning back, I turned around and took in a spectacular vista of the climb I had already accomplished. The new perspective made all the difference. It usually does.

"I find myself at the foot of The Trough again this week," I told the congregation. "I am uncertain how best to move forward. So, I'd like to concentrate instead on how far we've come."

For eleven years I had called Atonement's attention forward to the future and discouraged the sort of reminiscing that can mire a congregation in the past. But our final half-hour together was spent looking down the mountain.

God had given us good work to accomplish. The parochial reports reflected 385 baptisms, 75 funerals, 135 weddings, 275 confirmations, the reception of 1,375 members, and 550 (mostly) different sermons preached in 1,650 services.

But there was no place in the parochial reports to record many of Atonement's most vital ministries: the hungry who were fed, the hopeless who were inspired, the marriages that improved, the children who went to school with new backpacks over their shoulders, the women in Tanzania who were cared for in the birthing center we helped fund and construct. Atonement had always been a deeply compassionate congregation, but somewhere along the way, it had received an injection of missional steroids. The congregation delighted in giving itself away.

I chose for my text the often glossed-over prison break of Peter in Acts 12, a resurrection story at heart.

"I don't know what lies up the mountain for Atonement or me, but I know that there will be Easter, God kicking open locked doors and doing something new and life-giving."

At each service, I choked out the benediction around the huge lump in my throat, which only grew larger following the congregation's appreciation and applause. Yet even at that moment, as was the case in the bishop's Monday-night forum, scattered about the sanctuary were a handful of folks who remained seated and sour-faced with arms folded.

"What will you miss most?" someone asked at the reception.

"Oh, there is a long list," I said, "but preaching at Christmas Eve will rank near the top. I don't get to preach to two thousand people on Christmas Eve this year."

Then it hit me. Wait! I don't have to preach to two thousand people on Christmas Eve this year! For the first time in more than two decades, I could do as I jolly well pleased at Christmas. I was liberated to spend the holidays with Mom, worship in a colleague's congregation, or opt not to worship at all. There would be some sweetness swirled in with the bitterness of this new life chapter.

The books and office hangings were packed once again, and the building keys had been surrendered. Over the previous weeks, my lonely time in the sanctuary had been mournful and difficult. The final moments on this day were neither. I was too tired to mourn.

I wonder sometimes whether God looks forward in the same way we remember backward. When I uncovered the Atonement newsletter on my cluttered North Myrtle Beach desk so many years before, did God know that my saying *yes* to the Spirit's stirring would lead to this day? Had I misinterpreted that stirring? Did God have a different plan in mind? Did I miss a sign along the way? Make a wrong turn?

All I knew for sure was that I now had plenty of time to pray over questions such as these.

It was enough reminiscing for one day. I had absolutely nothing on my schedule and it was time to get to it. I offered one more quick prayer of thanksgiving, then turned and started down the mountain.

22

Fields & Floods

The Parable of the Man Who Sowed Good Seed — Part III

> The slaves said to him, 'Then do you want us to go and gather them?' But he replied, 'No; for in gathering the weeds you would uproot the wheat along with them. Let both of them grow together until the harvest. (Matthew 12:28-29)

The rains that fall in northwestern North Carolina are captured by the mountain streams and rivers and funneled southeastward toward the Atlantic. My childhood farm sat in the confluence of two such rivers, the North and South Forks of the Yadkin. When the Appalachians sent more water than the Yadkin cared to deliver, the river swelled beyond her banks and swallowed much of our property, including the gravel drive which provided the only way for us to access the outside world by vehicle. Until the river receded, life was inconvenienced. The river always overstayed her welcome.

On occasion, the Yadkin's timing was just downright rude. In October of 1964, the waters were above flood stage and still rising when Mom went into labor with Pete. (On second thought, maybe it was Pete's timing that was inconsiderate.) In a single afternoon, Mom endured a half-mile rowboat ride, the gondolier-like serenading of my father, and, several hours after arriving at the hospital, childbirth. She claimed they were all equally unpleasant.

The river was never so fierce as it was in 1973. Emergency personnel, family members, and even our pastor slogged down the hill through the muddy woods to help schlep furniture from the house to higher ground in the fields. We desperately dug trenches around our home's foundation to buy a few minutes back from the river.

At midnight, I sat cross-legged on the kitchen floor and shined a flashlight out the back door. Two days earlier, this water had dripped crystal clear from the leaves of rhododendron and mountain laurel. Now, it was muddy and threatening as it lapped across the threshold and into the house. I closed my eyes and prayed as passionately as my nine-year-old spirit was able. Twenty minutes later, the river crested.

I am not suggesting that my prayers halted the river. I am not suggesting they didn't. I only know that after the waters receded, the river was no longer just an inconvenience. It had become an *enemy*.

"Where did these weeds come from?" the slaves inquired of their householder. "How and why has evil infested the fields?"

"An enemy has done this," was the only response they received.

Even at nine years of age, I understood the slaves' frustration and helplessness. Unlike my enemy, their nemesis was unidentified. Was he a single person or a legion of evildoers? What was the enemy's intent? Was he simply making mischief, or did he have more sinister plans in mind? And speaking of plans, did the householder have a strategy in mind for dealing with the enemy should he decide to return?

For the moment, the slaves had no answers, but at least they could rid the field of the weeds before the enemy's handiwork caused more significant damage. Or could they?

The slaves followed protocol and approached the householder to secure a work order for weed eradication.

"Do you want us to go and gather them?"

"No," came the householder's reply, "for in gathering the weeds, you would uproot the wheat along with them."

Good thing they asked.

Our visual of this parable is still frozen where we paused it in chapter 14. Remember that the spokesperson for the slaves is presenting a small bundle of the weeds to the householder. Look again closely and you will notice something the slaves themselves have missed. Buried deep within that bundle are several heads of wheat which the slave accidentally ripped up in his haste to collect evidence.

"*There* is my concern!" the householder pointed out. "I have seen it happen too many times. Once you have collected the weeds and started the burning, *then* you will notice the bundles are full of wheat. Leave them alone."

Pragmatists have a difficult time with Jesus' parables.

"Who among you, having a hundred sheep in the wilderness and losing one, does not leave the ninety-nine in the wilderness to go in search of the one that is lost until it is found?"[1] Pose that question at a conference of shepherds, and every hand in the room will go up. No one would do this. Follow that advice and you end up with ninety-nine more lost sheep.

If you want to get a horticulturalist's heart racing, suggest that he or she allow an infestation of weeds to grow unchecked in a field of wheat. Better yet, ask the slaves. They understand that failure to attend to the young weeds will result in a bumper crop of weeds later. Their root systems will grow larger and stronger with time, making them considerably more difficult to eliminate.

The weed in the slave's hand is no ordinary, run-of-the-mill weed. It is bearded darnel, a noxious invader that, until it matures and is ready for harvest, is almost indistinguishable from wheat. The householder knows that the slaves have underestimated their ability to do damage in the field.

---

[1] Luke 15:4

In their zeal to eradicate the evil, the slaves will inevitably affect collateral damage upon the innocent.

"Let them grow together until the harvest." Those are the instructions.

Several months after starting my first pastorate, I set out to cleanse the church rolls. The process seemed simple, justifiable, and innocuous enough. To serve the flock, I needed to define the flock — or so I thought. Which sheep were I responsible for, and which sheep had moved on to other pastures?

I sent a letter to all members who met the constitutional stipulations for inactivity. In my rookie zeal, however, I unintentionally unleashed a firestorm.

"My parents and grandparents are buried in your cemetery. How dare you try to kick us out of our church?!" bellowed the voice on the other end of the phone.

"I am sorry to have upset you, Mrs. Jones. You haven't worshiped with us in three years, and I was just wondering if…."

"Well, wonder no more. Don't you dare remove us from the membership!" *Click.*

Even the best-intended laborers underestimate their potential to cause harm.

From the time I was old enough to shape sounds into words, I had campaigned for permission to operate my father's large deck push mower. This piece of machinery represented for me the rite of passage into young adulthood. Dad finally waved the white flag and relented on my twelfth birthday.

"Before you begin, make sure you…"

I interrupted, "Yeah, yeah, Pops. I've got this!"

I heaved on the chord, roused the monster, and then guided it back and forth across the small field of thick grass next to the barn.

Afterward, as I stood in the kitchen, wiping the sweat from my face and admiring my handiwork through the window, Mom casually asked, "You *did* mow around Dad's prized blackberry bushes that he just planted, right?"

Silence.

I watched as Dad got down on his knees and raked through the hay. He picked up what little was left of his plants, shook his head in disgust, and walked off.

"The plants looked like the rest of the grass," I rationalized.

I recognize the householder's expression of disappointment when the wheat is needlessly damaged. When healthy bushes get lopped off, it matters little that the laborer meant well.

"Let them grow together until the harvest," the householder ordered.

I can hear the unspoken protests of the slaves. Their objections are motivated by more than just their desire to save themselves unnecessary labor. There are matters of morality to consider.

"Then what are we here for if not to eradicate the weeds?" It is a common question of the righteous. "Isn't there right and wrong? True and false? Good and evil? We must take a moral high ground and stand opposed to the weeds. They will take over the world! Ruin our children! Infect our way of living!"

In my experience, those who become so militantly determined to rid the world of evil eventually end up resembling weeds themselves. One way the enemy accomplishes his work is by duping the slaves into sowing his evil for him. Unlike the householder, the enemy is willing to sacrifice a few of his own to recruit our help in eliminating his opponent.

As soon as the floodwaters receded in 1973 and the school bus could once again make its way up the muddy driveway to the farmhouse, Pete and I returned to school. We were the first passengers on a daily forty-five-minute route that eventually *crossed the tracks* to the formerly all-Black school where we sat in the desks of children who had been bused in the other direction to the formerly all-white schools.

Teachers told students that we were part of a larger cultural initiative the government called desegregation. But outside of the classroom, most folks just talked about "busing," usually in hushed conversations. Not everyone chose to whisper, however. Newspapers and television reports showcased hate-filled protestors wielding signs which called for the *undesirables* to be shipped home. Even a nine-year-old could see the awful consequences of trying to separate what God has joined together.

Two decades earlier, Joseph McCarthy set out to rid the nation of *pinko commies*. Vigilante groups formed. "If the Sheriff ain't gonna do it, then we'll take matters into our own hands!" There was the KKK, Bosnia, Ireland, the Middle East…wherever folks desire to cleanse by force, the innocent suffer.

The householder said, "Let them be."

We have all witnessed the trouble caused by taking such matters into our own hands. At the same time, we recognize the dire consequences of assuming a hands-off, turn-a-blind-eye attitude toward evil. Jesus' call is clear. Those who possess his heart are to respond to instances of racism, abuse, and social injustice. A lamp hidden under a bushel serves no purpose. Salt that does not season is worthless. Yeast that fails to leaven is no longer yeast. There is a reason that Jesus did not select passive images for his followers. We are people of action.

Let me reflect on the slaves' question by posing another question of my own. If the devil intended to inflict harm upon the field, why do you suppose he took the time to sow seed? Why go to the trouble to secure a specific weed, sneak into the field under cover of darkness, and sow that seed throughout the field? This plan took significant calculations and labor. Why not just run roughshod through the field with a scythe?

Could it be that the devil is ultimately powerless to harm the wheat? Jesus' kingdom has taken root in the field (world), and there is nothing the enemy can do about it. The devil must resort to more creative, manipulative measures such as stirring up confusion and enlisting the children of light to turn upon themselves. By taking matters into our own hands, we do the devil's bidding for him. The weeds have no power that we do not afford them. Evil can grow alongside the wheat and make life more challenging, but they cannot destroy it.

This parable addresses the larger issue of evil, not the acts of evil. Nowhere does Jesus suggest that we stand idly by as others rape, pillage, and murder. Resist evil. Just realize that, in the end, our efforts will not be effective in vanquishing evil. Only God can cleanse the field.

It is also worth noting that, as difficult as it is to distinguish the weeds from the wheat while they are growing in the same field, calling out the evil from the good that resides inside the same person is an even thornier matter. Anyone who has watched the sun come up knows that the division between night and day, darkness and light, is impossible to define precisely. Where does night stop and morning begin?

Our spirits are not "paint by number" where all the "fours" and "sevens" are evil and worthy of confession, but the rest of the numbers belong to our righteous selves. We are not so easily dissectible. Were God to remove all evil with one fell swoop, each of us would discover a portion of ourselves missing.

The farmhouse of my growing-up years no longer stands. After many decades of threats and near misses, the persistent, relentless enemy finally claimed it. Uninhabitable, the structure was recently demolished, and the rubble discarded.

Friends shared their consolations. "They can take your home, but no one can take your memories." True enough.

The rich images of life on the farm will always remain with me. Creeping cedar draped over Christmas decorations. Holiday feasts. Mom greeting my brothers and me as we got off the bus each afternoon. Getting lost in play and pretend in the forest.

But the memory I cling to most tightly may be the muddy procession of saints as they carried pieces of furniture like holy relics into the wheat field. The house is no more, but the field of God's kingdom will stand forever. That is the householder's promise.

God's Word forever shall abide,
No thanks to foes, who fear it;
For God himself fights by our side
With weapons of the Spirit.
Were they to take our house,
Goods, honor, child, or spouse,
Though life be wrenched away,
They cannot win the day.
The Kingdom's ours forever!

("A Mighty Fortress Is Our God" – Fourth Verse)

23

The Macchiato Revelation

We have a choice. We can embrace our humanness, which means embracing our broken natures and the compassion that remains our best hope for healing. Or we can deny our brokenness, forswear compassion, and, as a result, deny our own humanity.

~ Bryan Stevenson, *Just Mercy*

I am no longer afraid of becoming lost, because the journey back always reveals something new, and that is ultimately good for the artist.

~ Billy Joel

Coffee with the Interim .... Tuesday, July 17

For the first time in nearly a quarter-century, I awoke on Monday morning unemployed. There were no hospital visits to make. No staff meetings to plan. No worship to arrange. The only task on my schedule was *delete tasks from my schedule*. But before I had a chance to get busy doing nothing, I received a call from Russ, Atonement's newly appointed interim pastor. The contact was timely as most of the appointments and tasks being jettisoned from my calendar would eventually find their way onto his schedule.

Interim ministry is grueling, often thankless work. The pastoral minutemen and women who respond to these calls bounce like pinballs around the church serving for short stints in often troubled, highly anxious congregations. Since interims remain in place until a church calls its permanent pastor, churches are rarely excited when they arrive and are always pleased to see them go.

"Would you be willing to meet for coffee tomorrow?" Russ asked. "I would appreciate the opportunity to get your sense of the lay of the land at Atonement."

"Glad to," I replied, in a tone that sounded much more eager than I intended…or felt.

Russ was a pleasant soul. His demeanor and personality would take some getting used to on Atonement's part, I was sure, but he had the energy and drive to lead the congregation through the strenuous, necessary work ahead.

"So, where is home?"

"The Seattle area," he said. "I am eager to get back there. I would be there now, in fact, had Janice not approached me at Synod Assembly about this position."

I nearly spewed my caramel macchiato across the table.

"I am sorry, Russ. When did you say that you were approached?"

"At the assembly," he said, a little puzzled by my excitement. "Why?"

"Do you mind telling me what she said?"

"Janice asked me what my immediate plans were. I had just finished another interim assignment in the synod, so I told her I was headed home. But she asked me to change my plans as she had another assignment for me. That's when she told me about Atonement."

Synod Assembly — the annual gathering of pastors and laity from across Kansas and Missouri — took place in McPherson, Kansas, from June 7 to 9. On June 11, Jerry clearly stated to the vision board and me, "I will make no recommendations in this matter until I first interview members of the staff and have the results of Joe's evaluation in hand."

Yet, according to Russ, one week before any of the staff were interviewed and two weeks before the conference room drama in St. Louis, the bishop had already taken steps to secure my interim successor.

"Everything okay?" my new friend asked.

I assured Russ that I was fine and decided to keep this discovery to myself. He was not a party to the political shenanigans that were responsible for my new unemployment, at least not knowingly. I shared as much information about Atonement as a two-macchiato meeting would allow, wished him luck, and was on my way. Nothing I offered Russ was as revelatory as the information he had given me.

As Russ turned to leave, I called out, "Oh, one more thing. Watch your back."

The exodus of members from Atonement began immediately after my departure and continued over the ensuing months. Some members left to denounce what had taken place. Bonding with pastors and then watching them suddenly and unexplainably leave was just too painful. They were "done." The majority slipped out the back door quietly.

There is little that leadership in a congregation that size can do to slow the bleeding. Before staff realizes they have not seen the Jones family in six weeks, a letter arrives from another congregation requesting the transfer of their membership. The most significant casualties were the kingdom losses, those who were so embittered by the process and disappointed by the church that they did not resettle in any faith community. By Christmas, Atonement's attendance and offering had plummeted forty percent.

Like many of the members, I also spent much of the fall resentful and disillusioned. The more I reflected upon the events surrounding my resignation, the more intentional and choreographed they appeared. The beans which Russ unknowingly spilled suggested that, as stage manager of the process, Jerry had been insincere at best.

The other damning evidence regarded the requirements for my therapy. Throughout the Monday night congregational forum, members echoed the same request that I delivered eleven days earlier in St. Louis.

"Why was Pastor Joe not offered a leave of absence?" "After his work and therapy are complete, what is to prevent our pastor from returning to us?"

Jerry consistently volleyed back the same rehearsed response: "The work that Pastor Joe needs can only be accomplished by stepping away from his call and devoting considerable time and energies for renewal of life and ministries."

The moment I offered my resignation, the requirements for therapy shifted. The Consultation Center initially recommended six months of residential treatment. When all was said and done, much more was said than done. My therapy experience consisted of six one-hour office sessions with a local depression specialist. She uncovered no evidence of PTSD, no depression, and no reason that I could not return to ministry immediately.

By mid-August, before Russ had attended his second monthly vision board meeting, Jerry approved me for reentry. The only stipulation was that my next call could not be at Atonement or any congregation within easy driving distance of Atonement.

ONE MORE MEETING WITH THE BISHOP............ Tuesday, August 21

Unlocking the ministry gate was only the first step in finding my way back into the parish. Passing through that gate was an entirely different matter. I asked Jerry for one more meeting to clarify that process. And while I had his attention, I requested that he shed some light on a few other issues.

"Next week, I will begin visiting with other bishops, Jerry. It would be helpful to better understand your perspective regarding what took place at Atonement. I know how this works; they will call you for permission to talk with me and surely ask about my ministry. Can I ask what you will be sharing with them? Our stories need to match."

Curiously, Jerry had a difficult time with my question, so I posed it differently.

"Which of the vision board's presenting issues were most important for you? After the board shared them with me, we never discussed them again. Can we do that now?"

Again, awkward silence. For nearly a minute, Jerry stared off, trying to formulate a response. As I waited him out, the reason for his silence suddenly became apparent.

"You don't remember the board's presenting issues, do you?" I realized out loud. I could sense the pressure of the steam building in the kettle.

"I don't know what you want from me," he said sharply.

"You recommended my resignation, and I would like to know why," I said in a tone that I suspect was rarely used in that office.

Jerry could contain his exasperation no longer, and the kettle began to whistle. "Because that's what they wanted!" he snapped back.

Then, like in a scene from *A Few Good Men*, the room instantly turned silent again.

Had I been a little more composed — or a little less dependent upon Jerry's recommendation for my next position — I would have directed a few more questions to the witness.

"Who are *they*?" "Did it ever occur to you to ask what *I* wanted?" "When did we start basing our decisions on political expediency instead of faithfulness to the gospel?" But I had obviously pushed my luck far enough for one meeting.

Jerry's explosive confession confirmed what I had suspected: He had been little more than a functionary in someone else's plan to move me along. Maybe he was privy to that plan; maybe he wasn't. Regardless, I had to find a way to live with the mystery of it all…and hope that there was another bishop in the church willing to do the same.

SYNOD ASSEMBLY................................**Saturday, June 8, 2013**

The only item of personal interest on the 2013 Synod Assembly agenda was the "Election of Bishop." I half-heartedly tracked the local event from my apartment where I rested in bed with a rare, miserable summer fever. The early ballots suggested that, as usual, the incumbent would be a shoo-in victor for reelection. However, over the day, the race unexplainably tightened and was sent to a fifth and necessarily final ballot.

I forced myself from bed, tossed on a pair of shorts and a t-shirt, and rushed to the convention center just in time to secure a voting machine and cast a ballot. Several moments later, the assembly let out a collective gasp as the results were projected on the assembly screen. One year to the day after surreptitiously securing Russ to serve as interim pastor at Atonement, Jerry was defeated in his incumbent bid for reelection as bishop…by three votes.

24

WHEN THE FATHER COMES RUNNING

God creates out of nothing. Therefore, until a man is nothing,
God can make nothing out of him.

~ Martin Luther

Not forgiving is like drinking rat poison and then waiting for the rat to die.

~ Anne Lamott, *Traveling Mercies*

Once, when I was a young boy, I saw my father run. Just once. I was exploring down by the river on a warm, early spring afternoon when I heard someone scream for help. I raced on my bike back to the farm and reported to my father, "I think someone is drowning at the fork in the river!"

By reflex, Dad began sprinting. His stride was determined but awkward and gangly. I may have laughed had he been running for any other purpose, but this was a matter of life and death.

When he reached the water's edge, about a quarter mile away, Dad threw off his clothes without breaking stride. He called out to me, "Stay here, Joseph," and dove in headfirst. I watched from the bank and held my breath as Dad disappeared and resurfaced, again and again, frantically groping about the murky waters for any sign of life. After what felt like an eternity, he finally crawled onto the bank, heartsick and exhausted.

Hours later, the rescue squad recovered the body of a teenager somewhere downstream. The youth had accepted a dare from a friend to swim the swift currents.

"What a damned fool thing to do."

It was also the first time I ever heard my father curse.

When the prodigal son was still far off, "his father saw him and was filled with compassion; he ran and put his arms around him and kissed him."[1]

In order to run, a Middle Eastern man in Jesus' day had to hitch up his tunic. Because it was considered shameful for men to show their bare legs, they never ran. Never. Yet God, the father in this parable, disregarded convention and sprinted to greet the sinful, no-good, spite-filled, law-breaking son. Why? It was a matter of life and death.

The father in the parable of the prodigal son has a host of legitimate reasons *not* to receive his younger son back into the family. By requesting his share of the inheritance before it was due, the son essentially declared to his father, "I wish you were dead." The son then took the money — wealth that had taken the father a lifetime to earn — and quickly squandered it on dissolute, self-indulgent living, thus bringing shame to the family name.

Yet the father not only forgave the son, but he also made a grand community spectacle out of the pardon. He killed the fatted calf and staged a party to end all parties. His son had been lost but was found. He had been dead but was alive again.

Luther called this parable the "Gospel in miniature," because it reveals God's lavish and recklessly grace towards sinners. While its message offers

---

1 Luke 15:20

life for those who have wronged others or God, it goes down like castor oil for those who have been wronged.

Sometimes we suffer as a direct result of the choices we make. There are consequences for smoking two packs of cigarettes a day or accepting the dare of a friend to tempt fate foolishly. You may or may not consider such suffering *deserved*, but at least we know who or what bears responsibility for the resulting pain.

Much suffering, however, is not so easily explained. Take, for instance, my sister's congenital heart defect or the untimely death of a college student who hit a patch of black ice and then a utility pole. We call such suffering undeserved or *unjust*.

Unjust suffering is particularly treacherous because it threatens the soul. Those who do not have an answer for their pain often turn sour and bitter. As victims, we may lay blame or, more destructively, work to enact justice. The prevailing brand of secular justice is retributive and vengeful. Evil deeds get punished. If the punishment fits the crime, then we have achieved justice.

I wish I could tell you that I took no delight in Jerry's defeat. Yet there was a small part of me — a part of the smaller me — that understood the worldly desire for justice.

The election played out nearly perfectly. Jerry's fate was determined by an electorate of congregational delegates. The people he served looked at his body of work and decided, "You know, Jerry, you've had a good run as bishop, but it's time to move on." He would experience what it felt like to lose a job he dearly loved.

The vengeful me may have choreographed the process differently. In the perfect scenario, the final ballot is conducted by roll call. The moderator calls each congregation by name, and the delegates stand and deliver their votes for the entire assembly to hear. With the election deadlocked and only one congregation remaining, the moderator summons, "Atonement Lutheran." The delegates rise slowly, smile, and cast the deciding votes for Jerry's opponent.

It was a sweet, gratifying image…for a moment. But retribution can never truly heal our pain.

God utilizes a different system of justice. Richard Rohr claims that in response to our transgressions, "God will love you more than ever! God will love you into wholeness. God will pour upon you a gratuitous, unbelievable, unaccountable, irrefutable love that you will finally be unable to resist." God 'punishes' us by loving us more!"[2]

Jesus became the perfect example of *restorative justice*. "When he was abused, he did not return abuse; when he suffered, he did not threaten; but he entrusted himself to the one who judges justly."[3] To suffer and not judge in return is heroic. It is also extremely burdensome work.

INSTALLATION OF THE NEW BISHOP . . . . Saturday, November 2, 2013

Sixteen months after leaving Atonement, I remained unemployed. I missed the work. I missed the worship and the preaching. I missed the creative planning sessions with my staff. I missed helping members in their moments of crisis. Mostly, I missed *me*. My identity and sense of self-worth had become so intimately interlaced with my role as a pastor that they were nearly inseparable.

Fortunately for Atonement, and unfortunately for me, the church building sits prominently on a major thoroughfare in Overland Park. Thousands of people pass it regularly. So do I. Seeing someone else's car stationed in the senior pastor's spot evoked a visceral, awful response. Eleven years of muscle memory insisted, "Turn into the parking lot, stride through those office doors as if nothing has changed, pull a chair up to your desk, and get back to work!"

But when the first legitimate opportunity to re-enter the building presented itself, my spirit resisted.

Atonement's sanctuary is the largest and most centrally located

---

2 Richard Rohr, "Restorative Love," Center for Action and Contemplation, September 7, 2020, https://cac.org/restorative-love-2020-09-07/.

3 1 Peter 2:23

worship venue in the synod, so it was chosen to host the new bishop's installation service. Though I had no work, I remained a member of the clergy roster. So, unless I could manufacture a life-threatening medical condition, there would be no dodging this event. I would have to attend. And if I expected Jerry's successor to support my search for another position, I had *better* attend.

I dusted off my white robe and red stole — the same stole Bishop Michael placed over my shoulders on another stormy afternoon nearly twenty-five years earlier — took a deep breath and, for the first time in almost a year and a half, walked through Atonement's front doors.

It can be difficult to distinguish visitors from members in a large congregation. I used to instruct my greeters, "Visitors are typically the last to arrive at worship, hug the perimeter of the room while here, then look to exit quickly as soon as worship is over." I fit the description perfectly. Everything looked, smelled, and sounded the same. Nothing had changed, yet everything had changed. I was a visitor in a place that still felt like home.

I made a beeline for the holding area where worship participants were instructed to vest and receive instructions for the procession. At least here the gallery of other white-robed clergy folks would offer some cover.

The worship coordinator announced, "Before we talk through how all of this is going to work, I'd like to recognize our host, Pastor Brian, the new senior pastor here at Atonement."

"Here, here!" the group cheered and applauded.

I winced and braced for the stares of a roomful of colleagues eager to gauge from my reaction where I had landed on the "Woundedness and Resentment Scale." But something even more awkward happened; no one looked.

Rick summoned the magnificent pipe organ to life, and the festival procession began. Led by the cross and a parade of banners, the clergy streamed side-by-side into the sanctuary, parted around the large baptismal fountain, then rejoined and marched down the primary aisle. It was quite a spectacle — one hundred fifty pastors in all shapes and sizes, vested in red and harmonizing at the top of their lungs.

With his usual flare, Rick expanded the hymn to give all of us time to file into our pews. When the music stopped and the reverberations of the horns completed their final rounds through the space, I found myself in a familiar spot. There were nearly a thousand places I could have landed; I wound up in *my pew*.

When the sanctuary was quiet and empty, and the pulpit belonged to me, this is where I came for inspiration. I sat in this very spot and asked myself, "What will the next person who sits here most need to receive from the person who will speak from up there?"

But on this day, the sanctuary was anything but quiet or empty, and the pulpit belonged to someone else. Rev. Elizabeth Eaton, the Presiding Bishop of the ELCA, was the one speaking *up there*, and I, whether I confessed it or not, was the one in need of a word from the Lord.

To make matters even more awkward, months earlier, prior to being elected to her position atop the denomination, Bishop Eaton had been one of the synodical bishops who chose *not* to give me a second look. I interviewed and was a primary candidate for a position on her staff in Northeastern Ohio, but after having a sidebar powwow with her counterparts from Kansas, the good bishop promptly scratched my name from the race.

The pew that once had been my favorite place now felt like a prison cell. I was hemmed in by colleagues who pitied me, welcomed by the pastor who succeeded me, and surrounded by sheep who used to follow my voice but now belonged to someone else. I was compelled to sit through a sermon served up by a bishop who considered me unworthy of hire and delivered from a pulpit that used to be (and, as far as I was concerned, still should have been) mine.

Not since leaving Atonement had I been so hyperconscious of just how far my life had strayed from its intended course. My twisting, bumpy, and ever downward detour had reached the valley floor. I had no clue where I was heading and no plan for getting there, and the entire world seemed to be watching.

I may have crawled under the pews and made my escape had it not been for the knowledge that at least one person in the room was more uncomfortable than me. Jerry would soon have to surrender the mantle of his office to his successor. The primary player in this miserable chapter of my life was about to experience some public misery of his own. That seemed like something I might want to see.

Vengeful and filled with resentment, I leaned back, crossed my arms, and prepared to resist everything this preacher had to say. My body language veritably shouted to the Holy Spirit: "You might as well throw in the towel now and move along. You will find no room in this heart today."

There was only one problem with this defiance: I forgot who I was dealing with. The only reason I ever experienced any success as a preacher *up there* was that God was at work in the hearts of listeners sitting down *here*. The Spirit was not going to change tactics just because I changed seats.

I don't remember a single word that Bishop Eaton said that afternoon, but I vividly recall the message I received.

"My grace is sufficient for you."

These words were not part of the hymns we sang or the prayers we offered. You will not find them in the preacher's manuscript. I don't imagine that anyone else *heard* them. Yet, again and again, they found me.

I was not the first to receive this message. When Saint Paul appealed to the Lord to have his *thorn in the flesh* removed, this is the response he was given.[4] I knew the passage well and had preached on it many times myself. But on this day, I heard the words as if for the first time.

"My grace is sufficient *for you*."

The Lord was calling me by name. His words washed over me in irrepressible, merciful waves, slowly dissolving the bitterness that had all but consumed me. I whispered the rest of the passage from memory.

"For your power is made perfect in weakness. So, I will boast all the more gladly of my weakness, so that the power of Christ may dwell in me."

Of course! It is not my strength that commends me to God, but my weakness! God does not redeem my successes, but my failures. I knew this truth, but had I been so busy serving it up that I forgot to pull my chair up to the table and feast upon it myself?

---

4   2 Corinthians 12:9

I fished my phone from beneath my robe, opened the Bible to 2 Corinthians and began reading aloud to myself.

"Therefore, I am content with weaknesses, insults, hardships, persecutions, and calamities for the sake of Christ; for whenever I am weak, then I am strong."

That did it. The wall around my heart crumbled, and through the rubble, the Father came running.

After our sweet embrace, the Lord prepared a table. For over a decade, this had been my job. I stood on the serving side of this meal and promised, "This is the body of Christ, given for you." But on this day, the table was turned. I said nothing. I simply opened my hands and held them out as a beggar for grace.

My brother pressed the bread into my palm. My sister handed me the cup. And once again, the Lord called my name.

"This is for you."

I was no longer aware of anything that was taking place around me, only what was happening inside me. The blood of Christ was coursing through my veins, working to cleanse from my heart any remnants of the regret I had been lugging around for far too long.

God's message could not have been clearer:

"Look around. None of this ever belonged to you. It has always been mine; you just helped manage it for a while. Let it go. I have good work for you, work that you cannot complete if you are chained to this resentment. Loosen yourself from it. You can hand the pain to me if you like."

Then, for only the second time in my life, God's voice became audible. Above the organ, the choir, and the trumpets, God repeated the same three words I had experienced three years earlier and thirteen hundred miles away: "It is enough."

This time, however, "it" meant something entirely different. "It" was the power of God's grace that is perfected in such moments as these. In the painful and broken times of our lives, amid disappointment and suffering, we draw hope from God's accomplishments, not ours. "When I am weak," Paul says, "*then* I am strong because the power of Christ dwells in me."

Forgiving those who have unjustly wronged us is strenuous, demanding work. To add to the burden, the heavy lifting must be done by the one who has been wronged. It is too large a task for one person. On the cross, even Jesus had to ask for God's help to pardon his executioners.[5] How much more, then, do we need the counsel and encouragement of others to forgive those who have victimized us?

"My grace is sufficient for you. It is enough." These simple, poignant words released me from the shackles of a regretful past filled with resentment and the longing for reprisals, and helped usher me into the *something more* that God had in store.

I used to tell others, "It took a while, but I finally found the path that God intended for me. I only wish that I would have taken an easier route to get here."

But the truth is, God's path was never misplaced; I was. My journey was charted — straight, smooth, and ever upward. But here's the problem: It's impossible to follow Jesus down a path he does not travel, and the Lord spends precious little time on the road to success.

Years ago, I had a most vivid dream. I was lying atop a wood-paneled Chrysler station wagon as it sped down the highway. With one hand, I clung tightly to the roof rack, and with the other, I grasped the only remaining piece of luggage that had not yet set to flight: my vocational suitcase. With fists clenched and knuckles white, I held on for dear life. But as the journey grew longer and I grew weaker, something had to give.

Ultimately, I did not let go of the suitcase; it was ripped from my hands. As I watched it explode in the road behind me, a voice came from heaven, "Finally! Now I have something to work with."

---

5   Luke 23:34

25

THE ROAD TO JUMP OFF ROCK

Whatever ember of love for goodness flickers within us, however feeble or small…that's what the Spirit works with, until that spark glows warmer and brighter. From the tiniest beginning, our whole lives — our whole hearts, minds, souls, and strength — can be set aflame with love for God.

~ Brian McLaren, *We Make the Road by Walking*

Learn the rules like a pro, so you can break them like an artist.

~ Pablo Picasso

At the outset of the epic movie, *A River Runs Through It*, Robert Redford narrates the words of the author, Norman Maclean: "As a Presbyterian, my dad believed that man, by nature, was a damn mess and that only by picking up God's rhythm were we able to regain power and beauty. To him, all good things, including trout and salvation, come by grace, and grace comes by art, and art does not come easy."

If Rev. Maclean is correct — if art is the key to unlocking grace and all good things — then I have lived a good portion of my life spiritually challenged. The Creator who fearfully and wonderfully made me seems to have spent considerably more energy fashioning the left side of my brain than the right. As a result, I am genetically wired to work with syllogisms, remember facts, and tackle mental math problems. I am far less comfortable acting impulsively or chiseling away at a block or stone.

Not surprisingly, there is little demand for left-brained pastors. So, unless I intended to twiddle my thumbs and wait for a campus ministry position at an Ivy League university, I had to find ways to develop my inner dreamer, orator, and musician and coax them out of their cerebral hiding places. For me, art eventually came, but it did not come easy.

When it comes to grace, we are all challenged, left- and right-brained alike. It is not our genetics that handicaps us, but the prevailing, law-oriented culture in which we are immersed. The world demands something from us before it will love us. Its affection and admiration are conditional. Perform. Measure up. Prove yourself. Only then will the world recognize and reward you.

But God's ways are not the world's ways.[1] God does not love us because we are good; God loves us because *God* is good. God loves us because God can do no other. "God *is* love,"[2] epic, reckless, and relentless love. God loves prodigally, even when there is no assurance that we will love in return.

Even before I was old enough to put nouns and verbs together on my own, Sunday School teachers taught me to sing, "Praise Him, Praise Him, all ye little children. God is love. God is love." But singing about God's nature and picking up and living by God's rhythms are very different matters.

Eugene Peterson translates Jesus' invitation to the crowds in this way: "Come to me. Get away with me and you'll recover your life. I'll show you how to take a real rest. Walk with me and work with me — watch how I do it. Learn the unforced rhythms of grace."[3]

---

1 Isaiah 55:9
2 1 John 4:8
3 Eugene Peterson, The Message: The Bible in Contemporary Language (Colorado Springs: NavPress, 2005), Matthew 11:28-30.

When my life becomes arrhythmic and unbalanced — or, as Rev. Maclean puts it, a "damn mess" — it is most often because I have strayed from the heart of the Director and begun to tap my foot to the world's beat. In those moments, I have learned to be still and quiet and practice the art of holy listening, which, like other arts, does not come easy. But beneath the ruckus and cacophony of sounds that vie for my attention, I hear again the unforced melodies of that childhood Sunday School chorus and am reminded that God is love and that grace must always have the last and loudest word.

In larger congregations, pastors often recognize members long before learning their names. Such was the case for me with the Orr family.

For months, I knew Mark, the father of this attractive family, as the tall, self-assured man who occasionally played percussion in the contemporary ensemble at Atonement. Lori was a quiet and pleasant woman with a radiant, infectious smile. Each Sunday morning you could spot her with her sleeves rolled up, knee-deep in Sunday School children. Raegen, the elder daughter, was a cautious and quiet little girl when I met her. I had to carry our conversations. These days, I must fight to get a word in edgewise.

Isabel claims that I baptized her shortly after I arrived at the church, though I don't recall much about it. She has pictures and a certificate with a signature that looks like mine, so it must be so. I *do* remember teasing Isabel about her *pew swimming*. I was fascinated watching her little head pop up from behind the pew during worship…then disappear…then resurface about six feet away…then disappear again. She could swim pew laps throughout an entire twenty-minute sermon.

For the most part, the Orrs maintained a quiet, regular, faithful presence at church and blended into the sea of others who did the same. But in the winter of 2006, something happened that tragically distinguished Mark, Lori, Raegen, and Isabel from every other family in the congregation.

On Wednesday morning, the day after Valentine's Day, Mark hugged and kissed his girls goodbye and left with a coworker on what they intended to be an overnight business trip to Des Moines. Mark would not return home for eighteen months.

Highway Patrol and Thursday morning news reports blamed the accident on icy roadways left in the wake of a particularly treacherous, southwest Iowa winter storm. Mark had just started the return trip to Kansas City when the car in which he was a passenger lost control on a patch of ice and was sent careening across the highway median and into the path of an oncoming tractor-trailer. Remarkably, both drivers walked away from the scene virtually unscathed, at least physically.

Mark's fate likely would have been similar had it not been for the *second* impact.

Before leaving the hotel that morning, Mark tossed his bags and belongings onto their usual travel spot, the seat directly behind him. One of those items was Mark's laptop, encased in a brand-new protective metal shell which he had bought earlier that week.

When the vehicles collided, all the unrestrained objects inside Mark's car were immediately transformed into dangerous projectiles. The laptop struck Mark in the back of the head at an estimated force twenty times that of gravity.

The result of this second collision was a traumatic and permanent brain injury.

Victims of unjust suffering not only deal with the ostensible frontline pain and loss but are also left to process the *if onlys*. "If only I had taken a different route that day, then I would have avoided the accident altogether." "If only we had been more attentive, we may have noticed the signs of depression in time to help."

The tragic happenstances of Mark's accident were especially burdensome to reconcile. When you consider how drastically different life would be today for Mark's family *if only* he had placed his laptop on the floorboard or in the trunk, then you begin to sense suffering's cruelty and arbitrariness.

Mark spent most of the next year and a half in a rehabilitation facility in south-central Illinois, a twelve-hour round trip from Kansas City. When Mark finally returned home in the fall of 2007, doctors considered that he had reached the apex of his recovery. The accident left him unable to stand on his own or care for himself. He functioned cognitively at the level of a five-year-old, and his communication was strained. When I greeted him at church, I relied upon one of the girls to interpret his responses. Although I sensed that he remembered me, I could never be sure.

Mark's long-term prognosis called for a slow, steady decline.

The Orrs' Sunday morning experience changed considerably. In addition to the new handicap-accessible van and the motorized wheelchair, the family now required an ever-changing and ever-present cadre of around-the-clock caregivers to bathe, feed, and tend to Mark. They relocated to a new pew off to the far side of the sanctuary where they could care for Mark a little more privately. The new location made it difficult for me to keep up with Isabel's swimming, but from what I could tell, she appeared to be spending far less time in the water in those days.

With all of Mark's gadgets and support staff, the Orrs' new lifestyle outgrew more than their former pew. Mark required a larger, wheelchair-accessible home, which Lori found on the distant south side of the county. The new commute to Atonement became one more challenge in an already-overburdened schedule, so in 2009, the family reluctantly decided to connect with a congregation closer to home. I lost track of them for more than two years.

Late in 2011, I received a surprise phone call from Lori. In her quiet, cautious, slightly introverted manner, she said, "I was wondering if you would have time for a visit."

We met on a Saturday morning at Dunn Brothers Coffee, my office away from the office.

"I was sorry to learn of your divorce," she said as she shifted back and forth a little anxiously in her chair. "I heard the news last week at my dental appointment."

"I am a topic of conversation among dentists these days?" I asked.

Lori smiled and explained. "It turns out that my hygienist is a member of Atonement. Somehow, the topic of church came up. One thing led to another, and she mentioned that you sent out a letter. Anyway, I wanted to make sure that you were doing okay and catch you up on our lives."

So, for the next two chai teas and a bottled water, that is what Lori did. Though she chose different words, what she described was a long, arduous, deeply spiritual search for rhythm and grace. After seven years of living amid Mark's declining health and escalating needs, she sensed that God was preparing a different future for her. Lori was contemplating divorce. Not only did she want to know how I was doing, but she also needed to know *how I did it*. When the winds begin to howl, we seek the company and counsel of those who seem to have survived similar storms.

"We miss Atonement," she said. "The church we've been attending is just not the same."

"The congregation misses you as well," I assured her, "and would certainly welcome your family back with open arms. And if you move forward with your decision, they will quietly love you through the rough times. I know."

Several Sundays later, as if returning from an extended sabbatical, the Orrs rematerialized in their spot and instantly reconnected. From a distance, their lives seemed quieter and at least a little more rhythmic than they had in years.

A congregation of Atonement's size requires at least one staff person whose primary ministry is caring for those who are hurting. Our point person was John Frey.

Pastor John has a pastoral heart the size of Texas and a spirit that radiates such genuine compassion that I suspected members of manufacturing spiritual concerns just to collect a visit from him. He walks with a limp, the remnant of a childhood battle with polio, and speaks openly and often of his quest to understand the God who would allow such a disease to have its way with him. Yet despite his trials, or perhaps because of them, John has dedicated his life to caring for others on behalf of God.

Each Tuesday morning, the staff handed over into John's care the names of sick, infirmed, and lonely who needed his attention. One Tuesday in June of 2012, our sharing went something like this: "Pastor John, Rodney Cunningham is in St. Joseph Hospital again." "I saw Joyce Jones at the grocery store this week. She's lost her job and could really use our prayers…and food." "Janice Meyer is home from rehab and would love a visit if you have time this week."

Then, as I did each week, almost liturgically, I entrusted the list to John and said, "Let's pray for these folks."

On this morning, however, there was an addendum to the reporting.

"Oh, one more thing," someone interrupted. "I understand that Lori and Mark Orr are divorcing."

I unfolded my hands and looked up. Everyone in the circle was obviously concerned by the news, but no more so than they had been by Janice's knee replacement or Joyce's unemployment.

"I'll reach out to Lori this week," John said. And with that, everyone bowed their heads again…everyone but me.

How could such a life-altering, spiritually agonizing, hard-fought decision as divorce become just "one more thing" among any list of concerns? Did we not understand the hell that spouses go through to reach this point? Those in the circle with me were the most compassionate people I knew, yet they had processed this matter and moved on. What was I missing?

One of the staff awakened me from my trance. "Pastor Joe, would you like me to pray?"

"Thank you. I've got it," I said.

The reasons for my hypersensitivities were no mystery, of course. I reacted the same way John would have had the report been, "Oh, one more thing. I understand that one of our teenagers was diagnosed with polio this week."

I had been there.

Exactly two years had passed since the news of my own divorce became public. The announcement laid me bare. It was as if the entire world watched as I walked up and down the highway dodging cars and retrieving my dirty laundry from the ditches. I imagined friends and foes alike rolling down their windows and calling out, "Hey, look! Pastor Joe didn't 'tie the knot' tight enough!"

But not only had I been there; I was *still* there. My marriage to Atonement was rattling loudly atop the car and threatening to become the next suitcase to break loose. I could already anticipate the shouts from the next motorcade, "What's the matter? Can't hold down a job either?"

I knew firsthand the pain that Lori was experiencing. My dream marriage atrophied over years; Lori's changed in the blink of an eye. Neither of our partners had participated in the conversation about divorce. Carrie refused and Mark was incapable. Had Lori explained her decision to Mark, it would have upset him momentarily, but five minutes later would no longer have been part of his reality. So, out of compassion, she kept the matter to herself and bore the full weight of the decision's burden.

Lori and I suffered from the same arrhythmia. We were also in search of the same grace.

One camp of professional opinion believes it is never appropriate for a pastor to form a romantic relationship with a member of the parish. An alternate camp, comprised largely of pastors who married members of their congregations, heartily disagree. I don't know which position is *right*, only that it is more difficult for grace to have the last and larger word in any discussion where "never" is the first word. Grace always trumps the law.

So, late in the summer of 2012, after my separation from Atonement was complete, I reached out to Lori and volleyed back the question she asked me nearly a year earlier.

"Do you have time for a visit?"

She said, "Sure."

Several days later, Lori and I met for coffee for the second time, but for the first time as friends. A few days after that, we shared dinner and a movie, then dinner and an evening walk in the park. We laughed. We cried. We talked about disappointments and dreams. We prayed. Some evenings we became so lost in one another that darkness fell around us unnoticed. Then, we stargazed.

Like the weathered wooden porch swing at my parents' beach cottage, the park benches became places of God's speaking…only now I had a listening partner. On those starry autumn nights, the only thing clearer to us than the heavens above was our sure and certain shared belief that we were together because God had given us to one another. I had no job. No ministry. The future was more unclear than I had ever remembered. But life was slowly regaining its balance. I was tapping my foot once again. Lori and I had picked up God's rhythm.

On the outskirts of Hendersonville, North Carolina, at the edge of the little mountain community of Laurel Park, lies a magnificent stone outcropping known as Jump Off Rock. There, on a beautiful, fall color-drenched Saturday afternoon in late October 2014, with our families around us, the rest of the world and its laws 3,100 feet below us, and a simple communion table in front of us, Lori and I took one another's hands and received the blessing that I had spoken countless times to others:

"Inasmuch as Joe and Lori have given themselves to each other this day in the presence of God and loved ones here gathered…"

From where we stood on that precipice, we could see two long and winding roads leading up the mountain. The roads began in very different distant places, but the closer they came to the mountain and to one another, the more similar the roads appeared. Their twists and turns were nearly identical, their destination the same. It was obvious to everyone on Jump Off Rock that, at some point, whoever laid these roads intended for them to merge.

"…with the exchange of rings and the offering of solemn vows…"

In one of the final scenes of *A River Runs Through It*, Norman Maclean shares his own take on grace. Following the death of Paul, his brother, Norman says, "I know surely and clearly that life is not a work of art and that such moments (when we are free from life's laws) cannot last."

Lori and I had done nothing to deserve this moment or earn the next chapter in our life together. We had not discovered such joy because of our goodness, but because of *God's goodness*.

If we could, we would tell Norman Maclean that, despite its messiness, life most certainly *is* a work of art. It's just not *our* art.

"…I now pronounce them husband and wife."

And with that pronouncement, God signed yet another masterpiece. Something new and beautiful was finished. Something hopeful and wondrous was just beginning.

In our first act as husband and wife, we served communion to our family. There was a benediction, a flurry of pictures, and our time on Jump Off Rock was done.

Like most moments of grace, our ceremony was brief. Lori and I understand all too well that summit experiences are fleeting. We have each descended the mountain so many times that we know every switchback on the road by heart. But this time, we went home by another way. Two roads traveled up the mountain; only one road went down.

"What God has joined together, let no one separate."

26

A Controlled Fall

I sit, and moan,
Like one who once had wings.

~ John Keats

My whole life I have been complaining
that my work was constantly interrupted, until I discovered
that my interruptions were my work.

~ Henri Nouwen, *Reaching Out: The Three Movements of the Spiritual Life*

When someone tells me about a day that began for them "like any other day," I trust that their day did not end that way. "I was doing what I always do," they say, often "minding my own business," when something unexpected interrupts their usual routine.

I suppose the interruption could be welcomed, such as a letter of acceptance from an Ivy League school, the *you're going to be a grandparent* phone call, or a military father who surprises his children at the elementary school assembly. But welcomed interruptions are more likely to come on *You'll never guess what happened to me* days, not *like any other day* days.

I am thinking about *disruptions*, the sort of intrusions that hijack your spirit and alter your life, like the pink slip from the company where you planned to retire, the Special News Report about a terrorist strike, or the sudden jolt that results from the rear-end collision you never saw coming.

Shortly after Lori and I were married, I was at work in my home office, as I am most mornings — as I am right now — when I noticed the previous several paragraphs of work were hemorrhaging. The spellchecker had underlined every third word in red. My letter "a" had gone AWOL. *Repir keybord*, I tested, and then instinctively reached across with my right hand to inspect this vowel problem more closely: *aaaaaaaa*. The key seemed fine.

I resumed work, but again, the "a" refused to show up, and this time took the "q" with it. The keyboard was functioning well. The little finger on my left hand, however, was not.

Paul Simon provided the morning's background music. I joined in, adding a tabletop conga drum solo for "You Can Call Me Al." My desktop cadence and rhythm were perfect, for a moment. After a few measures, however, the left hand became slower...and slower...lagging farther behind. It was as if the little finger had passed its sluggishness up my left arm and into my shoulder. These symptoms presented for the better part of the morning and then resolved as mysteriously as they had appeared.

A few mornings later, they returned.

Over the ensuing months, I was poked, tested, medicated, questioned, tested again, and passed around from my primary care physician to several teams of neurologists to a chiropractor to physical therapists to spine surgeons, no two of whom supplied the same explanation, and not one of whom offered a diagnosis with any reassuring confidence.

Three neurologists separately administered nerve conduction tests (EMGs). Cumulatively, this amounted to ninety blissful minutes of having electrical charges passed through my limbs while technicians measured the degree to which my muscles lurched...or something like that. The sensation was reminiscent of sticking my finger in a light socket, only over and over. If my childhood memory serves me well — something I did not question *before* the shocks — my mother cautioned me *not* to do this.

"There is definitely something going on, or not going on, in that left arm," two of the neurologists reported. "It's not that remarkable, really. We just can't say what it is at this point."

The third neurologist disagreed. "Your results are normal."

Six months into this medical reconnaissance mission, it was the spine surgeon's turn to join the chorus of speculators. He seemed no more certain with his diagnosis than his neurological colleagues, just more eager to act on his hunches. A few X-rays and ten minutes of consultation were all he needed to begin sharpening his scalpel.

"I think your issue lies in the cervical spine," he deduced. "The X-ray isn't that remarkable (there was that word again), but we've ruled out the other possibilities." Pointing to the film, he explained, "I will fuse these two vertebrae here. Now, as a result, you can expect to live with some degree of pain for the remainder of your life, but your movement should return."

"Should?" I asked. "I think I will give physical therapy a try."

Nearly two years had passed since my "a" first went missing, and I still had no reliable answers. Each week, the sluggishness showed up more frequently and hung around longer. At times, I felt normal, but on most days, I endured a litany of frustrations. Typing was difficult. My left hand tired quickly and refused to cooperate with the rest of my body. When three of my fingers decided to go on strike the same afternoon, I had to resort to dictation software to finish my work.

Trudging through routine daily tasks required twice the usual energy. The lethargy migrated down to my left foot, forcing me to give up the air pedal bass drum. I am no spine surgeon, but that symptom seemed to rule out any cervical explanations. Each day I became more frustrated and immobile. Out of desperation, I circled back to the Department of Neurology at the University of Kansas Medical Center and the medical team that initially launched this expedition. My primary contact was Dr. Shanahan.

"Pastor Joe! Good to see you again."

In a metropolitan area the size of Kansas City, what are the chances that I would be assigned a neurologist who was also a member of the parish?

Dealing professionally with members of the flock comes with its share of rewards and risks. I have reluctantly opened my home to my realtor sheep and received tax advice from the accountant sheep. I am very pleased to patronize the establishments of my business-owning sheep. It's the stethoscope-bearing, "let's have a look at that" sheep that feel most invasive.

I have no issue when the engagement takes place on my turf. From the pulpit, I can control my vulnerability. I can even counsel the good doctor on ways to amend his life. It is another matter altogether when the engagement takes place in his office. When the clothes start to come off and the poking and prodding begin, I am no longer in control.

Eighteen months earlier, following the first round of poking, Dr. Shanahan prescribed a medication that had been worse than ineffective; it caused considerable side effects. That's understandable. But when two other neurologists noticed the medication listed on my chart, they audibly sneered.

"Not sure what he was trying to accomplish by prescribing *that*."

So, I chose to look elsewhere for answers and left his care the way most dissatisfied members choose to leave their congregations — I slipped out the back door and never told a soul.

I have often wondered if medical professionals are trained to interact with their patients in times such as these. Are aspiring doctors taught to read their patients' fears as well as their MRIs? Do they consider the heart as more than a muscle? Just as worshipers show up each weekend in search of answers for their nagging spiritual questions, patients come to doctors in hopes of explaining their pain. We are often frustrated and frightened.

If I were given the task of designing a medical school curriculum, I would require all first-year physician wannabes to take *The Art of Empathy 101*. In the spirit of the seminary course, *Ministry with the Elderly*, students would spend several days and nights confined to a semi-private hospital room as a patient. They would wear gowns, eat institutional food, and be roused throughout the night to have their vital signs taken. Instead of directing the nursing staff, they would have to ring the call button and wait to be served.

Doctors would learn to ask, "What does the person lying here most need to receive from me?" Then, I would recruit Dr. Shanahan to teach the course.

Instead of reprimanding me for abandoning the treatment plan or asking, "Where have you been?" Dr. Shanahan spent the next hour demonstrating the sort of grace congregations would do well to emulate.

"This must be getting pretty frustrating for you. How are you holding up?" "What were the results when you took this medication?" "Tell me about your sleep patterns." "Walk to the end of the hallway and back to me. Good. Again." "Grab my hand and squeeze as hard as you can. Do the same with your other hand."

When the exam was complete, my new friend closed his folders, pulled up a chair and calmly said, "Pastor Joe, I think that we may be dealing with Parkinson's."

In the movies, this scene often plays out in the doctor's study.

"I've called you in today because I'm afraid I have some bad news. It's a tumor, and it's located in a part of the brain that we just can't get to. It's inoperable. I am so sorry. I have done all I can do, but I have reached out to a specialist I know in..."

This moment was nothing like that.

I appreciated Doug's care and candor, but his suspicions did not land with the impact you might imagine.

There was no way I had Parkinson's disease.

I had done the research and ruled out the possibility a year earlier. Sure, I had a few of the markers — the unilateral sluggishness, some fatigue, and a very slight tremor in the left hand — but most of the *Signs to Look For* just did not apply to me. What's more, the other neurologists concurred. Lori was bold enough to ask them, even when I thought it unnecessary.

"None of the test results suggest PD," one doctor concluded. "I am certain. No need to worry about that."

"I am prescribing Levodopa," Doug continued. "Take a half pill three times a day for a week, then a whole pill the following week. If your symptoms improve at any point, then we will have our diagnosis. Parkinson's is the only condition this medication treats."

That approach seemed conclusive enough, and being conclusive, it was oddly unsettling. It is curious how quickly conviction waivers when tested *conclusively*. Co-existing with a nameless irritant might be preferable to living with the enemy I could identify.

Here is what I knew about Parkinson's disease (PD): If I had it, then I had been living with it for years, perhaps as long as a decade and a half. The dopamine-producing neurons in the substantia nigra portion of the midbrain are responsible for bodily movement. In persons with PD, these neurons degenerate and die. By the time this iceberg peeks above the water's surface and symptoms become detectable, about eighty percent of those neurons have been irretrievably lost. Doctors have not determined the cause for PD, nor do they have a cure.

Life with Parkinson's is a controlled fall. The most patients can hope to do is stave off the symptoms and manage the condition for as long as possible, but the disease inevitably worsens.

It is an awkward feeling to will part of your body to move and have it defy you. It is nearly as awkward to take medication and hope that it *doesn't* work. For seven days, I snapped the little yellow pills in half, swallowed, closed my eyes, and shifted the petitions of the previous two years into reverse. I prayed that this course of treatment would be unsuccessful.

The prayers worked. The medication didn't.

For the second week, I titrated up to a whole pill as instructed. Again, the results were the same — a glorious nothing!

Cautiously, but with growing confidence — almost optimistically — I began the trial's final stage on day fifteen. Ready to lay the Parkinson's theory to rest in peace, I increased the levodopa dosage to one and a half pills.

Twenty minutes later, as I rose from my desk to report the good non-news to Lori, a strange and awful energy suddenly surged across my left shoulder, down my arm, and into my fingers. It was electric, as if someone had flipped a breaker switch in my brain.

My body shouted, "Move!"

My heart stilled me. Slowly, I tested my fingers as the doctors had done a dozen times in their offices, tapping each in turn against my thumb, faster and faster. They performed perfectly. I drummed on the dresser top. My arms responded without hesitation.

I sat back down at the keyboard, took a deep breath, and began typing, *Oh God, please don't let my fingers work!* But they flew effortlessly across the keys. My "a" had returned.

Seven hundred fifteen days had passed since the symptoms first appeared. This day began like any of those, but it would not end that way. This day had stolen my spirit.

I lay on the bed and wept. Lori held me. Neither of us said a word.

27

Why Me? Why Not?

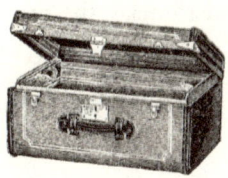

He must be very ignorant for he answers every question he is asked.

~ Voltaire

The unwounded life bears no resemblance to the Rabbi.

~ Brennan Manning, *Abba's Child*

The wretched *clacking* started as soon as the chain engaged and began pulling us up the lift hill. I was at once exhilarated and terrified.

"We're all going to die, aren't we?" screamed the teenaged boy in front of us, which set the child in the car ahead of him to whimpering.

"I wanna get off, Daddy! Now!" she begged.

But there was no getting off. Once the attendant locked the bar tight across our laps, there was no escape. No turning back. Passengers may choose to endure the ride white-knuckled and shrieking or throw their arms in the air and enjoy the thrills, but the ride determines when you are done.

My father was in his mid-sixties when the family finally persuaded him to brave his first roller coaster ride. We drew straws to choose his co-passenger. I don't remember if I won or lost, only that I wound up sitting in the car next to him.

I think of our experience together from time to time, but never more intently than I did in the days leading up to my fortieth birthday. The roller coaster became a perfect metaphor for my pushing back against time.

I convinced Dad to wait for the last car.

"There is a reason the line is longer in the back, Dad," I told him. "The ride is better there."

The truth was, I wanted to delay the first drop as long as possible. Sitting in the last car gave me a few more seconds to watch the screeching souls ahead of me raise their arms and disappear before I also got whipped "over the hill."

All the grandchildren were waiting at the exit gate, hopping up and down and squealing like groupies.

"How was it, Paw Paw? Whaddya think?"

He replied calmly, "It was the most unnecessary feeling I've ever had."

Turning forty caused me no real angst. They were just numbers. What horrified me was the prospect of living in the past tense, of cresting the hill and realizing that the best of what I could accomplish was behind me. So, I resolved to inaugurate mid-life — or better yet, delay it — by accomplishing something new and epic, a feat that would demonstrate endurance and stamina.

One month later, on Labor Day morning, three days before my fortieth birthday, as the gray, dank skies of northern Utah spit snow, I straddled my yellow and black composite and aluminum-framed Raleigh road bike at the start line in the little town of Logan, on the southern edge of Idaho's Cache Valley, and prepared to make my statement. Six hours and 104 miles later, I crossed the finish line of my first cycling century and staved off worries of over-the-hill whiplash for…a while.

But a roller coaster has only so many cars. So, at some point, all passengers must crest the hill. I don't recall when that exact moment occurred for me; it must've been in the middle of the night. I just woke one morning suddenly aware that the NBA was never going to call with a contract offer, thru-hiking the Appalachian Trail was off the table, and any aspirations I had of becoming an ultramarathoner would go unrealized.

I was surprisingly okay with all of this.

Those of us who are goal-oriented by nature are also resourceful and creative. As our abilities diminish, we simply establish new goals. We adapt. Instead of joining the PGA, we endeavor to "shoot our age." I may never drive a fastball out of Yankee Stadium, but I can coach the Little League youngster who might one day.

As I listened to the wretched clacking of the roller coaster chains marking time, my only thoughts had been of delaying the initial drop. It never occurred to me that there may be life beyond the bottom of the hill.

You may find it odd that, in the moments after learning that I had an incurable, neurodegenerative disease, my first thoughts were of cycling and mountain climbing. I lay in Lori's arms, quietly sobbing, and dreamt of the Cache Valley.

If you share my passions — if you are a fellow pedal pusher or trailblazer — then you *may* understand. But if you share my battle with Parkinson's, even if you have never mounted a bike or stepped foot on a mountain summit, then you absolutely get it.

I can spend hours on end glued to reruns of the Tour de France and the Giro d'Italia.

"What could possibly compel you to watch other people ride their bikes?" you ask.

The art. The form. The cadence. The sound of chains switching rings. I am obsessed with the sport. I am not watching other people ride; that is *me* rising from the saddle and weaving through the peloton.

Road racers tuck and rocket down steep, winding mountain passes so fast they must snug their knees against their bike's top tube to keep the frame from shimmying. I have done that. I can close my eyes, concentrate, and recreate the experience of cycling into the zone, those rare moments when even uphill climbs seem effortless and the pressure of my feet against the pedals is nearly imperceptible. I have been there.

But if my diagnosis was correct, those experiences were over. Screaming down twisting mountain roads at fifty-five miles per hour with only two half-inch-wide strips of rubber connecting me to the pavement is foolhardy anytime. With compromised balance, it is essentially a death wish.

My heart was still reeling and working to process my new limitations. My brain, however, was ecstatic. The medication had ripped through all the roadblocks of a two-year construction project and reopened the neurological highway on the left side of my body. My fingers were obedient once again. I returned to the computer, closed the dictation software, and typed at a furious and medically induced seventy words per minute. It was a wonderful, awful feeling.

As soon as my brain and fingers were reacquainted with one another, I began clicking through my digital library of photos and pining over pictures of past hikes and climbs. I created a new folder, labeled it *Top 10 Hikes*, and spent the early part of the afternoon filling it with images from the Cascade Mountains; Torres del Paine in Patagonia; two assaults on Longs Peak in Rocky Mountain National Park, my first fourteener; and the family's epic rim-to-river-to-rim hike of the Grand Canyon.

In the northwest corner of Wyoming is an area where God decided to show off during creation. Years ago, on a perfect vacation day, while the rest of the family chose to go horseback riding, I hopped the first morning shuttle boat across Jenny Lake in the Grand Tetons and began hiking up Cascade Canyon. All day, I hiked. My only destination was *up*.

Late in the afternoon, at an altitude no other hiker had yet attained that day, I rested on the shore of a small glacial lake and was absorbed by the reflection of a snowcapped mountain in the crystal water. When Jesus needed reenergizing, he would go to his *lonely place* on the mountain and spend time with his Father. As storms raged below him, the Lord prayed and was renewed. This was that place. I was sure of it. I also prayed. Then, I descended.

The best days are often the simplest.

I was now four hours into what had become a significant project. Once again, my clicking and dragging began to slow, a telltale sign that the neurons in my midbrain needed a little encouragement. I reached for the bottle of yellow pills. Fifteen minutes later, right on cue, my fingers began to dance again.

Kansans who have a passion for climbing must also possess a love for travel. Fortunately, I appreciate the journey to reach the trailheads almost as much as the adventure that begins once I arrive. The research. The planning. The road trips. I labeled the next folder *My Favorite Trips*.

I spent the rest of the evening foraging through thousands of images that carried me north to the roof of Norway and south again to the tip of Argentina. I returned to the wild plains of the Serengeti, relived my hot air balloon ride over Turkey, and strolled again down the Champs-Élysées in *La Ville Lumièr*. Israel, Italy, and Ireland. Canada, Cancun, and the Czech Republic. I completed thirty-six country folders before the alarm on my watch signaled *medicine time* once again. Road-weary and a little jetlagged, I shut the laptop and snapped another pill in half.

As the first day of this new life chapter drew to a close, I sat in the middle of the office floor surrounded by items from my treasure chest: A pair of threadbare Keens, a DVD of the Tour de France, pictures of Lauren and Grant stumbling up the Bright Angel Trail in the Grand Canyon, and a short stack of tattered passports.

Cycling, hiking, and traveling demand mobility, balance, strength, and endurance, the very capacities which Parkinson's slowly scavenges and depletes from the body. Levodopa, the drug of choice for treating the disease, did more than open the neurological floodgate in my brain; it also reoriented my world. I had been a pedal pusher, trailblazer, explorer, and adventurer. Now, I was also a *PwP*, a person with Parkinson's.

How would I set new goals and adjust expectations now that the future promised a day when simply getting out of bed would require mountain-climbing levels of energy? More muscles will stiffen over time and begin to defy me. One morning, I will wake to discover that the disease has migrated to the right side of my body. My gate will become choppy and unsteady, and my balance will fail me.

The manifestations of the disease extend beyond the physical. PwPs battle emotional and cognitive challenges, depression, insomnia, and hallucinations. Medicine can help decelerate the freefall, but only for a season or three. Over time, the effectiveness of levodopa diminishes and PwPs are left with dyskinesia, the uncontrollable shaking and gyrating so often associated with the disease.

The first stage of grief is *denial*. For the moment, my neurons had been teased back into their assigned brain stations, so the following morning, I put away my favorite things and returned to the computer to resurrect the PD research which I had begun half-heartedly a year earlier. My first goal was to disprove the outcome of the levodopa experiment. The doctor claimed these results of the levodopa test would be "conclusive." Well, how conclusive was "conclusive?"

I recalled reading about a DaT scan, a diagnostic brain test that utilizes a radioactive tracer injected into the bloodstream. Assuming the patient can reconcile using *radioactive* and *brain* in the same sentence, the tracer travels around the body for a few hours. Then, the patient lies in an MRI-like machine that photographs the dopamine uptake activity in the midbrain. According to the first website I consulted, "There are situations in which DaT scans can be beneficial in securing a diagnosis when neurologic exam findings are not clear-cut."

My neurologist was less optimistic.

"The DaT results are often unreliable," he warned. "Additionally, the test runs around ten grand, and I am rarely successful getting insurance companies to fund it."

"Can we try?" I urged.

The request was submitted. Ten days later, it was authorized.

The injection was given on the morning of the procedure; then the technician released me from the hospital.

"Go have lunch and kill a few hours," he said. "But don't lose track of time or run out of gas on the way back. If we miss our testing window, no one gets a refund check."

The following week, Lori and I met with the movement disorder specialist for a readout of the results.

"There is a moderate diminishment of dopamine uptake in the right side of the brain," he reported. This made sense as it is the right brain that impacts the left side of the body. "And there is a slight diminishment in the left side. The results are very consistent with your symptoms and our diagnosis."

And just like that, the first stage of grief was over.

Thirty years of walking alongside the hurting and bereaved have convinced me that we all process disappointment and pain differently. I become quiet and reflective. Lori, on the other hand, conducts research. She opened a brand-new binder labeled, *Joe's Medical Records*, and prepared to take notes during our next appointment.

"What is the best course of treatment for Parkinson's?" she asked the specialist.

"We just don't know. We'll have to determine that together over time and with some trial and error. It is different for each patient."

"And how long has this disease been shacking up in my body?" I asked. *Shacking up*, derived from the English word for *shaky*, seemed like an appropriate descriptor.

"We can't say for sure. Patients can have the disease for ten to fifteen years before they show symptoms. We just don't know."

"And the cause?"

Same response. "We don't know."

Only about ten percent of PD cases are genetically traceable. The other ninety percent are, like mine, idiopathic, which is medical jargon for "We don't know." But the doctor's first three questions to me suggested that science at least has theories.

"Did you grow up on a farm?"

"Check."

The twenty-acre field just outside my childhood bedroom window was regularly doused with herbicides and pesticides which likely leached into the groundwater.

"Have you had much exposure to chemicals?"

"Check, again."

When my father was not avoiding amusement parks, he was developing polybrominated diphenyl ethers, compounds used in the flame retardant treatment of textiles and manufactured products. PBDEs have been proven to increase the risk of neurological diseases such as Parkinson's.

"Have you experienced much stress in your life?"

"I'll send you a copy of my memoir when it's done."

"Why do evil and suffering exist in the world?"

I didn't ask this question of my neurologist, but probably should have. When it comes to addressing the theodicy problem, theologians and preachers might do well to take their cue from doctors and simply admit, "We just don't know. Evil and suffering are idiopathic." After all, if Jesus was reticent to respond to *Why?* questions — and his own "Why?" from the cross fell to the ground unanswered — then our chasing after explanations for evil seems like a waste of good, and in my case, depleting energy.

Early in my ministry, my mother gave me a framed, limited edition print of a "Hägar the Horrible" cartoon. In the first panel, the tubby Viking stands stranded on a rock in the middle of a stormy sea as his ship smolders and sinks in the background. He looks to heaven and cries, "Why me?" In the second panel, a voice answers from the cloud, "Why not?"

I don't know if Mom considered the print's theological possibilities when she selected it, or if Dik Browne pondered the theodicy problem when he created the strip. But Hägar's lament reminds me that, were it not for God's mercy, every day could look like Hägar's day.

Maybe the question most worth asking is "Why do we ask 'why?' only in times of trial?" Why not also during times of grace? We are quick to challenge God on difficult days when nothing seems to go our way, but what about days when the skies are sunny, the traffic signals are all green, and the news is good? Why do we so seldom turn our grateful eyes heavenward and ask, "Why me?"

After returning home from the Movement Disorder Clinic, I lay again in my favorite place, the arms of my lovely researcher, and we processed the visit together. Lori had saved a few more questions for me.

"Well, what did you think?"

I did not sob on this day or slip away to cycle the Cache Valley or climb Longs Peak. I thought of none of my favorite things.

Instead, in a profound moment of déjà vu, I flashed back five years to a conference room in St. Louis where I sat at table with a psychologist, a nun, a social worker, and a bishop. They had asked the same question. After delivering a report which essentially resulted in the loss of a job I dearly loved, the team wanted to know what I thought. I thought and felt that day much as I did *this* day. I thought the report was unjust and unfair. I felt victimized and powerless.

There was no turning back from Parkinson's. No reverse. The disease determines when you are done. What did I think? Like my father after his first, and last, roller coaster ride, the experience seemed random and unnecessary.

But before I could translate any of this into words, Lori asked another question. It is her favorite question. Mine, as well.

"How is your heart?"

I cannot tell you when it happened, but sometime during the day, my grip on the bar in front of me had relaxed and the color was returning to my hands. Although I wasn't yet ready to raise them in the air and shout, I turned my palms toward heaven and silently prayed. I thanked God for giving me such a beautiful partner as Lori to share this frightening, uncertain ride, and asked that we both find the strength and courage for the rest of the ride.

My spirit was curiously calm. And, for the first time in days, the wretched *clacking* stopped.

The screaming teenager in the car in front of my father and me had been spot-on. All of us are going to experience death. The grave awaits each of us as surely and unavoidably as the other side of the hill.

But so does God's grace.

I had experienced the initial drop and survived. I was still breathing. By all indications, the sun would rise again the next day and winter would soon give way to spring. Life continues, even when it doesn't.

I breathed deeply, held Lori tight, and whispered, "My heart is fine."

28

Thin Places

The Lord did not create suffering. Pain and death came into the world with the fall of man. But after man had chosen suffering in preference to the joys of union with God, the Lord turned suffering itself into a way by which man could come to the perfect knowledge of God.

~ Thomas Merton, *No Man Is an Island*

When you pass through the waters, I will be with you;
and through the rivers, they shall not overwhelm you;
when you walk through fire you shall not be burned,
and the flame shall not consume you.

~ Isaiah 43:2

Over countless millennia, God has used the powerful, patient waters of the Linville River to carve out a spectacular thirteen-mile stretch of a steep-walled canyon in western North Carolina. The Cherokee name for these waters is *Eeseeoh*, or the *river of many cliffs*. The land between these cliffs has always been rugged and untamed. To preserve its character, Congress designated the area as the Linville Gorge Wilderness in the Wilderness Act of 1964.

No one needed to convince John Linville or his son William that the land was wild. While trapping fur above the falls in 1766, these two frontiersmen awoke one morning to find themselves in the unfortunate company of a Shawnee war party. Both men were killed and scalped, not necessarily in that order.

In the hearts of the early settlers to the region, such a sacrifice was worthy of namesake status for the river. Those who drive through eastern Avery County will discover that the gorge, falls, the local town, and caverns also bear the pioneers' name.

The wilderness is slightly more hospitable these days, though the crags and crevices along the walls of the gorge are home to rattlesnakes, black bears, and, if you believe local lore, the last remaining cougars in Appalachia. It was largely the mystique of the wilderness, and the prospect of finding danger there, that lured me to Linville as an adolescent.

Backpacking in the Blue Ridge backcountry required a little creativity and cunning (translated, *deceit*) on my part, as there was no way my parents (translated, *mother*) would have permitted me to undertake a solo wilderness trip as a teenager. I cannot recall where I was supposed to be on the Friday evening following my sixteenth birthday, only that when my Carolina blue VW Beetle headed west toward Linville, my backpack and gear were buried out of sight.

The sun had already fallen low behind the mountain by the time I reached the trailhead. I shouldered my gear and quickly scampered several miles down the rocky path to the river's edge where I intended to set camp. Scouting level ground on the side of a mountain is challenging enough during the day; it is futile in the dark. So, I called an audible and pitched my tent on an apartment-sized boulder in the middle of the river. It was miserably hard, but flat. After rustling up enough dry kindling to feed the fire for the rest of the evening, I settled in and prepared to do nothing.

It was in the middle of nothing that I remembered my reading assignment. Hours earlier, as I breezed through the backcountry office to secure my permit, the ranger handed me a packet of information along with the explicit instructions, "Be sure to look over the brochure before you begin your hike." Hmm.

There was very little in the brochure that I didn't already know. I was aware of John and William's early misadventures and how the wilderness came to be named. I knew how to store food to discourage unwanted visitors in the middle of the night. And in the unlikely event that I encountered an aggressive bear, I knew how to behave and how not to behave. What I *hadn't* realized was the importance of context. The things that cause us no concern in the light of day can nearly paralyze us with fear when we are in the dark…in the wilderness…all alone…for the first time… with no way out.

I was reasonably confident that the Shawnee were no longer a huge concern, but for the rest of that interminable, sleepless night, every snapping twig, rustling leaf, and falling pinecone announced another hungry predator lurking just outside the tent.

By the grace of God, I survived both the darkness and my imagination…barely. Long before the sun's first morning rays spilled over the canyon rims, I was packed and ready to begin my climb out of the gorge and head home. But by the time I shifted my little VW into fourth gear, I was ready for the next adventure. The wilderness becomes considerably more appealing as soon as it appears in the rearview mirror.

A decade later, it was Grant's turn to experience Linville. Overnighting in the gorge was not recommended for a six-year-old. That information was not in the brochure; it's just something that every parent who must entertain a six-year-old knows. Backpacking would come later. For our initial trip, we would be hikers.

At the base of a mountain, a hiker can always choose not to climb. Once on the summit, however, only one good option remains — to descend. At the bottom of the gorge, the arrangement is inverted. Once you have snaked your way down to the river, the long climb out is not optional. Neither is staying the night without gear. But Grant was scrappy and energetic and, with a little encouragement, would do fine.

When my father learned of our trip, he insisted on joining us. Linville held a special place in his heart as well, though his affection had much more to do with brown trout than backpacking. Negotiating the gorge trails was a necessary inconvenience for reaching the river. Hiking them for any other reason seemed nearly as unnecessary as riding a roller coaster.

Dad was remarkably well-preserved for seventy-one and, on good days, outpaced me on level ground. But age was finally beginning to tame his stride. The trail out of the gorge, on the other hand, was as steep as ever. But come hell or high water, rattlesnakes, bears, or rocky cliffs, Dad would not miss his grandson's first experience of the wilderness.

The ancient Celts spoke of rare and holy places where the membrane that separates heaven and earth is almost nonexistent. In these *thin places*, as they were called, the transcendent and the ordinary meld into one another and become indistinguishable. Anyone fortunate enough to be near a thin place when the veil is lifted may be transfigured by a glimpse of the Divine.

The summits of biblical mountains became thin places for Moses, Elijah, and the inner circle of Jesus' disciples. But the Lord who delights in inhabiting the ordinary is just as apt to appear in any simple, unassuming space. The midpoint of the Babel Tower Trail as it climbs out of the Linville Wilderness is such a place.

The morning of our hike was crisp and perfect, the kind of made-to-order late October day that caused the Appalachian Tourism Department to gloat. The colors of fall were at their peak as a gentle breeze separated the first crimson and yellow leaves from their limbs and presented them against a cloudless Carolina blue backdrop.

"Be on the lookout for God," I told Grant. "The Creator is obviously in a mood to show off today."

Dad was the consummate teacher in constant search of subject matter for a lesson, but today he yielded that role to me. I decided to hold class on our descent while Grant's attention was still available.

"See that mountain in the distance, Grant? That's Mount Mitchell, the highest peak east of the Rockies."

"Yeah. Hey, Dad. Where are the Indians? And when's lunch?"

We shed our packs and made a table out of one of the boulders at the river's edge. After a game of rock hopping and an exhaustive search for Indians, because, according to Grant, this was "exactly the kind of place the Cherokee would hang out," we began our climb out of the gorge.

Though we retraced the exact path of our descent, nothing about the trail looked or felt the same. The skies darkened, the winds picked up, and the temperatures plummeted.

Any concerns about Grant's stamina vanished as he toddled along ahead of us, yammering to himself and searching for anything that crawled or had more than two legs.

Dad, however, labored quietly but heavily.

"Joseph, I need a minute," he whispered.

This was the first time I ever recalled my father asking to rest. He seemed almost ashamed as he leaned against a boulder, lowered his head, and panted. The roar of the whitewater had disappeared by this point on the trail. For a moment, the winds diminished, and the leaves ceased their rustling. We were as still and quiet as we had been all day. As we waited, the place around us began to grow thin.

It is impossible to carry a thin place with you and trying to communicate its intensity would frustrate the most gifted poet. Maybe it is enough to say God was undeniably present in that moment. I stood on the mountain in the middle, between my son, who refused to slow down, and my father, who could not summon the energy to continue. I looked ahead to where I had been and then behind to where I was headed.

God was more real and palpable than the shirt on my back. My favorite place had become holy ground.

In my current consulting work with churches, I have a regimented process through which I learn a congregation's heart and DNA. After wringing the data from member surveys and distilling the leaders' visions, I pull up my consultant's chair and, for the better part of three days, listen to members' dreams, hopes, and frustrations. It is exhausting, wonderful work.

I recently engaged in this process with a beautiful congregation in northern Iowa. After two full days of listening, and with notes from nearly forty interviews logged on the laptop, I checked what was left of my crinkled paper schedule. Only two forty-five-minute sessions remained.

There is generally little of me left by this point in the process. I am eager to wrap things up and head home to begin writing my report. The computer is often closed. After listening to over one hundred people, I don't anticipate hearing anything new.

My penultimate interviewee was an energetic young adult in his mid-twenties who breezed into the conference room and grabbed a seat before I could stand and greet him.

"Let's see…(rechecking my schedule)…Brad. I appreciate your coming in, Brad. Before we launch into our conversation about ministry, what can you tell me about yourself? How do you spend your time when you're not at the church? What are your passions?"

The sessions are much more productive when I demonstrate an interest in the interviewee. But in this case, I was just eager to divert the conversation away from church talk to *any* other topic. After two solid days of listening to folks share, "I come to this congregation because it feels like a family, and I love the sermons," even Saint Paul would need a reprieve.

"I am an avid backpacker," he replied. That was all the encouragement I needed. For the next fifteen minutes, our conversation left the building.

"Tell me about your most epic hikes. You probably don't have a bucket list at your age, but what's next?"

We reviewed our equipment and commiserated over the challenges of being Midwesterners with an attitude for altitude.

"I can't wait for my son to be old enough to join me," he said impatiently and then listened in return as I mourned the hikes that my health no longer allowed me to undertake.

Eventually, and reluctantly, I reined in our sidetracked sharing and returned to the task at hand. Not surprisingly, our time ran over.

Fifteen minutes after my final interview was scheduled to begin, as I stowed my laptop and prepared to strike out early for the airport, an elderly couple struggled through the door. It was evident that my ultimate session would also be unique. For starters, the husband was in a wheelchair. Flustered and frazzled, his wife, Kathleen, apologized as it took several approaches to maneuver the chair into place underneath the table.

"I am so sorry. We haven't been out in a while, and I forgot just how long it takes to get Roger from one place to another."

My heart rose to my throat. Roger's hands were twisting and gyrating with the unmistakable dyskinesia of Parkinson's. I felt myself turning white.

Roger attempted to offer his own apology, but the disease would not permit it. He labored and fought to shape his sounds into words but eventually lowered his head and gave up. Kathleen was his translator. Kathleen was his everything.

Roger was not the only one who struggled to communicate. I considered taking our conversation offline, as I had done with Brad, and asking about Roger's passions. But I stammered and stuttered, afraid of what Roger may be unable to say.

Perhaps I would explore our common battle with this disease. I could remove the consultant's hat and, for a moment, be a pastor again. More than that…a brother. Instead, I punted and defaulted to the questions I was there to ask.

"Roger and Kathleen, you have been members of this congregation for quite some time. What is it about the ministry that has kept you here for so many years? What is the church doing well?"

"You know, Pastor, Roger used to be a Lutheran minister as well."

I turned whiter still.

"You've obviously noticed that he has a neurological condition. It just got to be too much, and he had to give it all up. We have our struggles, but the church has surely been there for us. *That* is what they do well. This congregation is there for people who need them. After all those years of giving to others, I suppose it's Roger's turn to receive back now."

As Pastor Roger arrested his tremors long enough to nod his head in approval and smile, the place where the three of us sat became conspicuously thin. At once, I was transported to the mountain where I stood between Brad, who shared a common but fleeting passion, and Roger, who shared a present disease. I found myself again in the middle, looking in one direction to where I had been and in the other direction to where I may be headed.

And despite the unsettledness of that thin place, God's presence was unmistakable. I was again on holy ground.

"Roger," I said. "There is something I would like to share with you."

29

A God Who Shudders

The Parable of the Man Who Sowed Good Seed — Part IV

"...and at harvest time I will tell the reapers, 'Collect the weeds first and bind them in bundles to be burned, but gather the wheat into my barn.'"

Then Jesus left the crowds and went into the house. And his disciples approached him, saying, "Explain to us the parable of the weeds of the field." He answered, "The one who sows the good seed is the Son of Man; the field is the world, and the good seed are the children of the kingdom; the weeds are the children of the evil one, and the enemy who sowed them is the devil; the harvest is the end of the age, and the reapers are angels. Just as the weeds are collected and burned up with fire, so will it be at the end of the age. The Son of Man will send his angels, and they will collect out of his kingdom all causes of sin and all evildoers, and they will throw them into the furnace of fire, where there will be weeping and gnashing of teeth. Then the righteous will shine like the sun in the kingdom of their Father. Let anyone with ears listen! (Matthew 13:29-30; 36-43)

In addition to their extraordinary talent, Mickey Spillane, Richard Peck, Edgar Allan Poe, J.K. Rowling, Agatha Christie, Graham Greene, John Irving, and Margaret Mitchell had something in common: They wrote backward.

Mitchell started *Gone with the Wind* by conceptualizing the ending, then penned the rest of her novel with that ending in mind and already on paper. "This is the best way to write a book," Mitchell explained. "Then your characters can't get away from you and misbehave and do things you didn't intend them to do in the beginning." She understood the essential role that last words play in charting the course of a narrative.

In the same way, last words can shape movies, sermons, letters, and lives.

Each time I stopped to pray with Rose, I found Lane, her husband of fifty-five years, in the same spot. For the better part of two weeks, he kept a constant vigil by Rose's side, stroking her hair with his fingertips and wiping her brow with a cool cloth. One of the seven grandchildren often read from Scripture or their Nana's favorite poetry as Lane reminisced, "Momma, do you remember the time when we all…?"

At least once during each visit, Lane would softly ask, "Sweetheart, is there anything you want to say?" Then, he would lean close, turn his ear to her lips, and strain desperately to capture her every whisper. Those whispers were shaped into words, and the words were collected and stored away. The family would rely upon them to help assuage their loneliness in the years following Rose's death.

Last words are treasures.

In the fall of 2009, it was apparent that my father's health was steadily declining and that he would not survive long into the new year. Though no one said it out loud, we all knew what this meant for Pete and his family as they prepared to return home to Buenos Aires following their Christmas visit to North Carolina.

Pete, Kendra, and the children stood with Mom and Dad in front of the farmhouse and exchanged their treasures. I do not know what was shared. I have never asked. But even from a distance, I knew their words were measured and heartfelt. When you know the words you speak are *last* words, the treasure is especially rare and valuable.

According to John, Jesus' last word was *tetelestai*, "It is finished."[1]

"Finished" was spoken often during Holy Week. Pilate pushed himself back from his judgment bench and sighed, "Jesus is finished. Another political troublemaker out of the way." The religious leaders said to one another in hushed tones, "He is finished. One more heretic silenced." As the soldiers turned to leave Golgotha, they murmured, "Our work is finished for the day, and so is he."

But *tetelestai* is a different kind of "finished." It has a deeper meaning that conveys intentionality and describes the resolution of a plan. "I have seen it through to the end." "It is completed." *Tetelestai* is not the muttering of a victim but the confident proclamation of someone who is in charge.

All who heard Jesus' last word were undoubtedly perplexed by it, particularly the enemy. The kingdom movement which Jesus launched had ended in utter failure. "It is complete?" What could *it* possibly be?

Mitchell, Christie, and Spillane were not the first to write backward. The landowner in our parable (the Author of Creation) had already conceptualized and penned the end of the age. God's plan for dealing with evil went like this: The executor (the Son of Man) would summon the reapers (his angels) at the harvest (end of the age) to separate (judge) the wheat (the righteous) from the weeds (the evildoers). The weeds would be bundled and burned, and the wheat taken into the householder's barn.

The plan failed to answer many of the hearers' questions about evil, but at least it communicated an eventual reckoning. The strategy had an evident and fundamental flaw, however. The One responsible for executing the plan had himself been executed. It is difficult to summon the angels when your arms are pinned to a tree. Jesus could cry, "Tetelestai," all he wanted, but the only thing that was finished on Golgotha was Jesus.

Easter changes everything. Standing on this side of the empty tomb and looking through the prism of the resurrection, we see what those

---

[1] John 19:30

beneath the cross could not — the events of Holy Week were authored by the householder, not by the Jewish and Roman leaders.

The triumphal entry into Jerusalem was not an impromptu parade but a deliberate and strategic political procession intended to frustrate the Romans and raise the religious leaders' ire. Jesus marched the "Hosannas" from the city gate directly to the Temple, the one place where he could create enough unrest to ensure his death.

By the time he finished toppling the moneychangers' workstations and disrupting the system that provided monetary kickbacks to the Romans, there could be no doubt that Jesus was picking a fight. If Jesus upset the chief priests, he got whipped, beaten, and thrown out of town, but kicking sand on the Romans would have lethal consequences.

Jesus was no victim during Holy Week; he called the shots. On Good Friday evening, as Jesus breathed his last, the plan was complete.

John Irving explained, "You have to know what your voice sounds like at the end of the story because it tells you how to sound when you begin." First words are as essential as last words.

Right out of the ministry starting gates, Jesus put the world on notice that the kingdom of heaven had not come as we expected. The first word of his public ministry was *metanoia*. "Turn around. Change your heart, your mind, and your perspective."[2] According to Jesus, those who failed to re-posture themselves before the kingdom ran the risk of missing it altogether. Had we truly heard Jesus' first word, then his last word would not have taken us by surprise.

Until we adopt a new heart, God's plan for dealing with evil remains hidden. Jesus compared the kingdom to a treasure hidden in a field and a fine pearl hidden in the sea. Elsewhere, he used images of a lost coin, a lost sheep, yeast, and a mustard seed[3] — all small and seemingly worthless items.

But the kingdom's most clever disguise was a carpenter turned itinerant rabbi who hailed from a no-account town, was followed by fourth-string

---

2   Mark 1:15
3   Matthew 13:44-45, Luke 15

disciples, kept company with drunkards and prostitutes, picked fights with the rulers of the imperial kingdom, took a dive in the first round of a fight he incited, and died a blasphemer's death. This plan's power was made perfect in weakness.[4] The world does not honor weakness, or for that matter, any plan that finds completion on a cross.

Consider our typical Easter celebrations. We pull out all the worship stops, strike up the brass, and generate as much Alleluia volume as our sanctuaries and most sound-sensitive members can tolerate. The first Easter, on the other hand, was intentionally hushed. We attract the most impressive crowds of the year. The first Easter was essentially private. Preachers labor and fret over what we consider to be the most important sermon of the year. The first Easter sermon consisted of five simple words; "I have seen the Lord!" Amen. The crowds that pack our worship spaces are joyous and expectant. The first Easter ambushed the first witnesses and sent them scurrying in all directions, frightened and confused.

Can you imagine how differently the first Easter might have played out had it been choreographed by anyone other than God? Within an hour of sunrise, all of Jerusalem would have known of the Lord's victory.

As Jesus' publicist, I would have arranged a series of surprise drop-by visits. Dressed in resplendent victory white and leading an army of vindicated followers, the Savior would march into Pilate's headquarters, awaken the prefect and invite him to finish their earlier conversation about truth. Next, we would stop by the chambers of Caiaphas and Annas and ask, "Now, what were you saying about blasphemy?" The final appearance would occur publicly at the Temple, just ahead of a perfectly timed flyover of angels in formation.

But Jesus kept Easter contained. His victories over Satan, Caesar, and death were muted and reserved for a small, privileged band of Jesus' closest followers. Now, I ask you, is that any way to run a resurrection?

We would choose to handle the enemy and his weeds quickly, decisively, mercilessly, publicly, and, if necessary, forcefully. God's ways have

---

4   2 Corinthians 12:9

never been the world's ways,[5] and God's kingdom has never conformed to our expectations. Why would we believe that the householder's plan for dealing with evil would be anything other than mysterious? To eradicate suffering and evil by worldly force would require a different god with a different heart from the One who loves us through Jesus Christ.

As I sit at the keyboard this morning ruminating and theologizing about evil and suffering, Lori is thirty miles away on the front lines of the battlefield. Her mother, Ruth, is in the last stages of her battle with amyotrophic lateral sclerosis — Lou Gehrig's Disease.

Lori is helping her father, Richard, rearrange the hospital bed, regulate medication, administer breathing treatments, and prepare meals for the week ahead. Later this afternoon, the gravity of the inevitable will become weightier as the family arranges for Ruth's funeral. Ruth and Richard have met this illness with considerable courage, but the days ahead will become longer and increasingly more challenging.

Ruth will have died by the time Richard reads these words. What have we uncovered in this parable that might bring him comfort? Have our four chapters of foraging around in the Landowner's field given Lori truths to lean upon when the days ahead become long? What have we learned?

First, God welcomes our questions, frustrations, and even anger. Second, God is not responsible for Ruth's illness. Third, God promises to deal with evil and suffering once and for all.

While these takeaways seem helpful, the Landowner's plan poses one more substantial challenge — the need for patience. Justice will eventually be doled out, but not until the end of the age. Until then, we must find ways to coexist with evil and suffering.

On the front lines, the Landowner's words are a little underwhelming.

"I know this is painful, Ruth, and it seems unfair, but God will take care of this. There is a plan to end all suffering at the end of the ages."

What consolation does God's promise offer Ruth and her family if all the life-saving battalions are being reserved for the final showdown?

---

5   Isaiah 55:8

The promise also rang disappointingly hollow for Martha as she stood in front of her brother's sealed tomb.

"Lord, if you had been here, my brother would not have died. But even now, I know that God will give you whatever you ask of him."

Jesus pointed to the future: "Your brother will rise again."

"I know that he will rise again in the resurrection on the last day," said the sister of the dead man.

"I am the resurrection and the life. Those who believe in me, even though they die, will live, and everyone who lives and believes in me will never die."[6]

When Jesus saw Mary weeping, he was "deeply moved." The Greek word John chose here is *enebrimēsato*, which means *shuddered all over*. The same word is used to describe the quivering of a horse when it snorts. Jesus is not whimpering in this passage; he is veritably convulsing. Why?

The Jews supposed Jesus was mourning. "Look how much he loved Lazarus." But the sisters will tell you that this interpretation doesn't hold water. It had taken Jesus four days to reach Bethany. His lack of urgency did not exactly convey concern.

Maybe Mary and Martha were not the only ones who felt disappointed that day. They may have waited four days for Jesus to arrive, but the Lord had waited three years for the world to receive him. The power of the resurrection stood in their very presence, yet no one in Bethany perceived him.

Jesus knew the implications of a power display. You could speak publicly with a Samaritan woman in Jesus' day and get by with it. You could even give sight to a blind man on the Sabbath and live to tell about it. But raising a four-day-old corpse from the tomb catapulted Jesus to the top of the Religious Right's *Most Wanted List*.

Calling Lazarus forth from the grave would seal Jesus' fate, yet he shuddered and asked, "Where have you laid him?"

Why was it necessary for Mary and Martha to languish for so long before Jesus showed up? Why are we left to twiddle our thumbs until the

---

6 John 11:22-25

end of time before God acts decisively to finish off the enemy he has already defeated? Why does God seem so silent so often when we pray?

The parable of the weeds among the wheat gives us Jesus' most complete teaching regarding the presence of evil and suffering in the world. Yet as we push *STOP* on our study, many of our questions remain unanswered, and the theodicy problem is far from solved. At best, the parable appears to give us *eventual* answers.

But when we read the parable backward, as God wrote it, several significant truths come to light.

First, God is, by nature, a keeper of promises. Second, God always eventually shows up, even if not according to our schedules. Third, the next time Lazarus entered a tomb, he knew what to expect.

And, finally, the One who wore our flesh, bore our suffering, and endured our death — the God who shuddered — has earned our patience.

30

Repacking

Before Christianity was a rich and powerful religion, before it was associated with buildings, budgets, crusades, colonialism, or televangelism, it began as a revolutionary nonviolent movement promoting a new kind of aliveness on the margins of society.

~ Brian D. McLaren, *We Make the Road by Walking*

I'm not afraid of failure; I'm afraid of succeeding at things that don't matter.

~ William Carey

The full moon over Kansas this morning was shrouded by an ominous dark amber haze. It was the sort of spectacle that a century ago may have sent parents rushing to collect their children and praying over the end of the world. But according to satellite radio news, the menacing sky was the result of three million wildfire-charred acres that burned in California earlier this week. The smoke which they churned up arrived in the Midwest just before daybreak.

In other news this morning, waves from the latest Gulf Coast hurricane began pounding coastal communities from Louisiana to the Florida Panhandle. Forecasters predict that the storm will displace tens of thousands of residents.

Racial tensions are mounting in cities across the nation, and signs of increasing social and political polarization are everywhere.

I changed the station to *Classic Rewind*. For a predawn trip to the airport, I would much rather keep company with Tom Petty and Van Halen than CNN reporters who are live and on location.

Since Mark's accident, my carry-on bag rides beside me on the front seat of the truck. I slipped my hand into the side pocket to check for the essentials: wallet, phone, Parkinson's meds, face mask. Check.

For airline travel during a pandemic, masks are as essential as photo IDs. Since my last TSA screening, the lives of nearly one million people worldwide have been claimed by a merciless, microscopic virus. The suffering and death show no signs of relenting; neither does our fear. These days feel eerily apocalyptic.

From a historical perspective, our current crises are not unique. People living in sixteenth-century Saxony, for example, would have described life similarly. Due to the Black Plague, tuberculosis, smallpox, and syphilis, life expectancy in northern Europe in the early 1500s was thirty-eight years. Nearly one-third of children died before their tenth birthday. Where pandemics migrated, poverty and famine were sure to follow. The offshoot of this harsh cultural climate was deep, pervasive fear.

The Catholic church exploited that fear by managing and brokering the prospect of salvation. Armed with a rediscovered gospel of grace, Martin Luther, a particularly feisty Augustinian monk, protested ecclesiastical abuses, including the sale of indulgences. With the help of technological guru Johannes Gutenberg, the Steve Jobs of Luther's day and inventor of the printing press, Brother Martin's writings captured the attention and hearts of the German people and ignited a reformation.

Sweeping, substantive reform in the church is rare. Noted feminist biblical scholar and American author, Phyllis Tickle, suggested that the church historically "cleans house" twice each millennium by holding "five-hundred-year rummage sales." We decide what to dispose of, what to keep, and what to collect.[1]

The initial sell-off took place during Jesus' ministry. Established patterns of understanding had to be jettisoned to make room for his new teaching. The collapse of the Roman Empire and the beginning of the Dark Ages took place five hundred years later. At that sale, the church lost its nature as a vital movement, became institutionalized, and went underground. Not all rummage sales are profitable. The *Great Schism* took place in 1054 when the church divided into eastern and western branches. The Protestant Reformation occurred five centuries later, right on cue.

That brings us to today. It is once again time for reform.

The great suffering and pain caused by these disruptions beg for a heftier image than "rummage sale." The Great Schism weakened what was left of the Roman Empire and eventually led to its downfall. The religious and geopolitical Thirty Years War that followed the Protestant Reformation resulted in the death of eight million people or nearly twenty percent of the German population. Whether church reform takes place at higher doctrinal or institutional levels, or in the local congregation, loss is inevitable.

In the late 1970s, my denomination published a new hymnal that many congregations less-than-affectionately referred to as the "Green Book." When the pastor of my childhood church announced that our congregation would be making the transition, members immediately crossed their arms, leaned back in their pews, and resisted.

"We don't like the Green Book!" they protested.

As a teenager, I wondered, "How do you know?" The hymnal had not yet been distributed! The jury rendered a verdict before the defendant had even been properly introduced or taken the stand. We knew only one thing for certain about the Green Book: It wasn't the beloved Red Book. That was enough.

---

1   Phyllis Tickle, The Great Emergence – How Christianity is Changing and Why (Grand Rapids: Baker Books, 2012), 20.

Members did not fear change as much as they mourned the prospect of loss.

John the Baptist oversaw the kingdom's rollout strategy. "Metanoia!" he preached. "Turn around. Change your mind, for the kingdom of heaven is on its way."

When Jesus appeared on the ministry scene, he took the homiletical handoff from his cousin and proclaimed the same message. "Metanoia, for the kingdom of heaven is now here."

In most faith communities, the call for metanoia is essentially an invitation to scuffle, and a three-year scuffle is precisely what Jesus' sermons stirred up with religious leaders.

Those in power did not need to review this new kingdom agenda to know they disliked it. They immediately crossed their arms, sat back in their pews, and resisted. The current arrangements worked quite well for them, "thank you very much." And when the leaders learned that Jesus' kingdom initiative called for those at the head table and those at the servants' table to relinquish their seats and join one another at the same table, they disliked it even more. Change always requires that we let go of something — the familiar hymnal, our usual seat, a former understanding. We do not like letting go.

Even before Tickle called our attention to the five-hundred-year reformation rhythm, the church had entered an era of substantial change. Mainline Protestantism continues to hemorrhage members at an alarming rate. Each successive generation demonstrates markedly diminished interest in institutional religion. Seventy percent of the senior generation (ages seventy-five to ninety) will attend corporate worship somewhere this week. However, only ten to fifteen percent of their grandchildren will do the same. We do not need cultural pundits or religious prophets to tell us where this trend is headed.

The church is languishing.

Once again, I will lay my theological cards face up. The church is not suffering because it is losing members; the church is losing members because it does not know how to suffer.

All that I have suggested regarding our personal pain and loss may be applied to the church. The Body of Christ is an organism. Congregations live and breathe, get wounded and heal, grow, and diminish. They are born and they die. Like us, congregations fear uncertainty, mourn loss, resist change, and seek to avoid the pain necessary for reform.

Jesus could not have been more explicit regarding the cost of discipleship. He asked his followers to pick up their crosses, go where he went, love as he loved, serve as he served, and lay down their lives for one another.

"Very truly, I tell you, unless a grain of wheat falls into the earth and dies, it remains just a single grain; but if it dies, it bears much fruit. Those who love their life lose it, and those who hate their life in this world will keep it for eternal life."[2]

For too long, church leaders have been pressing the defibrillator paddles to the church's institutional heart trying unsuccessfully to shock it back into some semblance of life. Perhaps it is time to allow that heart to die. The metanoia which the body of Christ now requires is resurrection, not resuscitation.

Without loss, or unless something falls apart, rarely will we go to new places.

Tomorrow, thousands of Californians and Floridians will begin combing through the scorched and flooded remains of what used to be their homes. Will these victims attempt to restore life as it was before the devastation, or will they be encouraged to new places?

"Having our building burn down was the best thing that ever happened to this congregation." As a young pastor, I was taken aback by my colleague's comment. "Oh, it was painful, for sure," he said, "but starting over forced us to determine who we were and who God was calling us to be. Our new building ended up looking nothing like the old one. The same was true with our people. We allowed God to remake us as well."

God does not cause catastrophic crises, but a pandemic is just the sort of leavening agent the Holy Spirit can commandeer to help the church initiate reform. We are living in the early days of what *could* become

---

2   John 12:24-25

Christianity's next great reformation *if* the Body of Christ will sit with its suffering long enough to learn from it.

I described my initial call to ministry as "so gentle and unobtrusive that I almost missed it." My second call story is so radically different that I sometimes wonder how the same God could have authored it. This time, God's speaking was precise and unmistakable.

It came with exclamation points!

In November of 2013, in one of the last places I wanted to be (Atonement) and doing one of the last things I wanted to do (attending a bishop's Service of Installation), the Holy Spirit veritably pushed me through a portal to the second half of life. I am not sure exactly when my further journey began, but that was the moment I became aware of it.

This journey called for new luggage, a new destination, and a different travel plan. I had cast my line in nearly every synodical pond in the church and received barely a nibble.

I knew why, of course. Jaded by my experience with the church hierarchy, I imagined groups of clerical-collared leaders off in the corners of bishop conferences comparing notes and asking, "What can you tell me about this guy?"

"Crowther? Trouble. Nothing but trouble."

I was certain the professional roadblocks were politically motivated. But the actual explanation was even more disappointing.

Church representatives universally assumed that I was still on my *former* journey — straight, smooth, and ever upward — and that any pastor who had shepherded a large congregation would only be willing to serve another large congregation.

"I am sorry, but this is a synod of smaller churches." This became the predictable, standard reply from bishops and their staffs. "We will keep you in mind if one of our few larger ministries opens up."

Perhaps I should have led with, "You should know, Bishop, that I lost all my luggage years ago and have finally made it to the second half of life. I have redefined my standards."

Of course, that messaging makes little sense for church officials who are still in the first half of life. Moreover, traveling the straight, smooth, and every-upward trajectory leaves little time to listen to others' metanoia stories. I know. I used to keep such a schedule.

Initially, I volleyed back, "Thank you, Bishop. Please know that I am willing to interview with congregations of any size."

That's inevitably where the conversations ended.

Finally, a bishop who was also a friend confided, "Joe, you may want to reword that response. It sounds a bit desperate. Bishops don't like desperate."

But I wasn't desperate. I was repacking.

Do you recall the conversation that Jesus had with Peter following the resurrection? Can you reimagine it through the lens of the second half of life?

"Do you love me?" the Lord asked. "Then feed my sheep." In other words, "Journey a little further into your second calling. When you were young, you used to dress yourself and go where you wished. But when you grow older, you will stretch out your hands so that someone else may dress you and take you where you do not wish to go."[3]

In the first half of life, *I* chose the career suitcase and all its contents. I tried on the clothes that *I* liked, glanced in the mirror, then turned to the world and asked, "What do you think?" If I got a thumbs-up, it went in the suitcase.

In the second half of life, the process is radically different. I hold my arms up to the Lord and say, "Surprise me!"

---

3   John 21:15-18

As the baristas lock the cash register and begin the Sunday evening closing routine at a small Christian coffeehouse in downtown Overland Park, Kansas, four millennial musicians in dark t-shirts and knit hats take seats on stage, tap their mics for sound checks, and begin to play. Several people who have the gift of hospitality make rounds in the café, greeting patrons and alerting them, "Just want to let you know that we are about to begin worship, but we would love for you to stay and hang out with us awhile."

I am busy connecting my laptop to the jerry-rigged projection system. If this is one of the weeks that the technology works, I will cast images onto the screen behind the musicians. The first slide reads "Welcome to The Table."

I organized The Table as a missional community for others who, like me, were spiritually repacking. Many of our participants were disenchanted with traditional expressions of church. Ask them why they became a part of our group, and they will tell you, "My former congregation wasn't spiritual enough," or "didn't meet my needs," or "disappointed me," or "hurt me" in some way.

"This community was the religious caboose for a lot of your folks," described an official of the Episcopal Diocese after interviewing our participants. "Had they not climbed aboard the faith train here, they just weren't getting back on. Period."

There are two tenets to The Table's mission that seem to pique people's interests.

First, we intend never to own a building. It is a nimble, mobile ministry that refuses to become identified with a single location. We currently worship in a coffee shop. Next season our venue may be a warehouse or a community center.

Second, in our effort to love neighbor as self, The Table strives to give half of its offerings in blessing to the community. It is an ambitious goal but much more attainable because of tenet number one.

Recently, one of our participants invited a macchiato-drinking, laptop-consumed, hipster-type patron of the coffeehouse to hang around for worship.

"What do you folks believe?" he inquired.

"Well, let me tell you what we *do*," she said. "We provide meals for the homeless, partner with two area middle schools to help care for the needs of students and staff, hold appreciation events for local public safety personnel and first responders, visit hospice ministries, assist Meals on Wheels, and support area prison ministries and a Tanzanian medical mission. I guess we just believe in giving ourselves away to anyone who is not here."

Good answer.

At an inner-city congregation in Minneapolis, a hospitality team member removes a handful of change and small bills from the wicker donation basket on the coffee and doughnut table while other volunteers clean the urns and mugs and stow the table supplies away for another week. They don't especially care for the job, but they wish it took them longer to complete. The number of dirty coffee mugs is ever-dwindling.

On the other side of the lobby, church leaders scratch their heads and wonder what they can do to entice more people through the front doors. Like most mainline congregations these days, this church is languishing.

The leadership decides to invest in the "build it, and they will come" philosophy. They devise a plan to ramp up hospitality by reconfiguring and enlarging the entrance to the stately, stone, gothic building. They also decide to build a deck behind the church for increased fellowship space and hire an additional staff person to watch over all the programs they plan to start as soon as the throngs of visitors begin flooding in the front doors.

Lastly, the leaders interview consultants who will help them think through their plan and raise funds to make it happen.

I'm "that guy."

Since being hired by the congregation eighteen months ago, I have averaged one trip per month to Minneapolis to help guide this inner-city congregation through a process of discovery. We studied the heart and spiritual DNA of the membership inside the church, surveyed the community's needs outside the church, and considered God's desire to dissolve the walls that exist between the two.

I convinced the leadership that the growing population of lonely, hungry, and unhomed people in the immediate neighborhood could not care less about what kind of coffee they served or the sort of Hospitality Center the church maintained. What they most cared about was being cared about.

We reimagined the project to include program space for community support groups and an area to shelter and care for people who are unhomed. To keep the new front doors swinging in *both* directions and encourage the deployment of members into the community, the leadership added a Director of Community Outreach position to the staff. Then, once the vision was cast, we raised nearly three million dollars to support the initiatives.

When folks ask, "What do you do?" I used to say, "I spend half of my professional life serving a missional community that will never own a building, another half helping congregations construct new buildings, and a third half helping churches live more faithfully out of the buildings they already have." Now, I just tell them, "I am helping prepare the church for the next big rummage sale."

Most people consider that I am far less professionally successful than I used to be. By first-half-of-life standards, they are right. But I am also privy to a truth that most of the culture has yet to discover: What looks to the world like failing, falling, sacrificing, and losing is really part of the mystery of dying…and dying is requisite for rising.

And the last time I checked, rising is "winning."

The few remaining pieces of my old, tattered, duct-taped luggage are sitting somewhere near the "Priced to Move Quick" table at the rummage sale. Make me an offer if you wish, or just take it all. The suitcases may serve you well…for a while.

But eventually, you will tire of schlepping all that unnecessary weight around. Perhaps I can save you some heartache and time by sharing what I have learned the hard way: The more stuff you feel compelled to pack, the less interesting the journey will be.

Repacking

My bags are considerably fewer and lighter these days. So is my spirit. I spend very little time checking the rearview mirror or questioning my knots. If the Spirit urges me to turn around, I don't hesitate. And quite frankly, I am having far too much fun stumbling upon the mystery of God to worry about the world's yardstick for success, or how I measure up.

That's what I thought about this morning on my way to the airport… on my way to Minneapolis. I looked at the amber moon, smiled, and thought to myself, "Things are changing."

31

The Difference a Good Ending Can Make

This sermon was preached during the season of Easter.

And the one who was seated on the throne said, "See, I am making all things new." Also, he said, "Write this, for these words are trustworthy and true." Then he said to me, "It is done! I am the Alpha and the Omega, the beginning and the end. (Revelation 21:5-6)

Good books. Unforgettable movies. Effective sermons. Meaningful conversations. Games with buzzer-beaters or walk-off home runs. All have something in common. They end well.

Endings are critically important. Good endings can surprise us, cause us to bite our nails, warm our hearts, and leave us wanting more.

For some of us, our love of endings is more than our patience can bear. We read just enough of the early chapters of a novel to become acquainted with the characters and determine the plot, then flip forward to the final pages. We watch movies in the same way.

There are times when the ability to see the future would be tremendously helpful. Each autumn I work with engaged couples who would love to peek ahead at the weather forecast for the outdoor ceremonies they have planned in the spring.

A member of the parish is currently battling a rare disease. Doctors have offered to include her in a clinical trial that *might* provide healing.

The Difference a Good Ending Can Make

However, if the experimental treatment is not successful — or if she is part of the control group that receives a placebo — then our dear friend will have missed out on months of traditional treatment. If only she could have a look at the results of the clinical report now.

When life offers you the option to keep what you have or trade it for what's behind *Curtain Number Two*, we long for the gift of foresight.

Yet such a gift is not without peril.

I hear tell of a preacher who began his sermon by placing a table in the middle of the worship space. On the table, he stacked boxes of various sizes, each bearing the name of a member of the congregation. Instead of boxes, some members were assigned thin envelopes.

"These boxes contain one index card for each day of the rest of your life," the preacher said. "Would you like to see yours?"

In a sense, Saint John is helping me do something similar this morning.

The library of Scripture ends well with The Revelation of John. It is a unique, mysterious, and often misused book filled with images of creatures, battles, horsemen, dragons, beasts from the sea and the earth, and fiery lakes. Despite its oddities, Revelation has significantly impacted Western culture through its influence on art, literature, and music.

But it is not the search for great literature that most often lands a reader in Revelation. Rather, we desire to look ahead. We want a glimpse of the final chapter.

Will the world end because of war in the Middle East? What does Revelation have to say? Nuclear holocaust? What about global warming, pandemics, spiraling economies? Would you not like to know?

There is a unique spot in the Bering Strait off Alaska's far western shore. There, you can stand on the deck of a ship, look in one direction and see yesterday, then turn your head in the opposite direction and see tomorrow.

Revelation is also such a place. Stand in its pages, and you can look in one direction and see the life of Christ. Turn around, and you may see the future made possible by Christ. From this unique perspective, John offers hope to those wrestling with their present trials, whenever that *present* might be and whatever those trials might entail.

In the spring of 2008, I spent a week in Coventry, England, studying the emergent church there. Most of my work took place at a modern cathedral. Built in the early 1950s, one of the cathedral's most unique and striking features is the massive south wall which is made entirely of thick glass. Etched into the glass are huge figures of saints and angels partying, frolicking, blowing trumpets, and dancing across the wall.

If you stand in the worship space and gaze only at what is *on* the glass, the scene seems almost inappropriate, perhaps irreverent. You might question how artists could conceive of such heavenly merrymaking in a time of world hunger, war, and the widening gap between rich and poor. However, worshipers who take time to look *through* the glass wall have a completely different experience.

In November of 1940, Coventry suffered the most sustained aerial bombing campaign of any English city during World War II. Most of the metropolitan area, including the original cathedral, was left in ruin. Some of those ruins remain as a memorial to the city's pain and suffering. When architects designed the modern cathedral, they chose the theme, *Resurrection through Sacrifice*. As you look through the cathedral's glass wall, you can at once see both the saints and dancing angels and the ruins of the original bombed cathedral.

These architects were marvelous theologians. The challenges, trials, and ruins of our present lives are best understood when viewed through the prism of what is yet to be.

Of course, the Coventry architects were not the first to use this approach. The Apostle John invited his readers to view their suffering through the looking glass of his Revelation so that we might understand our present in light of what is yet to come.

Look again at John's art with me.

> "Then I saw a new heaven and a new earth; for the first heaven and the first earth had passed away, and the sea was no more. And I saw the holy city, the new Jerusalem, coming down out of heaven from God, prepared as a bride adorned for her husband.

And I heard a loud voice from the throne saying,
> 'See, the home of God is among mortals.
> He will dwell with them;
> they will be his people,
> and God himself will be with them;
> he will wipe every tear from their eyes.
> Death will be no more;
> mourning and crying and pain will be no more,
> for the first things have passed away.'

And the one who was seated on the throne said, 'See, I am making all things new.' Also, he said, 'Write this, for these words are trustworthy and true.' Then he said to me, 'It is done! I am the Alpha and the Omega, the beginning and the end. To the thirsty, I will give water as a gift from the spring of the water of life.'" *(Revelation 21:1-6)*

There are around eight hundred folks in our congregation who will look at John's artwork today, which means there will be around eight hundred different interpretations of that art. Such is the nature of art. The same sculpture, painting, song, or sermon will speak differently to each of us. I can only tell you what *I* see in John's portrait.

"The sea is no more." This is the first phrase that leaps off the canvas for me. Now, this may not seem like especially good news to anyone who enjoys a good day at the beach, but for John's community, the sea was not a place of recreation. It represented turbulence. The sea was unpredictable and treacherous. Remember how astonished and frightened the disciples were when they saw Jesus walk atop the sea and tame its raging waves with a word.

"Peace!"

No one commanded the sea! In Jesus' day, the sea was the enemy.

If we could ask Andrew and Peter, James, and John about the sea, they would tell us about its perils. Before they were fishers of people, they made their living on the sea. Ask the wives who prayed every morning for their husband's safe return from work. They respected the water. They feared it. "The sea will be no more."

"A story that ends with no more sea is a story that ends well," the disciples would say.

I also notice that something is missing from this art — tears. In John's image, not only will God wipe away the tears that rest upon our cheeks on the last day, but God will also reach back through time and remove all the tears of our pasts.

"Everything will be made new." That is what the one seated on the throne says. Jerusalem will descend from heaven as a new creation.

Some years ago, our Good Friday service ended powerfully. If you were present that evening, then I do not need to remind you what took place. If you were not, I apologize because, as with any fine art, my description will not do justice to what Lisa conveyed through her liturgical dance.

As "Adagio for Strings" slowly crescendoed on the organ, Lisa danced the crucifixion. The other dancers who joined her were draped with dark rags, symbols of despair and sin. Lisa carefully took those rags from the others, placed them upon herself, and bore those burdens up the chancel steps and to the foot of the large cross suspended above the altar. Then, as the organ swelled to the piece's climactic point, Lisa pulled the heavy, dark veil from the cross and collapsed beneath its weight.

Truth be told, I was a little apprehensive about the dance. The movement never quite worked during rehearsal. But in the moment, it found perfect expression. Worshipers were transfixed. We had heard of Jesus' bearing our sins to the cross, and most of us believed it, but that night we looked back through time and witnessed it.

On Easter morning, Lisa's rags were exchanged for four large one-hundred-foot white linen cloths that swept out from the altar, through the cross, and over the congregation. The Savior was not resuscitated. The graveclothes proclaimed that he had been raised to new life. John's vision declares that there is more in store for us than the healing of our bodies. God will make of us something completely new.

The late Dr. S.M. Lockridge, a prominent Black preacher, rendered his interpretation of Saint John's art, titled, "It's Friday. But Sunday's Coming!" I have experienced this art as a poem, a sermon, and a song, although in the African American preaching tradition, it's sometimes difficult to know where one artform stops and another begins.

The Difference a Good Ending Can Make

"IT'S FRIDAY BUT SUNDAY'S COMING!"[1]

It's Friday. Jesus is praying. Peter's a sleeping. Judas is betraying. But Sunday's comin'.

It's Friday. Pilate's struggling. The council is conspiring. The crowd is vilifying. They don't even know That Sunday's comin'.

It's Friday. The disciples are running like sheep without a shepherd. Mary's crying. Peter is denying. But they don't know That Sunday's a comin'.

It's Friday. The Romans beat my Jesus. They robe him in scarlet. They crown him with thorns. But they don't know That Sunday's comin'.

It's Friday. See Jesus walking to Calvary. His blood dripping. His body stumbling. And his spirit's burdened. But you see, it's only Friday. Sunday's comin'.

It's Friday. The world's winning. People are sinning. And evil's grinning.

It's Friday. The soldiers nail my Savior's hands to the cross. They nail my Savior's feet to the cross. And then they raise him up next to criminals. It's Friday. But let me tell you something Sunday's comin'.

It's Friday. The disciples are questioning. What has happened to their King. And the Pharisees are celebrating that their scheming has been achieved. But they don't know It's only Friday. Sunday's comin'.

It's Friday. He's hanging on the cross. Feeling forsaken by his Father. Left alone and dying. Can nobody save him? Ooooh It's Friday. But Sunday's comin'.

It's Friday. The earth trembles. The sky grows dark. My King yields his spirit.

It's Friday. Hope is lost. Death has won. Sin has conquered. And Satan's just a laughin'.

It's Friday. Jesus is buried. A soldier stands guard. And a rock is rolled into place. But it's Friday. It is only Friday. Sunday is a comin'!

The purpose of this art, these stories, and John's Revelation is not only to encourage us to hold out and hold on because help is on the way. Neither is John simply trying to convince us that life eventually gets better. The fact that Sunday is coming changes the way we live on Friday.

If you live with Sunday hope, even during Good Friday, that hope becomes contagious, and those around you start to live differently. And

---

1 "It's Friday But Sunday's Coming!" YouTube, uploaded by Carpenter Missions, 2 April, 2020 https://www.youtube.com/watch?v=QS2wPotScZY

when those around you live differently, then entire communities change. And when whole communities change, then culture may be next.

Can you imagine a world living amid Friday's suffering with Sunday's conviction? Have I oversimplified what it takes to ignite a revolution?

You do not have to preach to be a revolutionary. Love one another. Sit with those who suffer. Dry someone's tears. Feed those who hunger. Clothe those who are naked. Teach someone to read so they can also appreciate John's art. Tell those who are lonely that you will pray for them, then do it. Better yet, pray *with* them.

Dance with the angels and party with the saints. These are the sorts of things you do when you've seen the future. We know how the story ends. Spoiler alert! We win! So, live as victors. Sunday is coming.

32

THE ART OF SALVATION

You don't make a photograph just with a camera. You bring to
the act of photography all the pictures you have seen, the books
you have read, the music you have heard, the people you have loved.

~ Ansel Adams

But Jesus steps into that world of inevitabilities and says to Hell with
causes and conditions. Whatever your circumstances, there is always an
opening to new life, which you can access through faith.

~ Karen Mitchell

Growing up in the buckle of the Bible Belt, I was regularly interrogated in the interest of salvation. "Are you saved?" "Have you made a decision for Jesus?" "Have you found Jesus?" "Accepted Jesus?" "Invited him into your heart?"

Responding "yes" to any of these questions, in the estimation of my inquisitionists, saved me.

Even as an adolescent, I realized that salvation is much broader, kinder, and less manageable than my Southern friends may have considered. More than what we believe, salvation is something we experience.

Biblically, *salvation* can mean deliver, set free, redeem, restore, make whole, keep whole, keep safe, make complete, or heal. We may experience salvation when a war is won, a sickness is remedied, or someone lays down his life for a friend. Generally, salvation takes place whenever God provides a way where there had been no way…when ellipses replace the periods in our lives.

"Tell us what is saving your life now." Barbara Brown Taylor received this invitation years ago from the host of a congregation where she was speaking.

"It was such a good question," she wrote, "that I have made a practice of asking others to answer it even as I continue to answer it myself."[1]

A beautiful, disarming question such as this can reframe the matter of salvation and turn what might feel like an interrogation into a generous conversation. So, as we approach the end of this part of our journey together, I am glad to adopt Taylor's practice and pass the question forward to you.

"What is saving your life these days?"

Some of us know what is saving us. According to Taylor, most of us know what is *killing* us. Diseases. Our busyness. Materialism. Poverty. The list of *killing things* seems endless.

Though I may have described it differently at the time, this book arose out of my yearning to better understand the things that kill. Thirty-some odd chapters later, the primary revelation of my journey may be that the *killing* things and the *saving* things are often the *same* things. That which threatens to harm us today is often the very thing that will save us tomorrow.

Life springs forth from death — not just the one big death, but also all the smaller daily ones. Christ won by losing. He succeeded by failing. His power was perfected in weakness. It is by letting go of our lives that we gain them, and only by going down that we learn what *up* really means.

---

1 Barbara Brown Taylor, Leaving Church (New York: HarperCollins, 2006), 225, Kindle.

Jesus could not have been more explicit in the parable of the prodigal; it is our imperfections that bring us to God, not our good deeds. Jesus has always gotten along famously with sinners; it's the self-proclaimed righteous folks that give him fits.

These truths reveal the heart of the Christian faith, yet they still take believers by surprise. They seem edgy and radical yet are hidden in plain sight on every page of the Gospel. But even if we accept these truths intellectually and regard them as biblically indisputable, we push back at them. I did. On all but my best days, I still do. Death. Loss. Failure. Weakness. Letting go. The world has conditioned us to resist and despise the very things that, according to the Gospel, bring life.

We know how forcefully the world pushed back against Jesus and Paul. When Paul and Silas brought their message to Thessalonica, the Jews angrily dragged some of the believers before the city authorities claiming, "These people have been turning the world upside down."[2] We don't take kindly to those who mess with our worlds. We prefer the world right side up, just as we like salvation that is predictable and controllable. There is a part of us that prefers the type of salvation that proceeds from our saying "yes" to Jesus. It is much more manageable than the salvation that comes from God saying "yes" to us.

Few of us will adopt a reordered way of thinking and turn around unless some force from the outside — namely, suffering, or failure — compels us to stand on our heads. But if you can tolerate the rush of blood to your brain and the dizzying disorientation of inversion long enough, then the Holy Spirit may topple you over the threshold and into what Carl Jung and Richard Rohr call the "second half of life."

When our mother turned ninety, my brothers and I dutifully planned a surprise party. We devised a scheme for getting Mom to the fellowship hall at her church where a gathering of family members and friends were lying in wait in the dark. The plan worked flawlessly up until the very last moment. The guest of honor became so suspicious of stepping through the

---

2 Acts 17:6

doorway into that darkened room that she braced herself against the door frame. Aware of the joy that awaited her on the other side, I decided to provide a little encouragement.

I had to push Mom across the threshold and into the surprise celebration of her life.

Richard Rohr writes, "Most of us are never told that we can set out from the known and familiar to take on a further journey."[3]

Even those who *are* told are, at first, unwilling to embark. With a wall full of diplomas, a certificate of ordination, and a career of doling out spiritual counsel to others, I knew the further path existed; I just enjoyed the straight, smooth, and ever upward path more. But my resolve to live right-side-up had been so weakened by the *killing things* that the Spirit needed little elbow grease to push me through the passageway into the second half of life.

Today, it is the killing things that are saving my life.

Kintsugi is the centuries-old Japanese method of repairing broken pottery. When a vase or bowl is cracked, rather than discarding the pieces or attempting to rejoin them with camouflaged adhesive, the Kintsugi technique uses a unique tree sap lacquer dusted with powdered gold to adhere the fragments to one another. The flaws, imperfections, and scars become highlighted and made more conspicuous by these golden seams, yet the result is much more beautiful than the original. The artist does not repair the vessel as much as she uses it to recreate something completely new.

In 2008, I presented the Atonement art team with a challenge: "Kintsugi. Lent. Easter. Go!" An hour later, we had our theme and artistic backdrop for the season.

Ash Wednesday service began a little unusually that year. A woman dressed in stained, white overalls and wearing a dark apron stepped out

---

3   Richard Rohr, Falling Upward: A Spirituality for the Two Halves of Life (Jossey: Bass: 2011), xvii.

from behind the altar, took a seat at a spotlighted table, and began to work. Worshipers craned their necks to see what our unannounced visitor was doing. She flipped a switch, and the table started to turn.

"Oh…she's a potter," folks whispered. "Oh, yeah."

We borrowed our seasonal theme from Isaiah. "We are the clay, and you are our potter; we are all the work of your hand."[4]

Our artist was in residence for six weeks as she fashioned her clay into one beautiful ceramic vessel after another. By Holy Week, there was barely room to move about the chancel as it was filled with bowls, vases, pitchers, and chalices of all shapes and colors. The artistic centerpiece for the season was a magnificent, royal blue, marbled prayer bowl, which was placed next to the altar atop a six-foot-tall square-topped wooden pedestal.

At the climax of Good Friday's service, the liturgical dancers — dressed entirely in black — interpreted Jesus' death as they carefully weaved their way in, around, and through the fragile pieces of art. As their dance concluded, the dancers jostled the wooden pedestal, and the centerpiece unexpectedly crashed to the tiled floor, where it shattered into dozens of jagged pieces. The congregation let out a collective gasp.

A little girl seated on the front pew tugged at her mother's sleeve and whispered frantically, "Did they have an accident, Mommy? Did they?"

Without releasing her gaze from the altar, the mother responded, "I…don't…know, dear."

As was the case on the first Good Friday, spectators left the crucifixion uncertain what they had witnessed. Was this incident part of the script or a choreographic blunder? (Score one for the worship planning team.)

The mystery was solved early on Easter morning when the dancers — now dressed in resplendent victory white and gold — returned to the scene of the *accident*. They pirouetted and glided down each aisle and met beneath a veiled wall hanging at the front of the sanctuary where, on cue, they removed the covering to reveal a tremendous mosaic of a phoenix rising from flames to rebirth. Placed throughout the mosaic were the repurposed shards from the prayer bowl.

---

4   Isaiah 64:8

The Lenten series held the congregation's rapt attention from the moment the potter sat down at her wheel and reached for her first handful of clay. The power and creativity of the art explained some of the appeal, but there was more.

From the midst of his suffering, Job reminded God, "You fashioned me like clay."[5] If Job and Isaiah are to be believed, then the process of centering, shaping, reshaping, trimming, and firing is not only happening to the clay, but it is also happening to us. We do not just behold the art; we *are* the art.

We may be clay in the Potter's hands, but we are impertinent clay. Our lives resist the intense heat of the kiln and the Artist's constant reshaping. *We* know best where the Artist's fingernails should apply pressure and when the grip needs to be relaxed.

But Isaiah warns, "Woe to you who strive with your Maker, earthen vessels with the potter! Does the clay say to the one who fashions it, 'What are you making?' or 'Your work has no handles'?"[6]

Clay does not instruct the potter. As C.S. Lewis wrote in *Mere Christianity*, "When you argue against Him, you are arguing against the very power that makes you able to argue at all: it is like cutting off the branch you are sitting on." Of course, these truths do not keep us from advising God, nor do they make surrendering control to the Potter any easier.

Consider, then, the role of suffering.

Rohr writes, "I define suffering very simply as 'whenever you are not in control.' Suffering is the most effective way whereby humans learn to trust, allow, and give up control to Another Source."[7]

Once again, that which kills us is also that which can save us.

The further journey to abundant life must pass through suffering, failure, or loss. I wish this were not the case. Ever since Jesus first set his face towards Jerusalem, his followers have searched for ways to reach the Promised Land without traveling through the wilderness. Every year, throngs of

---

5   Job 10:9
6   Isaiah 45:9
7   Richard Rohr, "Transforming our Pain," Center for Action and Contemplation, February 26, 2016, https://cac.org/transforming-our-pain-2016-02-26/.

worshipers turn out for the palms, trumpets, lilies, and "Alleluias," but only the faithful inner circle brave the funeral.

The Triumphal Entry and the Resurrection work out swimmingly for us, but when it comes to the cross, we would just as soon take a pass. Jesus' explicit, unqualified directive was "Follow me." He didn't say, "Toddle along with me for a while until the journey gets rugged, then meet me at the empty tomb whenever you can." There is no bypass around Golgotha.

What is saving you today?

In her book, *Learning to Walk in the Dark*, Barbara Brown Taylor answers her own question as she contemplates her experience of darkness. "The monsters have not dragged me out of bed and taken me back to their lair. The witches have not turned me into a bat. Instead, I have learned things in the dark that I could never have learned in the light, things that have saved my life over and over again, so that there is really only one logical conclusion. I need darkness as much as I need light."[8]

Darkness is the supreme instructor. It teaches us through disorientation by stripping us of our bearings and forcing us to reconsider the dangerous illusion that we have something of value to contribute to the things that are saving our lives. As my marriage atrophied, as Carrie and Grant battled their emotional demons, as my hand mysteriously twitched and tremored — as I spent time in the darkness — I became keenly aware of what is all too easily overlooked in the light: "My help comes in the name of the Lord."[9]

I did not choose Jesus; I was chosen. I did not find Jesus; I was found. I did not invite Jesus into my heart; the Spirit convinced me that I have a place at the center of God's heart. We are not the primary actors in matters of salvation; we are acted upon. That which is concealed in the light of the day becomes apparent in the middle of the night.

When the soldiers apprehended Jesus in the garden, the eleven disciples scattered like a covey of flushed quail. They found one another again behind a locked door, and there they remained, cowering in fear and

---

8   Barbara Brown Taylor. Learning to Walk in the Dark, (New York: HarperCollins, 2014), 5.
9   Psalm 124:8

sheltered in place. The door was unlocked only to send out reconnaissance missions. The brothers drew lots, and the loser was released into the darkness to determine the lay of the land. When he returned, there was a secret knock. Then, the inquisition.

"Did you see anyone? Did anyone see you? Were you followed? Are you sure? Are they still looking for us?"

But what the disciples most wanted to know was, "Did you see *him*?"

There was much to fear outside in the dark. The Jews. The Romans. The unlikely prospects of finding their way back to life as they knew it before Jesus. But what most unsettled the Eleven was the news that the women brought from the tomb that morning.

The disciples abandoned Jesus when he needed them most. "Were you there when they crucified my Lord? When the ground shook, the rocks split, and the temple curtain was ripped from heaven to earth? Were you there when Jesus breathed his last?" Of the Twelve, only John could answer, "Present." If Jesus had truly escaped the tomb and was on the loose, then the disciples had a great deal of explaining to do.

The greatest miracle of Easter is not that Jesus rose from the dead. God had demonstrated authority over death on several occasions, most recently at Lazarus' tomb. The greatest miracle is that, after rising, Jesus came back.

No one would have blamed the Lord had he ascended directly from the grave into heaven to spend the rest of eternity at the right hand of God's throne. But Jesus returned to Jerusalem to enact justice on his executioners and settle accounts with his followers. But remember, God's justice is transformative, not vengeful. Jesus punished the disciples by loving them more.[10]

For the disciples, Easter took place in the dark. It was evening when the Resurrection found them. Jesus walked through locked doors and showed the brothers his scars — proof that he had survived the long night. He did not greet them with reprisals or reprimands. Despite their faithlessness, he said, "Peace." Jesus' first word was one of forgiveness.

---

10 Richard Rohr, "Restorative Justice," Center for Action and Contemplation, September 8, 2020, https://cac.org/restorative-love-2020-09-07.

When Thomas saw Jesus' scars, he responded with a most beautiful declaration of faith, "My Lord and my God!"

Jesus then made a world-reorienting proclamation. "Have you believed because you have seen me? Blessed are those who have not seen and yet have come to believe."[11]

You and I are more blessed than Thomas, Peter, James, Andrew, or any of the apostles who, for three years, had a front-row seat to witness Jesus' life, death, and resurrection. We are blessed *not* to have seen Jesus multiply the fish and loaves or exercise the demons from the possessed. We cannot place our fingers in Jesus' side or recognize his voice. We did not watch him raise Lazarus from the grave. We believe without seeing. Blind belief, by definition, is *faith*.

This is exceedingly good news, for regardless of what is saving our lives today, there are ultimately only two things that God asks from us on the last day: our death and our faith. Nothing more is necessary. Nothing less will do. The Artist who fearfully and wonderfully fashioned us from dust — who shaped and formed and hardened us into beautiful, unique vessels of grace — asks that we surrender our broken selves. God wants the shards.

There is no need to showcase your good works. They may please God, but you will not find them on the list of saving things.

Do not bother accounting for your sins. Mention them if you wish, but God forgave them the first time you asked. They have been forgotten.

Instead, surrender all your messiness, shame, and pain. Hand over the images that you have kept guarded and concealed, even from yourself. Submit your weaknesses and flaws, your suffering, and failure. Hand over all the tattered luggage that you have retrieved along the way. Do all of this boldly.

Finally, add a measure of faith that the One who has walked with you through the darkness will call forth from your final death a completely new, exquisite, and eternal creation. Trust the Artist of Salvation. There is nothing more to do.

---

11 John 20:29

Epilogue

My brother and I spent our afternoons differently growing up on the farm. Pete stepped off the school bus and made a beeline for his room where he stayed until his homework was finished. I admired my brother's discipline; I just didn't share it. As long as there were balls to dribble, a forest to explore, television to watch, rocks to skip across the river, or mischief to make, homework could wait until I got to school the following morning.

But there came a point each fall when both of our afternoon routines changed. The end of Daylight Savings Time meant Dad could no longer make it home from the lab in time to feed the birds before dark. So, from the end of October until the beginning of spring, the pheasants, peacocks, and the rest of our father's fowl menagerie became our responsibility.

Pete took all of this in stride, of course. He simply detoured by the feed shed on the way to his room.

I, on the other hand, resented giving up my playtime for turkeys, so much so that on an unusually warm and enticing mid-November afternoon, I pushed my chores aside and headed instead for my favorite playground — the forest beyond the far edge of the wheat field.

"Don't forget to feed the birds," my mother cautioned. "And you'll have to be home before sunset!"

"I know," I called back over my shoulder, then broke into a sprint across the field.

"Joseph?"

"I know!"

Earlier that June, Pete and I spent a morning combing the woods for the sort of spot a bear might appreciate. Then, we committed a good portion of our summer vacation to digging a grizzly-sized hole. The plan was to cover the hole with brush, just like we had seen on television, and capture an unsuspecting bear. We abandoned the project when school started, so the snare wasn't quite ready to set. It seemed like a good idea to have a look anyway, just in case some especially clumsy bear had happened by and stumbled in. No such luck.

I skipped and ran and played about the woods, bouncing from one adventure to the next. I commanded an armada of stick warships in our favorite little creek, then climbed someone's abandoned deer stand to scout for mountain lions. I imagined that the airplane circling overhead was the enemy and I had been spotted. So, I took cover next to the field in a bunker of newly fallen leaves. Using my walkie-talkie, I communicated my position to central command.

"I'm at the east edge of Crowther field near the really big oak tree. Send help quick!"

But my transmission was suddenly cut short by a familiar sound in the distance; the tires on my father's International Harvester Scout were churning up the long gravel driveway toward home. This was normally a welcome sound, but not on this day. The sun was setting. The pheasants were hungry. I was in trouble. And central command was going to be no help at all.

I crawled back into the deer stand and watched across the field as my father pulled into the drive. A few moments later, a beam of light emerged from the farmhouse and waved back and forth across the backyard toward the feed shed. I swallowed hard, then began the long walk home.

I was sent straight to my room. No discussion. No argument. No supper.

Sitting alone in my room, I imagined that I was in the outer darkness that the Bible talked about where the wicked are banished to weep and gnash their teeth. Though I wasn't exactly sure what teeth-gnashing looked like, it sounded horrible, like something one might be encouraged to do while sitting in the dark listening to their stomach rumble.

Weeping, on the other hand, came without effort. In fact, I couldn't stop it. I think it had something to do with how wonderful the food smelled in the dark and how joyous my family's conversations sounded. The tears just began to flow.

Then, for the second time that evening, I heard my father approaching. His footsteps across the living room floor were unmistakable…heavy and deliberate. Never one for knocking, Dad threw open my bedroom door. Light spilled around his silhouette and flooded my prison.

"We're about to have dessert," he said. "It's your favorite. Why don't you come join us?"

T.S. Eliot writes, "We shall not cease from exploration, and the end of all our exploring will be to arrive where we started and know the place for the first time."[1]

I am sitting in my office where our journey together began. There have been a few small changes to the room since we were last here. The walls have been painted a deep brown, and a large pin map of the United States hangs where the metal prints used to be.

My passion for cycling has been replaced by an addiction to the sport of disc golf. I discovered that slinging plastic through the woods helps preserve the balance that Parkinson's is trying so desperately to rob from my body. Before that happens, I intend to play at least one top-rated disc golf course in each state. I call it my "basket list." The map helps track my progress.

But for the most part, the images and diplomas on these walls are the same. What *has* changed is my enthusiasm for showing them to others. Those who visit our home these days rarely make it to my office. The images here no longer necessarily display the *me* I am most eager for others to see.

The last time we were here, I suggested that there are consequences for ignoring our suffering. Unresolved, unredeemed pain will eventually

---

1   T.S. Eliot, "Little Gidding," Four Quartets, part V, lines 867-869.

re-collect and embitter us. Until we find a sacred place for our wounds, we run the risk of transmitting our bitterness to others.

Over the past months, *Home Before Sunset* became an unexpectedly sacred place for my wounds. I dared to trust you with the parts of my story that, before this project, I kept hidden from everyone, even myself. Such sharing is risky. It is also transformative.

I also trusted God.

Richard Rohr reminds us, "When we trust that suffering can be part of God's great pattern to change all things, and that God is *in the suffering*, our wounds become sacred wounds. The actual and ordinary life journey becomes itself the godly journey. We trust God to be in all things, even in sin and suffering."[2]

We should not be surprised to find God in our pain. After all, if neither hardship, nor distress, nor persecution, nor famine, nor nakedness, nor peril, nor sword, nor death, nor life, nor angels, nor rulers, nor things present, nor things to come, nor powers, nor height, nor depth, nor anything in all creation can separate us from Christ,[3] then how could our woundedness possibly deter God? In Christ, God chose our suffering!

I find that people are usually eager to expose their physical wounds, even before those wounds have healed. I have learned to prepare myself during hospital visits.

"How did your surgery go?"

"Well, let me show you, Pastor."

We wear our wounds like badges of honor. They testify to the trials we have endured and give an accounting of all we have survived. When Jesus appeared to the disciples following the resurrection, the first thing he showed them were his wounds. Then, the disciples rejoiced, for they knew it was the Lord. His wounds gave him away.

My wounds are more visible from the pulpit these days. Like the depression of war veterans, the onsetting confusion of former NFL players,

---

2 Richard Rohr, The Wisdom Pattern: Order, Disorder, Reorder (Franciscan Media: 2020), 67-68.

3 Romans 8:35-39

or the tears of those who mourn, the spiritual wounds of those who bring good news suggest we have endured something formidable. This evangelist has survived the long night and, therefore, has something to say.

Locked away on death row in Herod's rancid prison, John the Baptist began to doubt his most resolute convictions. He dispatched two of his disciples to Jesus with a question: "Are you the one, or shall we wait for another?"[4]

Jesus responded, "Tell John what you hear and see."

The blind were stargazing and the lame were dancing. The poor were living with newfound hope. Jesus responded to John's doubt by sending him witnesses.

While I have at times questioned the Lord's judgment in delivering this calling to me, I am, by God's good grace, a preacher. Some of my colleagues are passionate about caring for their flocks in times of crisis. Others teach, direct staffs, or lead small groups. These are all meaningful parts of my work, but my heart belongs to preaching. I have spent my career witnessing to the things I have heard and seen.

I was not with the disciples on Easter evening. I did not see Jesus walk through walls, nor did I put my finger in the marks of the nails in Jesus' hands or side. I did not hear him speak, "Peace," into the hearts of his frightened brothers.

But like the eleven, I *have* sat alone in my room, guilty and ashamed of things I have done and things I have left undone. Even as a child, I experienced the joy of having someone step into my loneliness and pardon me with a word of grace.

I was not at the cross when Jesus died. Had the roll been called, you would have heard Mary and John say, "Present." But not me. Neither was I in the congregation at Philippi when the Apostle Paul explained, "Jesus did not count equality with God as something to be exploited, but emptied himself, taking the form of a slave."[5]

---

4   Matthew 11
5   Philippians 2:6-8

But I *have* stood on the edge of a precipice, clinging for dear life to the face of a cliff. I watched my father remove his gear, drop to his knees, and take my danger upon himself in order to lead me back to safety.

I was not among those who had their feet washed by Jesus on the night of his betrayal.

But my mother and the saints in my childhood congregation taught me that "God is love! God is love!" and then listened as I sang that gospel truth again and again.

More than Norman Rockwell images or simple wrapped-up versions of "the truth," listeners long for the testimony of witnesses. Like the disciples waiting anxiously in the upper room on Easter evening, we want to hear from the reconnaissance team — from those who have experienced what it's like beyond the walls.

"You've been out there. What did you see? Is there a word from the Lord? What can we expect? Can you share something that helps us make sense of the world?"

"Well, gather 'round and let me tell you what I've heard and seen."

So, if you visit our home this evening, perhaps have dinner with Lori and me, I will not show you my office walls. Instead, I will invite you to sit around the table or the fireplace where we will simply tell our stories.

And when it is my turn, I may share with you some of the lessons I learned while growing up on a gentleman's farm in the South or describe the daily challenges of living with Parkinson's. Lori and I may tell you how we met or show you pictures of our wedding. But at some point, if you are willing to become a sacred place for me, I will tell you about a moment in my life that was truly unordinary.

This moment occurred in St. Louis on the first full day of summer in 2012. That was the day that a nun, a psychologist, a social worker, and a bishop sat around a conference table together evaluating the woundedness of a well-intentioned, cooperative, talented, intelligent, defensive, and possibly slightly depressed and emotionally distressed Lutheran pastor.

As our readout session ended, the psychologist stuffed my folder under his arm, pushed himself away from the table, and concluded, "I know you'd like to think you're okay, Pastor. But no one can go through what you've experienced and not have significant issues to work on."

It was then that I finally found the words I had been struggling all morning to express.

"Maybe," I said. "Or maybe I just believe what I preach."

Gratitude

Preachers preach and writers write because others are willing to receive their words. Therefore, I am chiefly grateful to you for picking up this book. A journey is never complete until it is shared with someone else. You have given this project purpose.

I am grateful for parents who, as I wrote in chapter 8, "were challenged and tried by life yet clung tightly to their trust in God. They responded to life's injustices with patience and steadfastness and taught their children to do the same."

I am also grateful for the Sunday School teachers and pastors in my youth who stayed up late on Saturday nights toiling over creative ways to present Jesus' story. We both know that I daydreamed through many of your sermons and lessons, but thankfully, the Holy Spirit made sure that the important stuff stuck. My picture hangs on the center block walls of Bethel Lutheran Church in Salisbury, North Carolina, where I was baptized, confirmed, and married. The saints there refer to me as a "son of the congregation." It is a fitting description and one that I carry with honor.

Ask any pastor, "Why ministry?" and they will tell you the story of at least one significant someone who, in God's good timing, helped do a little spiritual steering. Rev. Chris Heavner was one of my *someones*. I am grateful for his patience in counseling, for sharing the road trip to Chicago and his encouragement to attend the seminary there, and for his holy nerve to suggest that a little "growing up" might have been in order before striking out to study anywhere.

Ask any author, "Why did you start writing?" and they will likely tell you a story of someone who sparked an interest or an idea. I am grateful for Charisse Peeler for first suggesting that not only did I have something to say, but I also had a story worth writing.

Home Before Sunset took shape while a cadre of extraordinary souls read over my shoulder. Betty Bauer and Mary Ida Yost will always be my first content editors. "Did this chapter work? Fall short? Leave you scratching your head?" Mary Ida and Betty provided the thumbs-up, thumbs-down, thumbs-sideways feedback.

The invaluable work that we accomplished over the phone and across dining room tables was then translated to the computer screen and bantered back and forth across country. Alice Trego was my *fixer*. Each time I conversed with her, something in the manuscript changed — three paragraphs appeared where there had been one, descriptions became quotes, and chapters got reordered. Alice did not reduce the content of the book, only the time it took you to read it.

I am grateful for Kristine Spanier, my *finisher* and touch up artist. Had it not been for Kristine's extraordinarily insightful and confident work, and her assistance in navigating the maze of publishing, I would still be tweaking and adjusting and fretting over final details.

I am grateful for Brien Spanier's creativity with cover design and Diana Foster's photographic gift for seeing the small picture. You both are extraordinary artists.

I am grateful for my beta readers: Blair Anderson, Kristine Spanier, Lyle Niedens, Debbie Kanode, Judy Bakalar, Chad Huebner, and Candace Underwood. Your responses and feedback were essential in shaping this project.

I tell pastors, "The stuff that's on your heart inevitably gets on your congregation's heart." Much of what occupies my heart for ministry came from sitting at the feet of Reggie McNeal. I am grateful for Reggie's missional zeal and his dynamic way of spreading it. In my consulting work with congregations, I am often a retailer. Reggie is the manufacturer.

When a project sends me digging through my oldest sermon files, I close the folders with a deeper appreciation for anyone who endured what I had to say in the early years. I am grateful for those who listened to my preaching and had the moxie to ask, "Huh?" You helped me become a better storyteller.

I am grateful for my children's openness to remembering and their willingness to process the most difficult times. Lauren and Grant, you are wise beyond your years. You affirmed and challenged me in just the right places. Thank you.

Finally, I am grateful every moment for Lori, my best friend and loving wife. You have listened patiently and shared tenderly. I am so blessed that our journeys merged.

www.ingramcontent.com/pod-product-compliance
Lightning Source LLC
Chambersburg PA
CBHW020656060526
44119CB00090B/406/J